Masters
of Battle

Masters of Battle

Selected Great Warrior Classes

John Wilcox

ARMS AND
ARMOUR

My father was the youngest son of a large (seven brothers and seven sisters) working class family. All of the seven sons fought in the front line during the First World War and, unusually, all survived. To their memory and, in particular that of my father, Leonard Wilcox and his closest brothers, Alfred Wilcox, VC, Bernard Wilcox, MM, and Ernest Wilcox, DCM, this book is affectionately dedicated.

Arms and Armour Press
A Cassell Imprint
Wellington House, 125 Strand, London WC2R 0BB

Distributed in the USA by Sterling Publishing Co. Inc.,
387 Park Avenue South, New York, NY 10016-8810.

First published in 1996
This paperback edition 1997

British Library Cataloguing-in-Publication Data:
a catalogue record for this book is available from the British Library

ISBN 1-85409-454-8

Designed and edited by DAG Publications Ltd.
Designed by David Gibbons; edited by Michael Boxall;
Printed and bound in Great Britain by
MPG Books Ltd, Bodmin, Cornwall

Main jacket illustration:
Defeat of British Forces at Isandlwana by Zulus,
22 January 1879, painted by C. E. Fripp.
(Peter Newark's Military Pictures)

CONTENTS

ACKNOWLEDGEMENTS

W riting a book is a solitary business, but to a gregarious person like myself, a work of non-fiction provides the great compensation of demanding research which, for much of the time, requires the help of others. In preparing this book, I have been extremely lucky to receive such help and, in addition, an invaluable amount of encouragement from friends, family and colleagues.

The original concept took the form of an idea for a television series and I gratefully acknowledge the role of editor and publisher Peter Jackson in prompting me to develop it. Other old friends were kind enough to comment helpfully on sections at various stages, notably Nigel Cole, David Goodenday, Bryan Thompson, and, especially, Liam Hunter, who ardently debated the contents on many occasions but, alas, did not live to see the book published. I am grateful also to John Brushfield for the practical assistance he gave in the search for a publisher and to Roderick Dymott, of the Arms & Armour Press imprint of Cassell, for grasping the potential of the project and encouraging its completion.

I must thank the staff of the following libraries and institutions who gave me courteous and invaluable assistance: in Britain: the London Library, the British Library, the Imperial War Museum Library, the library of the National Maritime Museum, Greenwich, the library of the Royal Armoured Corps Tank Museum at Bovington, Dorset, the Royal Armoury at the Tower, and the Jorvik Viking Centre, York; in America, the library of the Saratoga National Historical Park, and the Handley Library at Winchester, Pennsylvania: and in Germany the Unterseeboote Traditionsarchiv, at Cuxhaven.

Individuals were remarkably generous. Chief Mangosuthu Buthelezi, Chief Minister of KwaZulu in South Africa, took two and a half hours out of a busy day to give me lunch and discuss the Anglo-Zulu war. Colonel George Connell, late US Marine Corps, introduced me to his neighbour in

Arlington, Virginia, Mr Donald Bills, who showed me his collection of 18th-century Kentucky rifles and explained the techniques of loading and firing them. And Herr Horst Bredow, of Cuxhaven, recalled his father's experience as a First World War watchkeeper in U-boats and his own as a submariner during the Second World War. To them all I am most grateful.

Once I had first drafts on paper I was fortunate in being able to secure the help of distinguished specialists who read and commented on the sections within their areas of expertise. I gratefully acknowledge the help here of Professor M. C. Prestwich, Pro-Vice-Chancellor of Durham University; Professor Sean McGrail, former Professor of Maritime Archaeology, Oxford University; Mr Paul Okey, Historian, Saratoga National Historical Park, and Ranger Joe Craig, also of the Park; Professor John Laband, of the Department of Historical Studies, the University of Natal, South Africa; Rear-Admiral Patrick Middleton, CB, formerly of the British submarine service; and Major Alistair Roxburgh and Lieutenant David Cole, both of the Queen's Dragoon Guards. Most of their corrections and suggestions were incorporated into the final MS, but on some rare occasions, I took the liberty of disagreeing with them. They should not be held responsible, therefore, for whatever errors have crept into the text.

Lastly, I owe a great debt to my wife Betty, who has not only stoically tramped over battlefields, proof-read 90,000 words and lived uncomplainingly with these warriors for the last three years, but has given me constant encouragement throughout.

JW
Chilmark, May 1995

INTRODUCTION

This book of war and warriors, of the distant and not so distant past, was – strangely – born of a conversation about sport. We fell into the familiar and perennial debate about who was 'the best ever'. The discussion ranged over cricket – could Bradman have handled the West Indian pace attack? football – was Pele better than Matthews? and boxing – could anyone, anywhere, have beaten a fit Mohammed Ali? We happened to be in London, but a similar conversation could well have been taking place contemporaneously in Manhattan (Ruth or diMaggio?) or Marseilles (Borotra or Forget?).

It was a matter of minutes only before the military history *aficionados* among us transposed the game on to the battlefield. And so *Masters of Battle* came into embryonic form.

The pages that follow describe the life style, methods of warfare and weapons of warriors whom I claim to be the best at their trade the world has ever seen. Not the great generals and admirals of the past – no Alexanders, Caesars, Marlboroughs or Napoleons – but rather their rankers and line officers, men who were so specially skilled that they tipped the scales towards victory. Ordinary men, in fact, who did extraordinary things.

The best thing about playing the game in a solitary way at the word processor, of course, is that one's choice cannot be gainsaid. Therefore, the heroes that are contained in these pages are my choice alone. It may well be that some readers will not agree that the English and Welsh longbowmen of Crécy and Agincourt were the best artillerymen who ever lived, or that the Zulus were the finest aboriginal warriors. But provoking a difference of opinion is part of the fun – and, of course, the choice must be highly subjective. Even so, the case must be made, and I have done my best to substantiate the claims I make for each warrior and I have described and analysed the effectiveness of the weapon or weapons which made him famous.

Here then, in addition to the medieval bowmen and the Zulus, I offer the Vikings as the best marines, the riflemen of Saratoga as the finest sharpshooters and skirmishers, the Kaiser's U-boat captains as the nonpareil among privateers and the Panzer commanders of the Second World War as the choicest of the 'armoured ones'.

In researching and writing the book, however, I have overlaid two other requirements for entry into the pantheon. Each warrior, by his deeds, must have changed the course of history in ways which affect his country, or even, perhaps, the world, to this day. Additionally, he had to be *interesting* – not just a killer who did his job well, but a man the minutiae of whose life and battles offers fascination to those who, like me, find such matters intriguing.

One reason for applying these additional qualifications is that they do, to some extent, overcome my paradoxical dislike writing about death and destruction, weapons and killing. I admire and have a respect for all of the men detailed in these pages. They were professional men of war in great danger themselves who, with some rare exceptions, did their work as humanely as conditions allowed. But I am not sure that I could have done that work myself and I am ambivalent about soldiering as a peace-time career. Therefore, I hope that the pictures painted in these pages of how these warriors lived and looked and of the events which shaped their lives will prove as interesting as the great battles which they dominated.

Although I have visited the sites of these battles, talked to experts and, where they exist, survivors, and attempted, usually across the centuries, to sniff the ambience and call up the ghosts which still linger there, much of the research has involved digging deeply into the published works of other writers and weighing and then re-cycling their words and opinions. This book is not, then, claimed to be an original work of scholarship. For that reason – and because I believe them to be an irritant – I have not used footnotes. The main quotations used in the book are attributed in the text and their sources are to be found in the selected bibliography at the end.

The warriors described are, I submit, all fascinating in their very different ways. For that reason it has been neither desirable nor necessary to gild them with the brush of imagination. It is true that I have created a composite figure for each class of combatant, usually based on someone who actually lived and fought at that time. I have done so the better to personalise the warriors and to describe their lifestyle. But the experiences attributed to them all are based on fact.

Of course, the choice of warriors is not exhaustive. No infantry? Well, it would be a brave man who attempted to make a case for any foot soldiers other than Caesar's legionaries – and they have rather been done to death by historians. What about cavalry? How do the mounted hordes of Genghis Khan weigh against the Cheyenne and Sioux who did for Custer? And the airmen? Who to choose between, say, the young men of von Richthoven's Flying Circus in the First World War, the Battle of Britain's Few from 1940, or the Mirage aces who were Argentina's only success story in the Falklands War?

Ah well, perhaps next time.

1
THE MARINES
The Vikings of the North

The common perception of marines is of soldiers who live on ships yet who fight on sea and land. It could be argued that the Vikings were more seamen than soldiers. In fact, by the 10th century this was no longer true. But if one had to categorise these Norsemen by modern terminology it would be difficult to find a more appropriate, if crude, definition than that of marine; probably the first true marine in military history and certainly the most effective.

They first swept down from the rooftops of the world 1,200 years ago to create the Viking Age, which lasted for nearly 300 years and re-shaped the ethnic pattern of the globe. Not since the Romans had any people so dominated the western world and left so firm a mark on history. Their name became a by-word for cruelty and banditry. In the 9th century, the abbeys, monasteries and churches of England, Scotland, Ireland and coastline continental Europe rang with a new and urgent prayer: '*A furore Normannorum libera nos, Domine*' – From the fury of the Northmen, deliver us, O Lord. The image of rapacity has lingered on. Play the word association game with 'Viking' today and the response will almost certainly be 'rape and pillage'. And yet, and yet ...

The scholarship of the last hundred years has gradually produced a modification of that simplistic view. The image remains coated with the evidence of a barbarity which was shocking, even by the rude standards of the day. Beneath it, however, has emerged evidence of Viking traits which tell a different, more rounded, story.

The Vikings conquered but they colonised, too. They fought but they fertilised as well, seeding and tilling the land as assiduously as they fished the seas. They were makers of artefacts whose surviving remnants reveal clear signs of exquisite taste. Their ships broke new ground in terms of seaworthiness, versatility and beauty. Their navigational techniques were hardly bettered by Columbus 500 years later and their sagas, even in translation, reflect a poetic imagination. They gave a lesson to the French in administration and they re-opened the coasts of England and Ireland to international trade after the Dark Ages. Their influence can still be detected at every turn throughout modern Europe.

In many ways, the Vikings fit awkwardly into the pattern of this book. It is impossible to feature one battle in which they changed the course of great events. Their main weapon could not be wielded by hand or fired – they sailed in it. Their most interesting achievement took place not on the battlefield but in Arctic seas, fighting the enemies of wind, wave and exposure.

For all that, and despite their multi-faceted achievements, they were primarily epic warriors, fit to stand alongside other specialist masters of war who changed the pattern of things.

THE RAIDS

Lindisfarne today slumbers and, in the winter, half freezes off the northeast coast of England. It is still called Holy Island, although it is not really an island because at low tide, a narrow isthmus connects it to the mainland of Northumbria, and notices warn motorists of the dangers of parking and dawdling along the causeway when the tide is turning. A friendly hotel, a less friendly pub and a cluster of cottages are scattered about the inlets on the island itself. Although there is a small museum, the remains of a rust-coloured sandstone abbey and the ruins of a castle on the promontory, there are few signs of serious tourism. No one is about. An almost sepulchral calm hangs over the place. It is here that in AD 793 the Vikings first left their imprint on history. It is as though Lindisfarne is waiting tremulously for them to come back.

They came, on a June day more than 1,200 years ago, directly out of the sea from the north-east. A handful of long, low, black ships, each with a single, bulging sail, headed straight for the shore and beached on the gently shelving shingle. Without preliminaries, the crews leapt ashore. This was no provisioning party. The ships disgorged tall, bearded men wearing conical helmets and wielding swords and huge axes. They made straight for the monastery, where monks from Iona in Scotland had settled in 634 to bring Christianity to the Northumbrians.

It is difficult, even imbibing now the uneasy tranquillity of modern Lindisfarne, to imagine the horror of that first attack. In 793 only monks and sheep inhabited the place – hence Holy Island. The monastery was a centre of learning and a sanctuary for contemplation. Jutting out into the black North Sea, the monks felt close to their God and free from secular intrusion. They spent the hours praying, chanting, tending the sheep and working on the scholarly tracts for which Lindisfarne had acquired an international reputation. There was not an armed man on the island when the Vikings struck.

The monastery, however, was a repository of great treasure. Over the generations, with bequests and gifts from rich merchants who valued their souls, the monks had built up a glittering collection of gold and silver crucifixes, altar dishes and candlesticks. The stone walls were hung with fine tapestries and the chapels housed beautifully illuminated manuscripts, studded with fine gems, and ivory reliquaries. The monastery was a place of beauty as well as contemplative reverence.

The big pagans from the north cared nothing for introspective theology. Their gods were martial and crude. Brandishing their weapons, they ran across the springy turf, scattering the sheep, and made straight for the monastery. The butchery was cruel and gratuitous. Many monks were cut down as they knelt. Some were taken to the sea to drown, others had their habits ripped away and were forced outside naked at sword point. The monastery was methodically stripped of its treasures and the booty taken down to the longships waiting on the shingle. Then, as suddenly as they had appeared, the raiders were gone. There had been no time to raise the alarm and to fetch help – if any had existed on that barren coast. The Norsemen slipped away, back over the horizon to be swallowed up by the North Sea. The Viking Age had begun.

The attack on Lindisfarne is the first recorded Viking raid, but there may well have been others even earlier. King Offa is known to have been arranging for the defence of Kent against pagan seamen in 792 and the *Anglo-Saxon Chronicle* records an incident in 789 when a royal official was killed at Portland by men of three ships who put ashore there. The *Chronicle* adds that 'Those were the first ships of Danish men which came to the land of the English.'

Although the Lindisfarne raid was a hit and run affair and by no means an invasion, its very ferocity sent shock waves round the then civilised world. The renowned English scholar Alcuin was teaching at the court of the Emperor Charlemagne at Aachen when the news reached him. He immediately wrote in sympathy and horror to the King of Northumbria:

'... never before has such terror appeared in Britain as we have now suffered from a pagan race, nor was it thought that such an inroad from the sea could be made. Behold the church of St Cuthbert spattered with the blood of the priests of God, despoiled of all its ornaments; a place more venerable than all in Britain is given as prey to pagan peoples.'

Alcuin had put his finger on the key point about the attack: 'nor was it thought that such an inroad from the sea could be made'. The enlightened world was not unused to savage raids by the heathen. The demise of the great Roman Empire at the hands of the pagan hordes was comparatively recent history and Europe still contained wild tribes who knelt at no altar. The point about the Vikings, however, was that they had come without warning from a faraway land *over the sea*. They had used their maritime skills to appear without warning, to strike before a defence could be prepared and then to sail away before any kind of retaliation could be mounted. For the first time since the galleys of the Phoenicians and Romans had dominated the Mediterranean, sea-power had become a key factor in warfare.

The success of the Lindisfarne expedition encouraged a party of Vikings, probably the same one, to return to the Northumbrian coast in the following year and raid a monastery at Jarrow. This time, the Viking leader was killed and a severe storm crippled the little fleet and for some time afterwards the raiders looked farther west for their spoils. In 795 Iona was plundered for the first time, as was an island off Ireland, to the north of Dublin. Other, unrecorded, attacks were almost certainly made on the northern coasts of Scotland and Ireland and early settlements were established in these barren places. As a result, the raiders became able to rely on a chain of provisioning stops and storm shelters along the sea routes from Norway to Ireland. These pirates, clearly, were resourceful as well as predatory. But who exactly were they and where did they come from?

It is generally accepted that these early raiders sailed from Norway, despite the reference to 'Danish Men' in the *Anglo-Saxon Chronicle*. In fact, the Anglo-Saxons were often confused about the distinctions between the Scandinavian races, not least because these peoples spoke in a generic tongue, Old Norse, and also because, later at least, Viking raiding parties and armies included men of various nationalities. The origin of the word Viking itself is multi-faceted. Etymologists have traced it to various words in the Old Norse tongue: *vikja*, to deviate, turn, or wander; or *vik*, inlet or fiord; or *vig*, battle. Some scholars have linked it to the Old English *wic*, meaning camp, or the Latin *vicus*, a trading town. Whatever its genesis, for the people of Europe and for the Norsemen themselves, it came to mean sea rover or raider. On the one hand, a pejorative term, redolent of terror and barbarity; on the other, a word synonymous with adventure, conquering and bravery.

The Vikings who made those first raids were fundamentally a single people who were just beginning to diversify into the single nations of

Norway, Sweden and Denmark. They were descended from Germanic tribes who swarmed over Europe for some 500 years after the death of Christ. From the quantity of indigenous flint implements found and from their impressive size and workmanship, it is clear, however, that southern Scandinavia had supported a rich culture much earlier – through the New Stone Age (late 3000 BC) and the subsequent Bronze Age.

From about 1000 BC the northern lands entered a period of decline. The climate began to lose its hospitality and take on more of its present characteristics: long, dark winters, ice and snow, storms and lowering cloud. The archaeological remains from this period are both poorer and rarer. Through the early Dark Ages, there was considerable migration south-wards from the Nordic lands. The Goths left eastern Sweden to settle in the Baltic provinces; the Langobards shook the pine needles of southern Sweden from their sandals to settle down the Elbe and ended up in Lombardy, northern Italy; and the Angles forsook Slesvig to colonise eastern Britain. The fighting qualities of the Norsemen were known and respected from the earliest days and this encouraged a mini-exodus of mercenaries. Vikings formed the private bodyguard of the emperors of Byzantium and helped maintain that dynasty for 400 years or more. In fact, what is now called the Viking Age, dating from about 770 to 1070, could well be re-defined as the last phase of a great migration.

Nevertheless, apart from the distinctive use of ships and the sea, there are two important features of the classic Viking Age which distinguish it from the earlier period of Scandinavian expansion. During the early part of the first millennium, everyone in Europe seemed to be on the move. The peripatetic nature of the Scandinavians, then, seemed not out of place. By the time of the great raids and the, later, colonisations of the 9th, 10th and 11th centuries, however, eastern Europe was comparatively settled and the Viking incursions stood out shockingly. The ferocity and anti-clerical nature of the attacks was the second distinguishing feature. This can prob-ably be traced to the fact that, unlike most of middle and central Europe, the far North had escaped the civilising influence of the Romans. The Vikings, then, although they had been skilled traders and merchants and were to prove themselves so again, ravaged with a barbarity and lack of dis-cipline which shocked the settled world. They looked and fought like bears, robbed, raped, traded in slaves and delighted in sacking Christian places of worship.

The set-back suffered by the Norwegians at Jarrow seems to have earned England a respite from the Viking raids for there is no record of fur-ther attacks until 835. But the rest of Britain did not escape unscathed.

From 795 the Norsemen launched a series of attacks on monasteries and settlements in the Orkneys, Shetlands, Hebrides, Isle of Man, Wales and, above all, Ireland. These continued throughout the first half of the 9th century.

Sometimes the Vikings struck the same places again and again. The great Irish monastery of Armagh, chosen by St Patrick as the seat of his church in the early 5th century, was plundered five times, thrice within a month in 832. Four years later, the attacks developed a new and more sinister aspect. In 836 a Norwegian fleet entered the river Liffey and established a permanent settlement on the 'Black Pool' *(Dubhlinn)* where a monastery already stood. So Dublin was founded – and colonisation had begun. In 840 the Norse leader Thorgils came to stay and become the first King of Ireland and overlord of Dublin. A chain of other fortified Viking towns was established – Limerick, Wexford, Waterford, Cork among them. They became Ireland's first trading ports and have survived to this day.

The Nordic wave also broke round the coast of continental Europe and swept, like a tidal bore, up the great rivers. The port of Dornstadt on the Rhine, at that time one of the greatest commercial centres of northern Europe, was attacked at least six times, according to one chronicler. In 841 Rouen was sacked, Nantes in 843, Hamburg and Paris two years later. In 844 Seville was held to ransom for a week and Pisa was put to the sword. It seemed as if nowhere was beyond the reach of the black longships.

The monks in their despair recalled the words of the Old Testament prophet Jeremiah: 'Out of the north evil shall break forth upon all the inhabitants of the land.' Many felt that the Day of Judgement was at hand. 'The wild beasts', wrote the French Monk Abbo, 'go through hills and fields, killing babies, children, young men, old men, fathers, sons and mothers. They overthrow, they destroy, they ravage; sinister cohort, fatal phalanx, cruel host.'

This terror was wrought by both the Norwegians and the Danes, the latter joining the party after the early raids on Northumbria, Scotland and Ireland. The Swedes, meanwhile, had been striking to the east and south. They had opened up a route to Byzantium and begun a rich trade in slaves, gold and silver with the Arabs. Sweeping south down the great rivers of central Europe, establishing settlements on the way, they seized Kiev and clashed with the Greeks at the very threshold of Constantinople. They eventually established themselves on the banks of the Dnieper, around Kiev. They were called the Rus – and so gave their name to Russia. Within less than a hundred years the Vikings had taken their longships to the corners of the known world.

These early raids were not always unopposed however. In 849, the Irish witnessed the welcome spectacle of dog eating dog as a Danish fleet arrived, via England, under the chieftain Orm and attacked the resident Norwegians. For the next few years the two Nordic tribes fought each other on land and sea until, in 853, Olaf arrived with a large number of ships in the Liffey and re-established Norwegian supremacy in Ireland. This internecine Nordic struggle seems to have been confined to Ireland. Elsewhere – and particularly in the Viking attacks on Friesland, Kent, Cornwall, and the coastline and estuaries of northern France – the two main Scandinavian streams, sometimes joined by a minority of Swedes, were united. But spheres of influence emerged. The Hebrides, Iceland, Greenland, Orkneys, Shetlands, Ireland and north-west England were Norwegian. The forces which landed in England, Frisia and France during the 9th century were largely Danish.

The early excursions – unlike the more planned invasions of the 10th and 11th centuries – were made by quite small forces: probably rarely more than a few hundred strong. Contemporary records were never specific about numbers of warriors but the *Anglo-Saxon Chronicle* refers more often than not to twenty-five ships or even five, although more are listed on the continent. As the 9th century progressed, the English Channel became the Vikings' main highway.

To make it easier, they now began to set up permanent, well-defended bridgeheads at strategic points along this sea-way, where they could winter safely and even bring their women from the north and so avoid the long journeys back to the fiords. They usually chose peninsulas or islands at the opening of estuaries. Three of these – there were probably more – were at Noirmoutier in the mouth of the Loire, occupied in 849; Thanet, in 850; and Sheppey, the gateway to the Thames and therefore to London and middle England, in 855. Unlike the storm havens created round the north coasts of Scotland and Ireland, these bases were mini-townships, provisioned to sustain continuous warfare.

Instead of migrating in the winter like locusts, the Vikings were becoming a year-round, indigenous blight. It was no longer sufficient to move treasures inland and hope that bad weather would keep the rovers at bay. Now the Vikings were turning their sharp bows up-river to strike at the very heart of European nations. Their longships seemed equally at home in shallow fresh-water as out at sea. Up the Somme and the Seine they sailed (Paris was attacked in 845, 856 and 861 and the city subjected to a year-long siege in 885-6); and the Scheldt, the Moselle and the Maas also saw the dragon-headed prows.

On both sides of the English Channel, as the Vikings' intentions of invasion became clear, so too did the need to organise a systematic way of dealing with them. It wasn't easy. Whether fortuitously or not, the Norsemen had attacked at just the right moment. On the continent, the great empire of Charlemagne had broken up in quarrels after his death and England was a collection of divided, ineffectual kingdoms. Two means of handling the invaders emerged: fighting them and buying them off. In 845 the French king, Charles the Bald, gave the invaders 7,000 pounds of silver, the first of thirteen such payments known to have been made in France up to 926. That bribe bought just six years of respite. It also created a new term, *Danegeld*, to describe a cowardly and ineffective solution to a problem. According to contemporary Frankish sources, some 865 pounds of gold and 43,042 pounds of silver found its way back to Norway and Denmark in loot and *Danegeld* during this period.

It was to little avail. A monk from Noirmoutier, who had fled the place after the arrival of the longships, wrote in the 860s:

'The number of ships grows; the endless stream of Vikings never ceases to increase. Everywhere the Christians are victims of massacres, burnings, plunderings; the Vikings conquer all in their path, and no one resists them; they seize Bordeaux, Perigueux, Limoges, Angoulême and Toulouse; Angers, Tours and Orleans are annihilated and an innumerable fleet sails up the Seine and the evil grows in the whole region. Rouen is laid waste, plundered and burned; Paris, Beauvais and Meaux taken, Melun's strong fortress levelled to the ground, Chartres occupied, Evreux and Bayeux plundered and every town besieged.'

Their success in France encouraged the Vikings to sail southwards, through the Bay of Biscay to one of the most splendid of Europe's kingdoms at this time: Moorish Spain. It is possible that early raiders had reached this rich coast late in the 8th century, but the first recorded attack is upon Seville in 844, when the city was taken and held for a week. The Moors were different from the timid burghers of France. They fiercely counter-attacked and the invaders were only able to escape with their lives by ransoming their prisoners.

In 859, Bjorn and Hastein set out from the Loire with a fleet of 62 ships on one of the most famous and protracted Viking raids. They sailed south and then east, through the Straits of Gibraltar, sacked Algeciras, and spent a profitable time harrying the North African coast. They wintered in a typical Viking 'nest', an island in the Camargue in the Rhone delta, which they used as a base for marauding operations up river as far as Valence. Then they attacked Italy, pillaging Pisa and Luna. It is thought that they sailed further south, possibly even to Sicily, before turning for home. They had a shock off Gibraltar, where a Moorish fleet was waiting for them in the Straits and the subsequent battle decimated the Viking flotilla. Even then, some survivors went inland and had the audacity to attack Navarre, where they captured its prince and ransomed him for 90,000 *dinarii*. Only about one-third of the ships that had set out finally got back to the Loire in 862. But their crews, in addition to acquiring battle scars and sun-leathered skins, had amassed great riches.

INVASION AND COLONISATION

Meanwhile, the little kingdoms of England were trying to fight. Dira, the southern part of Northumbria, fell between 855 and 867 and Bernicia, its northern part, by 875. East Anglia collapsed in 870 and Mercia, including London, between 869 and 874. Only Wessex stood firm. In 865 King Aethelbert had succeeded to a unified block of southern England, comprising Wessex (the central part of southern England), Sussex, Surrey, Kent and Essex. Aethelbert raised men from his small kingdom and fought valiantly. He was unable to prevent the sack of Winchester, but he held off the Nordic host which patrolled his borders until his death in 865.

In that year, however, the Viking presence in England took on a more permanent and threatening mien. 'There came', the chronicles record, 'a great heathen host to England and took winter quarters in East Anglia, and they were there provided with horses.' The horses gave the Norsemen a mobility on land to match that given to them at sea by the longboats and this united army began to operate as a single, formidable unit. It seemed that the whole of England must now become an extension of Scandinavia. The era of raids had been succeeded by that of invasion.

That star that later was to flicker so benevolently on the island in 1805 and 1940 now shone on the oppressed Saxons of Wessex. In 870, Aethelbert's grandson Alfred succeeded to the throne of Wessex. At 21, he was more a scholar than a soldier (he was later to translate several ecclesiastical works from Latin into the Saxon vernacular, and to invent a candle clock and a reading lantern). At first, there seemed little to celebrate in Alfred's succession. In the first eight years of his reign he fought a series of battles and smaller engagements with the Vikings, neither winning, nor being totally routed. To some extent, he was saved by the collapse of the other English kingdoms. This offered rich spoils – not least in land – to the conquering Danes and they laid down their axes and swords to absorb the vanquished territories of Northumbria and Mercia. The small, hard-travelling force of Alfred was able – just – to hold its line while much of the enemy's attention was elsewhere.

The main onslaught came in 878. The *Anglo-Saxon Chronicle* records:

'In this year the host went secretly in midwinter after Twelfth Night to Chippenham and rode over Wessex and occupied it, and drove a great part of the inhabitants oversea, and of the rest the greater part they reduced to submission, except Alfred the King and he, with a small company, moved under difficulties through woods and into inaccessible places in the marshes. And the Easter after, King Alfred with a small company built a fortification at Athelney, and from that fortification, with the men of that part of Somerset nearest to it, he continued fighting against the host ...'

The resistance which Alfred organised constitutes one of the most sterling and comparatively unsung episodes in English history. Somehow the young king, who had been hunted round his country like an outlaw, managed to attract to his banner at Ecgbrihtesstane (Brixton) on the Wiltshire border enough followers to challenge the Danish host to a pitched battle. Many of the west country Saxons were untrained men of the soil. The Danes were vicious professional warriors. Yet at Edington, just north of Salisbury plain, the Wessex army inflicted an overwhelming defeat on the Vikings. After a fortnight's siege the Danes inside Chippenham surrendered and the Danish king Guthrum submitted to Christian baptism at Alfred's own hands.

It was now that Alfred showed that he was a statesman as well as a scholar and soldier. He knew that, complete as was his victory for the moment, there was no guarantee that it would be lasting. In the past the Vikings had always come back. So he negotiated the Peace of Wedmore which secured for the Saxons the southern region of England. To those of the Danes who wished to settle, it gave them the chance legally to do so, under their own Danelaw. It bequeathed them – without the need to fight for it – a band of broad acres extending diagonally across the waist of England, with a long North Sea coastline offering easy access to Denmark and a shorter one on the Irish Sea, giving the same to the Norwegian settlements in Ireland.

Those Danes who accepted the offer stayed 'to plough the land and make a living for themselves'. It was a peace which lasted, although by no means did it see the end of Viking attacks. Alfred had gained time to build his kingdom upon a basis of a strong Church and an administrative framework which was the beginnings of the formal rule of law in England. At roughly this time the Danes who had conquered in the north were settling into their lands, trading across the North Sea, tilling the land and even re-building the walls of York which they had destroyed. The Saxon archbishop Wulfhere returned to York and converted many Vikings to Christianity.

Complete sweetness and light had not settled over the entire country however. A strong band of pirates stayed centred at Fulham on the Thames, preferring their longboats to ploughshares, and raiding across the Channel. The Norwegians in the North also remained hostile, and Alfred had to remain vigilant. In the decade 881-91, the king built a series of strong points across his country to offer protection to the local peasants. He created a standing army and built a fleet of ships to fight the Vikings before they could set foot on shore. This first English navy copied the style of the Viking longboats, of course, but sometimes exceeded them in size: some had sixty oars and were said to be swifter and steadier than those of the Danes.

These defences were tested in 892 when Hastein landed with an army from France and, with a strong contingent of Vikings who had not taken to the pastoral life in the Danelaw, made a new assault on Wessex. Once again it says so much for Alfred that he was able to contain this new attack, for the Vikings now operated in terms of armies, not raiding parties, and they tested and probed the King's defences with subtlety as well as courage. Starved out of Chester by Alfred's burning of the surrounding countryside, the Danes moved into Wales. From there they made the long journey to Essex, eventually pulling their ships up the Thames and then (avoiding London, which had become Alfred's territory in 886) up the Lea. But the English would not let them rest. Alfred blockaded the river and the Vikings were forced to move on, leaving behind ships and the fort they had built.

Eventually, after Alfred had won a modest naval victory in the Channel in 896, the Viking host dispersed. The *Anglo-Saxon Chronicle* records that some went to 'East Anglia, some to Northumbria and those without stock got themselves ships and sailed south oversea to the Seine'. That reference to 'stock' is significant. It refers, of course, to land holding. The Danelaw Treaty had given validity to land won by conquest and more and more of the Norsemen were making settled livings by farming and trading from coastal ports. They displayed expertise at both endeavours, being more alert and decisive than their Saxon neighbours. As events had shown, the old blood-lust was still never far from the surface and a call to arms and oars could still raise recruits from the settled territories. The English had not seen the end of longship invasions by any means, but, by the end of the 9th century, serious settlement had begun.

The Norwegians in Ireland and in the Celtic fringes of Britain were beginning to integrate, too. Ireland, in particular, had not settled passively under the Nordic yoke. But, by the mid 10th century, the Irish were beginning to tolerate the presence of the Vikings in their midst – not least because of their skill as traders. Dublin remained the strongest Norse settlement, developing into a great port, shipbuilding and manufacturing centre. In fact, the Norwegian (the Danes were very much in the minority) influence centred on the trading towns they had created, usually on the coast, while the Irish remained in inland, rural areas. Formal confrontation ended with Brian Boru's much lauded victory at Clontarf in 1014. In fact, this was not a clear-cut Nordic-Irish confrontation and, indeed, the defeated King Sigtrygg Silkenbeard continued to reign on in Dublin for another 20 years until his death. The Norwegians – outward-looking from their coastal communities – were now being baptised into Christianity and gradually integrating with the more insular Irish, leading them to trade from the Viking ports.

Events in Norway were contributing, in a convoluted way, to the Viking colonisation process. King Harald Fairhair began his long reign in the late 9th century and set about unifying his country, already so deeply fragmented geographically by fiord and mountain. He encouraged the settlement of Iceland and was strong enough at home to enforce laws based on long tradition. So it was that, for making a *strandhogg* or land raid in Norway itself, he banished from the country one Hrolf, son, it is said, of one of his best friends.

The offender was a huge Viking called 'the Ganger' (walker). Because no steed could bear him, he walked everywhere. Hrolf raided in the Hebrides and Scotland, where he acquired a Scottish Christian wife, and arrived in France at the beginning of the 10th century. His leadership qualities were such that he collected around him a small army of Norwegians and Danes – the latter probably refugees from the English Danelaw, anxious to live by the sword rather than the plough – and set about plundering the broad valley of the Seine in a part of north-west France named after the old Roman province of Neustria. It was a rich sector, full of orchards and lush meadows. Hrolf and his men liked what they saw and decided to stay.

By 911 the French king, Charles the Simple, grandson of the Bald who had attempted to buy off the Vikings, was in turn forced to parley with his country's old enemies. Hrolf – he had by now become Rollo – was firmly in possession of Neustria but was raiding voraciously up the Seine. So Charles made a virtue of necessity and formally ceded to him the country the Viking had already occupied and made him Count of Rouen. Later that title was to become Duke of Normandy and the Vikings' holdings to expand to the full size of the region we know today. In return, Rolf promised to stop raiding into Charles's realm, to swear fealty to the King and become a Christian. In effect, Charles was establishing a buffer state to deal with any further incursions from Vikings. Rollo, he reasoned, would be good at that.

This was one Franco-Viking treaty which held. Rollo was as good as his word. He was baptised and set about restoring the churches he and his warriors had sacked. He stopped his ventures up the Seine, cultivated the priests who made up the intelligentsia of his land and gained their help in establishing a disciplined state. At a time when most countries – Alfred's Wessex had been a notable exception – were like the France of King Charles, uneasy coalitions, with warring nobles bearing little allegiance to a central ruler, Rollo created the model medieval fiefdom. The basis was a strict hierarchical structure, with Rollo firmly at the top and lieutenant-nobles arrayed beneath him, giving loyalty in return for the land they held. As payment for protection against invasion, they also gave a percentage of their land's yield at harvest-time and supplied warriors when needed. Laws were made, policed and, on the whole, adhered to. It was a system which produced inequality but it also created an ordered state in which it was possible to improve the quality of life.

Rollo, the definitive, swashbuckling, Viking pirate, had converted from poacher to gamekeeper with a vengeance. He stoutly defended his shores from Viking incursions and he lent men-at-arms to Charles to help the king in his unremitting quarrels with his nobles. The Vikings of Normandy, perhaps more quickly than any of their fellows, quickly put down roots. In the space of a few generations they had even lost their old language and now spoke only French. Rollo established a dynasty of male descendants who, unusually for the times, all inherited not only his courage and martial skills but also his administrative flair. By the time the sixth generation Duke, William of Normandy, had inherited in the middle of the 11th century, Normandy was one of the leading powers in Europe, strong enough, in 1066, to mount the last successful invasion of England.

Rollo died in his bed. It is said that he asked to be buried in Rouen Cathedral and ordered large sums of gold to be distributed to Christian churches in Normandy. It is also said, however, that the old ruffian made provision, in addition, for human sacrifices to be made to the pagan gods. Like much that has been written about the Vikings, this may well be apocryphal. Nevertheless it sums up nicely not only the sly 'belt-and-braces' attitude of provident rulers like Rollo, but also the great changes which their lives had spanned.

The overriding image which the Vikings have imprinted upon posterity is undoubtedly that of the warrior/seaman; skilled, brave and savage. Yet the administrative skills which Rollo displayed in Normandy reflected no ethnic abnormality. In parts of the Danelaw of England at the same time, the Vikings were establishing a different but equally fascinating social order, dovetailing the working of the *sokes* (parcels of land given to Danish ex-warriors to develop for themselves) with a toleration of the defeated, indigenous Saxons and a respect for their independence and need to earn their own livings. A written code for the year 997 in the Danelaw provided for twelve local citizens, called thanes, to judge impartially under oath offenders before the law. This is the first recorded evidence of the establishment of trial by jury.

In Iceland, the Vikings had a completely virgin canvas on which to paint, although Irish monks had partly settled islands off the main island during the Dark Ages.

In no other country was the cultured, home-making side of the Viking character so clearly and quickly displayed. On this green and sea-girt rock, the Mr Hyde element which was never far beneath the Dr Jekyll exterior, took over and built the first true republic in modern Europe. It is ironical that the colonisation should have been carried out under royal encouragement. Some records imply that the early settlers fled Norway to escape the tyranny of King Harald Fairhair. But the King knew only too well of the crowded conditions existing in the few scraps of productive land fringing the fiords stretching from what is now Alesund down to Stavanger. These provinces of south-west Norway were cut off by mountains and sea and voyaging to the west offered the only hope of expansion. It had bred many of the Viking raids half a century before; now it led to exploration and colonisation.

By the 870s whole families were equipping longships to 'sail down the sun'. Iceland, which hitherto had seen only a few Irish monks, became the first stepping-stone to the West. At first, the Norwegians grabbed all the land they could and within a few months most of it had been taken. Instead of reverting to what, knowing the Vikings' respect for the property of others, might be considered the obvious road of violence and land-taking, the settlers quickly and unanimously established rule of law.

By 930, they had set up the Althing, the oldest national assembly in Europe. It met in the open air for two weeks each summer at Thingvellir – a plain, bounded by cliffs of lava, to the east of modern Reykjavik. It was at the Althing that the settlers of Iceland created a judicial procedure and settled forensic matters. Here they declared their independence of Norway and, in 1000, decided to convert to Christianity.

For the next two and half centuries this Viking colony flourished as an independent Christian democracy – flourished, that is as well as severe winters, a harsh land and stormy seas allowed. The island became a jumping-off ground for further explorations and, equally importantly, it bred a remarkably literary output, amazing in its quality and quantity given the remoteness of the country. The Sagas of Iceland provide a feast of poetic and narrative entertainment. They also preserve, albeit in a hyperbolic and therefore distinctly unreliable way, the early history of Iceland and Scandinavia. The little community's independence was preserved until the Icelanders were forced to submit to King Hakon of Norway between 1262 and 1264. It remains to this day, however, a country in which the Viking story is most clearly preserved, not only in its literature and people but in its architecture, archaeology and etymology.

But it is to England, where the Viking Age began, that we must return to trace its close.

King Alfred did not see out the 9th century. His son Edward succeeded him in 899 and showed that he had inherited much of his father's ability. With his sister Aethelfaed and her husband Ethelred, Earl of Mercia, he not only kept the Danes at bay but was able to push them back, winning the towns of Derby and Leicester and making peace with the dangerous Norwegians of York. The latter posed the greatest threat, not least because of the constant aid they received from their cousins in Dublin and the motley tribes of the far north. War flared up in 937, but the Saxons, under Edward's successor, Athelstan, won a significant victory at Brananburh. This broke the Norse-Celtic alliance and prevented what might have been the permanent exclusion of Cumbria and Northumbria from Saxon England.

Alfred's legacy did not last. Through the late years of the 10th century, southern England once again became weak and vulnerable. In 978, a 12-year-old descendant of the great king ascended the throne. Ethelred was blighted by poor advisers and a personal inability to be decisive. 'The Unready' (probably meaning 'heedless' or 'loath to take advice') is the epithet he earned then and how he is remembered now. In great contrast, two leaders of note were at the same time securing their realms in Scandinavia: the Norwegian Olaf Tryggvason, descended from Harald Fairhair, and the Dane Svein Forkbeard. The vulnerability of England – now made quite rich by the thrift of its citizens and the wisdom of Alfred and his descendants – was apparent.

Olaf was the first to strike. For the people of England it must have been like a nightmare from the past. Once again the longships appeared off

Saxon shores and in the estuaries. In 991 the Norwegian brought a fleet of 93 ships and attacked Folkestone and Sandwich. Next he landed 50 miles from London, at Maldon, and crushed local opposition. London and the whole of south-eastern England lay at his mercy. Ethelred's reaction was to pay *Danegeld*; ten thousand pounds of silver bought him three years of peace.

In 994, predictably, Olaf was back, this time allied with Svein Fork-beard. Their threats produced 16,000 pounds of silver and they returned to Scandinavia. Five years later Forkbeard sailed again for England with national conquest in mind. Ethelred, at last, made a feeble attempt to fight but his indecision prevented combat and, once again, *Danegeld* was paid. Svein departed but returned with the cuckoos and so it went on. In 1001 he levied 24,000 pounds of silver from the English king; in 1009 Svein com-prehensively defeated an English fleet off Sandwich; and he landed to loot comprehensively the whole of Ethelred's kingdom. In 1010, the Norwe-gians rejoined the sport and sailed up the Thames to tear down London Bridge with grappling hooks, so inspiring the 'London Bridge is Falling Down' chant of school-children for the next thousand years.

The Danelaw, though vulnerable because of its lack of leadership, had so far lain outside these attacks. Then in 1013 Svein sailed up the Humber and made a Danish call to arms. His army enhanced, he turned south and, quickly, Oxford, Winchester, Bath and London fell. Ethelred fled to Nor-mandy and Svein installed himself king of all England – only to die five weeks later. His son, Cnut, although only 18, was a true Viking. He imme-diately left Denmark to claim his inheritance, crushed what little opposi-tion Ethelred's son, Edmund, was able to raise and crowned himself as the first king of a united England.

This chip off the old Viking block also levied the highest *Danegeld* ever recorded: 82,000 pounds of silver from throughout the realm – 10,000 pounds from London alone. The difference now, however, was that Cnut (or Canute, as he became known, as 'an English king') did not hurry back north with the loot. He used it to pay off his army, many of whom settled in England. Canute became king in reality as well as name. He submitted to baptism, restored monasteries and, in a written code of law, established the Church as the faith of the land and required the population to support it with silver and crops.

Canute lived to be respected as a good monarch, giving England its first peace in a quarter of a century. He refuted personal flattery – famously sitting in his chair at the water's edge to prove to his sycophantic courtiers that he could not control the tides – and introduced a recorded taxation system. Alas, his death in 1035 ushered in a period of quarrels over the succession which left a pious, diffident son of the Saxon Ethelred, Edward the Confessor, to take the throne. Edward, saint-like and revered in his day, overdid the piety and refused to sleep with his wife. The resultant lack of issue produced yet another scramble for the crown which was settled, on a hill in Hastings in 1066, when that descendant of a true Viking, William of Normandy, took it firmly. He established a royal dynasty which, tenuously, has survived to this day.

The Viking Age was over. It tried to splutter into life again in 1069, when a Danish fleet once again sailed up the Humber in an attempt to support rebels against William, and in 1085, when a Danish king planned a formal invasion of England. But these came to nothing against the entrenched power of the Normans. Scandinavia reverted to being a trio of nations tucked away in Arctic semi-darkness on the roof of the world, busy with their own problems. The Vikings had sailed, fought, shocked and colonised for 300 years. Now they virtually disappeared from the world stage.

It had been a remarkable era, fashioned by men of stature whose character and way of life deserve closer examination.

THE VIKING AND HIS ENVIRONMENT

The Viking who looks out at us across the centuries – with the help of Hollywood, elegiac Victorian paintings and, much more reliably, ancient carvings, etchings and grave remains – is unquestionably formidable. He is tall for his time, about 5 foot 8 inches, and bearded. Satisfyingly justifying the legend, his hair is fair and his eyes are blue. They stare out from a face that has been seamed by hundreds of hours peering into salt spray.

One thing is missing: no horned helmet. He will only wear that, if at all, on ceremonial occasions. The helmet he is wearing now is conical and made of tough leather, designed to protect him from anything but a direct axe or sword blow. He wears simple, warm garments: a woollen shirt and breeches, with calf or goatskin shoes, laced round the ankle. In winter, he will be shrouded in furs, but now he wears a small cloak fastened with a distinctive penannular ring brooch, and gathered at his right shoulder to keep his sword arm free.

That sword is no toy. He calls it *Fotbitr*, Leg Biter. Two-edged and made of iron, it has been forged by the best French smiths and slipped out from France, despite the embargo on arms exports first imposed by Charlemagne to stop the arming of these barbaric Norsemen. He also possesses a *skeggox* or 'beardaxe', a fearsome double-bladed weapon which only the Vikings now use. And, for defence, a wooden shield with a round iron boss.

His wide shoulders and splayed legs bespeak a life spent out-of-doors and at sea. The general air of well-being also suggests a reasonably balanced, protein-filled diet. In fact, our man's daily food relies heavily on rye bread, oats and barley porridge, fish, boiled meat (particularly mutton) and plenty of wild fruit. He drinks sweet fermented mead, made with honey, although recently he has taken a fancy to the wines which he has tasted on his rovings to the south. He knows all about using ice and salt to preserve food on his long sea journeys and about drying fish and meat for the same purpose. Despite his outdoor life-style and good diet, his life expectancy is no more than about 40 years – disease, the perils of the sea and the dangers of his calling will see to that.

His name? Well, as this narrative has already demonstrated, the Viking names that have come down to us are mainly those of kings and chiefs: marvellously evocative, like Svein Forkbeard, Eirik Bloodaxe and Magnus Barelegs. But this story is not about kings. Our man must be a composite, representative figure of the Vikings who followed the kings and did the work, so we will call him Eirik – a name which, anyway, figures with distinction throughout the Viking sagas.

Eirik comes from Hedeby, then in Denmark, now – just – in Germany. About 1100 years ago, this was the leading metropolis of the Viking world, straddling the northern trade routes and, behind its ramparts, reasonably immune from attack. All that is left of those ramparts now is a semi-circular mound of earth round a patchwork quilt of fields facing the sea. Even today, however, these remains rise in places to 30 feet (9 metres) and they enclose an area of 60 acres. In the late 10th century, when they were built, they enclosed a bustling, near impregnable fortress; not so much a Viking 'nest', much more a permanent base.

Visiting Hedeby in the 10th century, Ibrahim ibn Ahmed Al-Tartushi, a merchant from the dazzling white domes of Moorish Cordoba, described it as a filthy place, smelling of fish. But, he said, it was 'a large town, at the very end of the world ocean'. In fact, Hedeby was built at the base of Jutland, facing east into Hedeby Nor, the inlet that provided both a sheltered harbour and access to the Schlei fiord and so to the Baltic Sea. The rampart was linked to the *Danevirk*, the system of great earthworks which ran east to west across the Danish isthmus, protecting the Danish border from incursions from the Germans and Frisians.

Hedeby owed its success as a market town and great port to its position. It had control over the most important trade routes from Western Europe to the Baltic. The *Haevej*, the northern end of the north-south continental land routes, passed through the *Danevirk* near Hedeby. Equally importantly, the short road across Denmark, at the base of the Jutland peninsular, used to avoid the long and dangerous sail around the Skaw, the northern point of Jutland, ended at Hedeby, which was used to ship goods further east, to the Baltic states and beyond. The town was also the source of a thriving import trade, receiving iron ore from Sweden.

Eirik lives in the centre of the town, beside a plank-sided stream which meanders down to the sea. This is of no great benefit for the ground around it is waterlogged, but it has preserved original house-timbers and helped archaeologists in the 1930s and 1960s to build a picture of the town. Eirik's house is timber-framed, with panels of wattle daubed with clay and dung to make them waterproof. The roof is of thatch, with a hole at the top to allow cooking smoke to escape. Set back from the slat-boarded path, the dwelling is rectangular in shape and, as befits a successful warrior, it is a fair size: about 50 by 20 feet. Sanitation is just a hole in the ground and Eirik's wife washes his clothes in cow urine – not an altogether daft idea, since it contains ammonia.

His wife and the sexual act are important to Eirik. He has three sons and four daughters and such potency is respected. Like most of his fellows he also has concubines and mistresses. The Danes are much less ambivalent about these matters than the Swedes to the north. (In his book *The Vikings,* Michael Hasloch Kirby quotes this list of 'touching fines' from the Gotland law of Sweden:

Touching a woman's wrist or ankle 4 ounces of silver
Touching elbow, or between knee and calf   2⅔ ounces
Touching a breast 1 ounce
Holding a shoulder or just above the knee 1⅔ ounces

Conventional morality is of no concern to Eirik but religion is beginning to bother him a little. Of course, all his life he has believed in Odin, the undisputed, principal deity in Norse mythology, and in the more down-to-earth and understandable god Thor. The new religion of Christianity, however, is creeping into favour and Eirik has had its tenets explained to him by a priest in Mercia. They don't seem so far removed from his present understanding of things – that evil one day will be vanquished and only the good deities reborn. In fact, when he dies, Eirik will receive a Christian burial but he will go to his grave still happily believing in Odin, Thor, Frey, *et al.*

All in all, Eirik has done well in life. He has been raiding for fifteen years now and has eighteen slaves, acquired from his expeditions. Much of his wealth, of course, comes from his share of booty and *Danegeld*, but he has also traded shrewdly in amber and has a small farm and a herring fish-ery, worked by his slaves. He is quite proud of the fact that seven of his older slaves have worked hard enough and been sufficiently thrifty to have earned their freedom. He gives his present slaves small patches of land of their own to cultivate and time during the day to do so.

In one way, Eirik is not quite typical. He is a Norwegian, born and brought up in Hordaland, a province of south-west Norway with a long tra-dition of Viking piracy. This helps to explain his fair complexion (the Irish used to define their Norwegian oppressors as the 'whites' and the Danes as the 'blacks'). He fell in with a Danish raiding-party years ago and married a Danish girl, with whom he now lives in Hedeby. His origin also helps to answer one of the great questions of the Viking Age: why did they do it? Why did these Norsemen suddenly descend on neighbouring – and not so neigh-bouring – countries and put them to the sword? What triggered it all off?

There are several answers and one of them lies with Eirik's place of birth. Norway is a land bisected laterally by deep fiords and high moun-tains. Then, as now, there were few rolling acres and any land that was cul-tivable bordered the fiords in narrow parcels. To a lesser extent, the same shortage of farm land pertained in Sweden, and much of Denmark was marshy and unproductive. As populations grew so did the pressure on the younger generations. There was no land to farm, so, like Eirik, they went a-Viking.

There was plenty of opportunity. The Vikings had always been shrewd and adventurous traders. For years they had been exchanging their furs, walrus ivory and amber for the gold, silver and other luxuries of the rich cities of the south. They saw for themselves the wealth of other lands. The Arabs, in particular, always wanted slaves. Piracy provided them – and gold and silver, too.

Banishment also helped to create the exodus. The Vikings may have been good farmers and lyrical poets. They were also uncommonly partial to a good fight – and the kind of family feuding which makes the modern Mafia resemble a charity commission. Without some kind of discipline, their society would have torn itself apart. So a code was created which ruled that, unless it was a duel or fair fight, 'man-slaying' was a crime, usually punishable by banishment. Other transgressions could also lead to being outlawed – as with Rollo. Banishment fuelled the departures, and often the outlawed ones – restless, violent, unwilling to conform – proved the best leaders in the brutal trade of piracy.

In the view of many historians, however, the most plausible reason for the Viking explosion is found in the development of their unique and elegant ships. The Scandinavians, with their comparatively poor farm land and long coastlines, had always been fine sailors. No one is quite sure when they converted their smallish, canoe-shaped rowing boats into ocean-going ships by adding a mast and a sail, slung from a single yard. But it did the trick. It provided the key which allowed longer voyages and unlocked the Pandora's Box of the Vikings.

The longship was as integral to the success of the Vikings as was the longbow to the English archers at Agincourt or the rifle to the American skirmishers at Saratoga. As well as a beautiful artefact in its own right, it was a flexible and swift means of travel, and it became, in effect, the Vikings' key weapon.

THE LONGSHIP

The knowledge which the world today has of the Vikings has been built over the years mainly from study of the Sagas, other contemporary writings, the fragments of carvings, runic symbols, tapestry and graffiti which survive, and from excavations on land and recovery from the sea. Discoveries over the last 120 years of buried and sunken longships have yielded what is probably by far the most reliable insight into the Viking Age and has enabled archaeological historians to understand how this important feature of Nordic life was built and sailed.

Many tourists will have seen the two Viking longships which ride in magnificent, suspended display in white, sepulchral rooms at the Viking Ship Museum at Bygdoy, just outside Oslo. They have been painstakingly reconstructed from remains found respectively at Gokstad in 1889 and at Oseberg – both in Norway – in 1904. A third, from Tune, is not so well preserved. We owe their existence to the Viking custom of burying prominent men and women (the Oseberg ship was a burial chamber of a royal lady) in their ships, complete with provisions for their journey to Valhalla.

The longships on display at Bygdoy are stunning in their elegance. Beautifully proportioned, with sweeping, clinker-laid planks rising to high prow and stern, the Oseberg ship in particular has superb carvings on bow and stern. These two 9th-century longships, however, were probably never meant to sail long distances or fight. They were special occasion vessels; rather like royal yachts. Of equal importance are the five 10th/11th-century longships excavated in 1962 from the bottom of Roskilde fiord, where they had been deliberately sunk as block ships to protect the Danish royal town of Roskilde from attack. One of them, *Skuldelev 2*, has recently been shown by dendrochronology to have been built in Dublin. These ships were all working and fighting vessels, unlike the Norwegian longships, and all of them, in partially reconstructed form, are now on display at Roskilde.

There have been other finds, but these Norwegian and Danish examples have provided the basis for the work of scholars in recent times who have made extrapolated assumptions from them and made replicas and carried out sailing trials. To them the present author is indebted for much of the information in this section; in particular to Professor Sean McGrail, formerly Professor of Maritime Archaeology at Oxford University, whose definitive section on 'Ships, Shipwrights and Seamen' in James Graham-Campbell's comprehensive book *The Viking World*, itself draws on the original research carried out in Norway by Arne Emil Christensen, of the Viking Ship Museum in Oslo, and, in Denmark, by Ole Crumlin-Pedersen, of the Institute of Marine Archaeology at Roskilde.

Detailed examination of the ships, and trials of replicas, have answered some of the basic questions of how the Vikings' vessels retained their dual-purpose capacity – the ability to transport men and goods safely across the most stormbound seas in the world, and yet also to slip quietly up rivers, some of them comparatively shallow in places, to attack inland towns.

The fundamental shape and simple method of construction gives the key to the vessels' resilience and versatility. The master builders who designed them have left no plans; they worked the natural material by hand and eye to ensure that each ship 'rode with the sea'. In other words, the timbers would work and groan, probably leaking quite a bit, but remaining reactive to, not fighting, the pressures placed upon them. The ship would flex in a heavy swell like a young sapling.

The equal-ended bow and stern, topped by high posts, had the effect both of splitting head seas and parting following winds and waves to reduce the risk of pooping. The light draft – usually no more than three to four feet, even in the longer vessels – enabled the ship to navigate coastal waters and estuaries. The thinness of the planking bestowed a lightness that enabled the smaller vessels to be manhandled overland when necessary. Yet the keel was heavy and T-shaped in cross-section. While not too deep, it stretched from prow to stern to give directional stability and was deep enough to prevent sideways drift.

Oak was the preferred timber, particularly for the keel, although ash, beech, alder, birch, lime and willow were also used for specific purposes. The carefully selected oak logs were split radially, more and more thinly – like slicing a cake – and the wedge shape was ideal for the planks of the clinker-built hull. It has been estimated that between 1,765 and 2,050 cubic feet (50–80 cubic metres) of oak was necessary to build a 65–80 foot (20–25 metres) longship – equivalent to about twelve mature trees. Key sections were made of either straight timber (keels, masts, yards, etc.) or naturally curved wood (stems, some keels, ribs and knees).

In the southern Baltic the planks or strakes were fastened together with wooden pegs and the overlaps made watertight with moss. In the west, iron nails and animal hair were used. The mast (which was never very tall) stood in a 'mast step', a mortise in the keelson. In early ships further support came from the 'mastfish', a massive central timber, replaced in later vessels by a crossbeam.

In warships, the masts would be unstepped for battle and ease of rowing. One rectangular sail, slung to swivel from a heavy yard, was carried. The combination of sail, rigging and hull was so unlike anything seen before that it was almost certainly developed in Scandinavian waters. Because the mast was stubby, the sail was cut in a wide rectangle to compensate, although in later vessels the shape became more conventionally square. It was woven from a coarse wool in a double layer to provide strength and was usually dyed red, sometimes patterned in squares or diamonds to give individuality to the ships and to shout their ownership to the world. It could become extremely heavy and hard to work when wet, but it generated great power.

Hard evidence about the rigging systems used is poor, but from examination of extant coins, seals and graffiti it is clear that the standard rigging was very simple, with a forestay to the bow, shrouds fastened to the top strakes or thwarts and a backstay that probably doubled as a halyard to hoist the yard and sail. The running rigging to hoist and lower the sail and to control the head and foot of the sail was almost certainly similarly straightforward.

In the merchant ships, sails were the main means of propulsion and oarports were only fitted forward for rowing to manoeuvre in harbour. The warships, however, were fitted for oars along their full length and the oarsmen – sometimes two to an oar – sat on sea chests in the early ships, graduating to thwarts later. The warships used their sail on passage, but in battle, or when approaching shore, the sail was lowered and the oars employed. Trials have revealed that high speeds could have been reached over short distances; sometimes in excess of nine knots.

The vessel was steered with a distinctive side rudder, looking rather like a broad oar and fastened at the right stern quarter with a leather thong so that it could be swung upward when beaching. The Norse word for steering board was *stjornbordi* so the rudder has ever since lent its name to the starboard, or right side of a boat. The blade of the rudder was carefully shaped to give it a cross-section similar to that of an aircraft's wing, so that the sideways thrust generated on the rudder blade by the water could be subtly varied and thus turn the vessel.

The ship, whether trader or warship, was always open decked, although there would be a central cargo section in the former and both ships had raised decks at the stern for the steersman and forward for the lookout. But the crew had no covered accommodation. The dimensions of the ships and their complements varied, of course. It is said that the fleet flagships, the great *drakar* or dragon ships, measured some 160 feet in length, with a beam of 25 feet. But no remains have been found. The average, larger warship was probably between 70 and 100 feet long and 15 feet in beam. She would have carried some 100 men and shipped about 50 oars on an invasion, but only 50 or 60 on a Commando-style raid.

So much for the fundamentals. What remains unanswered is how did these vessels perform, how were they navigated across vast distances and what was life like on board?

The Viking shipbuilders are known to have used a length/breadth ratio of approximately 4:1 for the wider, more capacious merchants ships, but 7:1 for the sleeker warships. The consequent deeper keel and the characteristic steepness of the lower strakes in the latter would have given them a good capacity to sail to windward. This would have been helped by the simple rig, the stability offered by the short mast and the use of a tacking boom to hold the leading edge of the sail taut. From reasoned supposition and on the evidence of trials of replicas it is felt that the better-handled ships could have sailed to within 75 degrees of the wind, making two knots or more to windward.

In 1893, a Norwegian replica of the Gokstad ship sailed from Bergen to Newfoundland in 28 days. Her skipper, Captain Magnus Andersen, was impressed by the vessel's handling at sea, even in bad weather. She responded well to the side rudder, which he found easy to operate, and she proved reasonably watertight. Recent trials of replicas of the Roskilde ships, using more authentic sails, proved that the Viking design produced seaworthy ships which could maintain good sailing speeds (up to 9.2 knots in good conditions and two knots at about 75 degrees into the wind).

Having said that, conditions aboard a longship must have been crude in the extreme. Even though the ocean-going ships had a good freeboard, both to give advantage in combat and some protection from the sea, there were precious few places to shelter from freezing spray and wind. In heavy seas, those not on watch would simply crouch on the slender deck bottom,

between the thwarts, wrap their cloaks around them and think of landfall
... and Odin. Some of them may have had the comparative luxury of two-
man skin sleeping-bags.

There were no passengers; every man was both a seaman and a soldier
and he had to be ready at all times to work the ship and to fight. Provisions
on long voyages were basic. Food was mainly dried, pickled, salted or possibly smoked fish and meat, with unleavened bread. For drink there was
water in skin bags and beer or sour milk in tubs. Some of these provisions
and other essential cargo may have been carried under the half decks.
Often, on tough passages, they would have been lost. Going to sea in the
Viking Age was not for the faint hearted.

And this raises one of the most important points about the performance of the longships. The Scandinavians were undoubtedly some of the
best seamen the world has ever known (they still are). From birth they had
lived by the sea and on it. They knew instinctively how their ships would
behave and they handled them with sensitivity and great skill. In other,
less practised hands, these high performance craft would almost certainly
have handled less well.

How the Vikings navigated their craft on long passages has concerned scholars for centuries. First, it must be said that, whenever they
could, the Norsemen limited their ocean voyages to the summer months,
when the skies were clearer and the seas calmer (hence the early respite
that the monasteries received in winter months). They knew about the
Pole Star and that its angular attitude changes as the ship moves north or
south. It is possible that they made a rough and ready measurement of the
height of a star above the horizon by using the outstretched hand: a finger's breadth is, say two degrees; a wrist's span eight degrees; extended fingers eighteen degrees and so on. There are indications in the Sagas that the
seamen used a form of latitude sailing, based on the known latitude of the
home port and striving to maintain a constant latitude as indicated by the
altitude of the Pole Star.

When skies were overcast, there were other indications for the experienced sailor. The flight line of migrating birds would show them the
direction of land. The angle to a steady swell from a known direction could
have been used, as could the relative direction of a prevailing wind: warm,
wet winds from the south-west, cold wet winds from the north-east. The
Vikings had no refined compass or accurate timepiece, but some authorities believe that they had discovered the sun-seeking property of double
refracting cordieritiolite or Icelandic crystals. In addition, the finding in
Greenland of fragments of marked wood and stone has provided circum-

stantial evidence, at least, that the Vikings did use bearing dials, using the sun's shadow to act as primitive compass cards for latitudinal guidance.

What is certain is that Eirik and his brothers were not dismayed to see a safe coastline drop astern of them and to head into the open sea. They were resourceful and inventive navigators, as unafraid to head into uncharted oceans as they were to beach on an unknown land and attempt to take it by force.

INTO BATTLE

In battle, the Vikings were not sophisticated strategists. They relied more on surprise and the ferocity of a frontal attack than on feints, ambuscades, investments and the other ploys in the medieval militarist's limited armoury. They were, however, shrewd as well as utterly fearless and they fought to their strengths, which were, of course, those of good marines: the ability to use the sea to strike unexpectedly, to debouch on to an enemy shore with speed and efficiency, and then to fan out inland and take objectives before the enemy had time to bring up support troops.

Later, when invasion rather than raiding became the objective, the Vikings adapted their marine outlook admirably to land battles. They used horses to give them mobility and they were among the first of the military powers emerging from the Dark Ages to recognise the power of archers. But even when engaged in manoeuvring masses of forces on land, they remained true marines; they never liked to be too far from a river or a beach where the longships would be waiting, to be used either in attack or defence.

European history is studded with Viking land battles, but there are few records of sea encounters between the Norsemen and nations outside Scandinavia. The few which exist – notably the confrontations with Alfred's embryonic English navy and clashes with the Moors in the Mediterranean – often show the Vikings coming off second best. But as often as the Vikings set upon alien peoples, they fought at home among themselves. These wars usually involved sea battles – probably the first real engagements ever witnessed in northern waters.

In 885, the great Harald Fairhair, one Saga records, secured his Norwegian crown by confronting a fleet mustered by seven rebellious noblemen at Harsfiord in south-western Norway and defeating them comprehensively. But what was probably the greatest sea battle in Viking history took place comparatively late in their day, in 1062, when Norway's Harald Hardrada (he who lost his life at Stamford Bridge in a vain attempt to invade England on the eve of Hastings in 1066) fought Denmark's King Svein Estridsson.

The battle took place at the Nissa, a river in western Sweden, and the Danish king seemed to have the advantage. His ships numbered 300 as against the 150 commanded by Harald. But the Norwegians won. The battle lasted throughout the night and the Saga records that 'more than 70 of Svein's ships were left behind'. The Sagas were written usually some 200 or more years after the event and, like Shakespeare's accounts of England's royal politics, must be treated warily as historical sources. But they are consistent enough to reveal how the Vikings fought afloat.

It is strange that such good seamen eschewed maritime skills on these occasions. Vikings usually fought in placid coastal waters or fiords, so that the sea should not interfere with a good scrap. Manoeuvrability and flexibility – the very attributes which so distinguished the Vikings in land battles – were deliberately negated. The defenders improvised floating raft forts by lashing their ships gunwale to gunwale, with the largest in the centre and leaving only a few smaller craft to ferry troops around the periphery or carry off wounded. The attackers would then assault the fortress, preceding the attack by an arrow storm. Sometimes ships were deliberately rammed. When the vessels were locked in combat, the king or ranking nobleman directed the battle from the stern of his flagship, surrounded by a protective wall of armed shieldsmen. With spears, swords and axes and even large stones, the Vikings would hack away until one side won. Quarter was rarely extended and even more rarely sought.

On land, the battle plan was simple: to attack frontally with great ferocity. If they were cornered, the Vikings would form a ring and with their massed battle axes swinging over their 'linden wall' of shields, they would hack a way back to their ships. Most attacking forces contained wild men called *berserkir*, or 'bear shirts'. They were usually big men who disdained the wearing of armour and who worked themselves up into a frenzy before a battle – whether by self-hypnosis or the taking of a primitive drug is not known – and hurled themselves into the fray. Usually they wielded the largest axes and with them virtually ran amok. English speakers still refer to wild behaviour as 'going berserk'.

On land the Vikings were certainly capable of conducting campaigns demanding resolution and a commitment far removed from their hit and run image. They laid siege to Paris for nearly a year in 885, showing tenacity and a knowledge of investment techniques. They would probably have taken the city if Charles had not arrived to buy them off. They could fight shrewdly on the defensive, too: witness their wriggling off Alfred's hook in their long marches around southern England in the 890s.

But it was their speed of strike, their courage and, above all their sheer audacity which shines down the years. When Olaf Tryggvason led the renewed attacks on England in 991, his messenger told the Saxons: 'Bold seamen have sent me to you and have told me to say that you must send treasure quickly in return for peace, and it will be better for you all to buy off an attack with treasure, rather than face men as fierce as us in battle. We need not destroy each other, if you are rich enough. In return for the gold we are ready to make truce with you.' They got their gold. The rich Saxons paid. Banditry, of course. But what cool, audacious, splendid cheek!

THE WAY WEST

As fighting men, the Vikings must rank a place in any military pantheon. Singling out their greatest achievement to demonstrate their skills, however, poses problems. No definitive pitched battle or even campaign springs to mind, although the 859 expedition of Bjorn and Hastein to the Mediterranean must stand out as a great and sustained marauding coup, outclassing in result and variety of military techniques used the epic voyage of de la Perière in *U35* in the First World War.

But we are short on detail of that expedition's sea and land battles, the attacks on North Africa and the excursion to Navarre – the minutiae that set the blood tingling and the imagination racing. So we must turn away from the bloodied beaches and battlefields to re-capture an achievement that sheds light on the more peaceful, explorative aspect of the Norsemen's complex character; an aspect that was quite as important as their martial skills in fashioning the mark they left on history.

Towards the end of the 10th century, the little independent Norwegian colony on Iceland received a new immigrant. He was not entirely welcome because he was in disgrace. Red of hair, beard and temperament, Eirik Thorvaldsson Raudi had been banished from his small village in Norway for man-slaying. The Icelanders had a liberal tradition, so they took in the big man and his family, probably carefully explaining the Icelandic code of behaviour to him as a precaution. If they did, it was to no avail because Eirik transgressed again and, once more, was banished, this time for three years.

Now he had no obvious place to go. He could join one of the marauding bands which were always sailing south, of course, but where was he to leave his family? He decided to take a risk. Eirik had heard of a great land to the west that had been sighted 60 years before by a seaman blown off course. A man named Snaebjorn, seeking to escape retribution for murder,

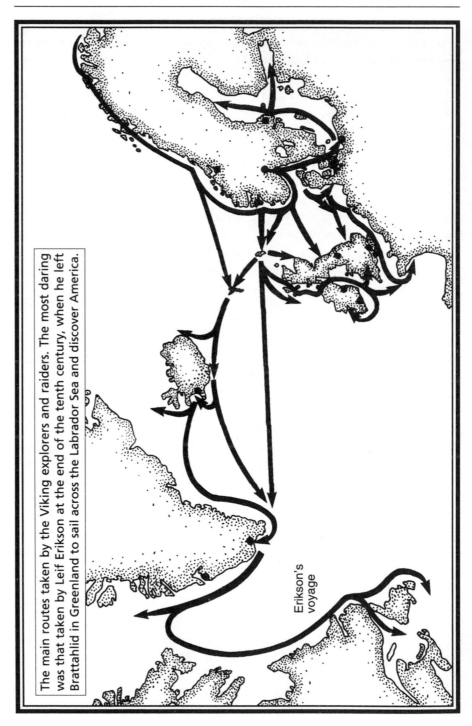

The main routes taken by the Viking explorers and raiders. The most daring was that taken by Leif Erikson at the end of the tenth century, when he left Brattahlid in Greenland to sail across the Labrador Sea and discover America.

Erikson's voyage

had later tried to colonise it but had died in the attempt. It was empty, somewhere in the west and it beckoned Eirik the Red. In 982, at about 32 years of age, he loaded his ship and set off.

He sailed due west, moving steadily with the prevailing easterly breezes of early summer, sighting the sun by day and Polaris by night. After logging about 450 miles he made the coast of Greenland – and frightening it was. Immense ice cliffs towered above the small ship and, beyond, the tips of mountains could be seen touching the clouds. Hesitantly, Eirik and his crew probed this savage coastline, sailing south and then west and then north again as they rounded Cape Farewell. Eventually, they came to a succession of fiords which reminded them of home in Norway. The waters teemed with fish, and grassy slopes carried a profusion of wild flowers: harebell, buttercups and pink wild thyme. At the head of one of these great inlets, Eirik made his home, calling it, of course, Eiriksfiord.

Resolved to found a colony, Eirik now displayed a cunning which surely makes him the first of the world's travel agents. He knew that Iceland was becoming over-crowded, but that men would only come to the new land if it had an attractive sound. So, although the winters were hard and he could hear what sounded like constant cannon-fire in summer as huge icebergs broke from glaciers that slid down to the sea, he called it Greenland and sailed back to Iceland for colonists.

In doing so he launched a series of epic voyages which, for courage and seamanship, have rarely been equalled. For more than a hundred years, colonists braved the Arctic seas to sail to Greenland the Good in response to Eirik's siren call. From a beach at Snaefellsnes, on the west of Iceland, broad-beamed *knarrs*, merchantmen – very similar to one of the craft raised from the harbour at Roskilde – would embark for the perilous voyage. They could take about 30 families with animals, household gear and frequently a cargo of timber as well – for Greenland, although it had pasture, grew nothing more substantial than scrub birch.

The voyage could take four days, if they were lucky. But it was often likely to last for two weeks – or for ever. Many ships simply disappeared. In the summer of 985 alone, one little fleet of 25 ships lost eleven of its number. The voyagers usually sailed only in the summer months but, even so, they had to pass through the lower reaches of the Arctic storm centre. Bailing was constant and sometimes desperate during squalls.

Enough of them made it to set up three small colonies on Greenland's south and west coasts. They endured for about 500 years, eventually being wiped out in about 1500. But while they were there they provided the springboard for the greatest single voyage of the Viking Age.

Brawling Eirik settled down at Eiriksfiord to become the respected leader of the colonists. His wife became a Christian, although Eirik steadfastly refused to desert Odin, and they raised fine sons, including one, Leif the Lucky, who regularly sailed the long and hazardous trading route from Greenland to Iceland, Scotland, Norway and back again. The stones of their homestead can still be seen at Eiriksfiord. From there, the old man and his son looked towards the setting sun. Some years before a trader had been blown far off course. At last he had fought his way back eastward to report sighting a long, low, wooded land. It was enough for Eirik. He and his son decided to find it. The Saga relates that, on the eve of sailing, Eirik fell and broke a leg. So Leif Eirikson, Leif the Lucky, sailed to the west without his father.

It was just about the start of the new millennium – as good a time as any to make such a voyage. Leif had no map, only the memory of the trader from 15 years before. With his crew of 35, he sailed due west until he came upon a dismal, glacier-topped rock pile which he called Hulluland, or Flatland. It is now known as Baffin Island, and is part of Canada.

He then turned south and eventually put ashore on a broad white beach, fringed by lines of tall trees, thick and sturdy enough to make a timber-starved Greenlander's heart sing. Leif named it Markland, Land of Forests. It was the coast of Labrador. But still they sailed south. After about two days, they landed on what is now Belle Island, off Newfoundland, and wintered on the main island a little farther south.

The source of most of this story lies in the Viking Sagas, those potent Nordic mixtures of myth and fable, fact and half-truth. What follows next in the Saga made historians doubt the story for years. Not only, it related, did Leif find an equable climate, with equal days and nights, no frost in winter and grass hardly withered – not only that, but he found grapes growing wild. Accordingly, he named this Vinland, or Wineland.

Newfoundland today, although much more benign than Greenland, is not the sort of country to offer wild vineyards. So was Leif's voyage just another fable? Another tall story from the tallest of tale tellers? Two facts now clearly prove that it was not. Most of us today believe that our Northern Hemisphere climate used to be much, much colder years ago: Englishmen cite examples of fairs being held on a frozen Thames, and so on. That is true of the years after about 1200, when the entire North Atlantic area entered what has been called the Little Ice Age. But a thousand years ago, it was warmer, the summer ice pack staying much farther north.

This does not explain the grapes, but it does explain the absence of frost in Leif's new land and the temperate nature of the climate. And perhaps the grapes were really gooseberries or cranberries, both of which grow in the north and can be used in wine-making.

The second point, however, is much more conclusive. After wintering in North America, Leif sailed home to run the family farm after his father's death. His brother Thorvald then took up the quest and spent two winters in Vinland. Others followed and a determined attempt was made to establish a colony on the original site. It failed and for years archaeologists searched for evidence that it did exist. Eventually – only a few years ago – they found it.

It was appropriately two Norwegians, Helge Ingstad and his wife Anna, who made the breakthrough. They followed the Saga closely and identified a spot called L'Anse aux Meadows, in the Sacred Bay area at the northern tip of Newfoundland, as an area which almost exactly matched the topography described in the story. They dug and eventually found artefacts and traces which have been accepted as proof that a little Nordic colony was established there many centuries ago. The diggings revealed eight or nine house sites, a smithy, cooking pits and hearths. Despite extensive searches, nothing quite like them has been found anywhere else in North America. Among the pits were definitively Viking artefacts such as a bronze ring pin and a soapstone spindle whorl.

It is not known why the little colony collapsed. It was probably a combination of hostile Indians, the increase of ice on the long journeys to Greenland and Norway and a general decline in Nordic sea power. But it had certainly existed.

The Vikings, then, got there first. They couldn't settle, and Columbus, who made the trip farther south nearly 500 years later, rightly gets the credit for opening up the New Continent, although we really shouldn't call him the discoverer of America. Nevertheless, who is to say that echoes of the Eirikson family's epic voyages hadn't filtered down to Genoa 500 years later to turn Columbus's eyes westward?

It is diverting, at the least, to think that at roughly the same time that they were fighting, laying waste and then colonising half of northern Europe, a company of these marines found time to discover America.

THE LEGACY

It would have been a fitting memorial to the remarkable dominance exercised for three centuries by the three small nations of Scandinavia if the Vikings had succeeded in colonising America. That they did not do so in no way detracts from their influence on our heritage.

This is a book about warriors and too many words, perhaps, have already been devoted to the Norsemen's achievements beyond the battlefield. It would have been inappropriate, then, to have dwelt more on the influence of the Sagas, which thrilled men throughout Europe in the Middle Ages with their martial tales, tall stories and rich passages of poetry. Or to have lingered on the visual brightness which the Vikings, through their love of jewels, lustrous robes and richly carved artefacts, shed on a drab world timorously emerging from the Dark Ages.

Their first achievement was to turn people's eyes back to the sea. They displayed, in a road-less age, the importance of the ocean as a highway first to trade and then to power. The wonderful mobility given to the Vikings by their ships and their peerless seamanship, enabled a few thousand swordsmen to dominate half a continent. They introduced amphibious warfare and used it with the skill of a 20th-century war supremo. Concentrating vast fleets from out of the northern mists, they could nearly always surprise and outnumber their victims.

They were cruel and barbaric – even beyond the standards of their time. At Peterborough one Viking killed 84 monks with his own hand. Another was said to have invented the terrible 'blood eagle': tearing open a man's rib cage from the back and ripping out his lungs so that they flapped like wings from the last breaths of the victim. It can be argued that this gratuitous cruelty had a purpose, in that word would be passed that it would be wiser to yield and pay than to oppose a Viking. Certainly, the cruelty seemed to diminish somewhat as their power increased and they absorbed some of the mores of their conquered vassals – not least, of course, the gentle teachings of Christianity. They revelled in and profited from slavery, but they gave their slaves the chance to earn freedom by hard work.

It was freedom which the Vikings respected perhaps most of all. 'Who is your leader?' cried a French count from the river bank as the great longships crept up the Seine. 'We know no masters,' came the reply. 'All of us are equals.' Not quite true, of course, but it neatly sums up the Viking's spirit of independence, which, with honour and bravery, he held most dear. As he inter-married with the Saxons, the Irish and the French of Normandy, this is one of the great genetic traits which he bestowed on his successors and which helped to nurture the small flame of democracy which survived the feudal systems in those countries and created their modern, distinctive national characters.

The Jekyllian side of the Norseman's nature came increasingly to the fore as he colonised, rather than destroyed. His sense of freedom and fair play produced the democratic sophistication of the Althing, led him to accept Alfred's terms at Edington, produce the jury system for trials and helped to create the ordered state of Normandy. The energy which had driven him to piracy spurred him into introducing new methods of agriculture to his Saxon neighbours in the *sokes* of the Midlands and northern England. And his wanderlust and sense of adventure established trading routes again for the English and the Irish, re-opening their coasts after the xenophobic dark centuries and sewing the seeds for the establishment of the British as a seafaring nation.

The Vikings were the first and the greatest of marines, of course, and superb warriors. One has the feeling that they would have acquitted themselves well at Dieppe, Anzio and even on D-Day. But they were also shipwrights of grace and skill, poets, pioneer navigators, administrators, explorers and colonists who put down vastly important roots in Europe and beyond. Whenever English-speaking people now use words such as 'die', 'law', 'egg', 'fellow', 'skull', 'skin' or 'sky', or refer to place names such as Wexford, Whitby, Longford or Russia, they acknowledge the existence of the Vikings in their past and their debt to them for their present.

2
THE ARTILLERYMEN
The Longbowmen of England

'ARTILLERY – Engines for discharging missiles: formerly catapults, slings, arbalests, bows, etc.' — *The Shorter Oxford English Dictionary.*

First, then, that definition. Archers as *artillerymen*? Bows as pieces of ordnance? Surely that is stretching things a little far? Over-pulling the bowstring, perhaps? In fact, no, not at all – and not only because the impeccable Oxford Dictionary says so. What follows will show that the remarkable feats recorded by the English and Welsh longbowmen of Edward III, the Black Prince and Henry V more than 470 years ago were achieved as a result of their deployment as artillerymen, using what were later to become classic artillery tactics in battle.

The danger in pointing this out, alas, lies in tarnishing that attractive and long-preserved image of the medieval English archer as an independent, Robin Hood type of figure. Was he not more a marksman than a mortarman? A hawk-eyed sniper who could split a shaft while it still quivered in the bulls-eye at a country fair, as readily as he could place an arrow through the slit of a helmet to kill a charging knight? Well, it is true that marksmen abounded. Most bowmen learned their trade shooting for the pot and anyone who has tried to hit a moving target today, even squinting through the sight of a technology-encrusted modern bow, must give respect to those 14th-century peasants who could pierce a rabbit at 100 paces using the fashioned branch of a yew tree. But the fact remains that it was as artillerymen that they notched their place in history.

And a firm place it is. In three battles during the brutal conflict between England and France which became known as the Hundred Years War, these proletarian warriors were consistently decisive in a way unmatched by modern artillery. At Crecy in 1346, at Poitiers ten years later and at Agincourt in 1415, the English and Welsh longbowmen were the key factors in routing armies many times larger than their own. Placed shrewdly and used to create arrow storms quite as devastating in their way as the cannon bombardments of the Somme, Alamein and Stalingrad, these archers emerged in the late Middle Ages as a new and disturbing fighting force.

Their weapon was far from new, of course. The bow had been part of hunting and warfare since man first sought ways of hurling things through the air. The earliest arrowheads were discovered in North Africa and are believed to date from about 50,000 years ago; proof that bows and arrows were in use when the ice of the last Glacial period covered vast parts of northern Europe. The war bow had marched with every conqueror from Alexander to Richard Coeur de Lion. In fact, on the continent by the 14th century it was considered a primitive weapon, superseded by the cumbersome but accurate crossbow, the tool by which thousands of mercenaries then earned their living.

What was different about the longbow was partly just that: it *was* long – and thick. No one on the continent of Europe used such tall bows and few had the strength and the skill to pull them as fast and as accurately as these English and Welsh archers. They could let fly twelve arrows in a minute and send them 200 yards or more. Without armour of their own, they had the courage and nerve to stand fast against the charges of the finest armoured cavalry in Christendom. And they had the audacity, when needed, to mix it in a hand-to-hand mêlée with armoured knights.

All of this earned most of them sixpence a day by the time of Agincourt (about 25 times more than they could earn on the land back home), and, more importantly, the respect of the nobles and men-at-arms. Before the advent of the longbowmen, the peasants and bondmen who made up the bulk of medieval armies possessed few real fighting skills. They were regarded as the precursor of the cannon fodder of later centuries. Their role was to hold a spear, stand in line and provide the homespun backcloth against which the nobles, with pennants, armour and broadsword, could perform golden deeds of chivalry. The longbowmen changed that.

By their deeds they earned respect, a degree of privilege and the simmering fear of the nobles. They emerged from feudal times as the first peasant fighting men to be treated as specialists of war in their own right. In this they sowed the seeds of that English proletarian independence which flowered centuries later under the threat of the Armada and Hitler's bombs. Because of their victories, they unleashed an era of national self-confidence and awareness which bound England together for the first time since the Conquest. It was an era which also produced the first English literature, the first definitively English architecture and the end of French as the official language of the country. Paradoxically, the longbowmen of England also were the catalysts in putting France, long torn apart by the enmity between the great dukedoms and the crown, on to the road towards unity and sovereign statehood. In short, they were the finest and most influential artillerymen the world has ever seen.

THE WAR

The conflict which gave the longbowman his stage lasted longer than a hundred years. In fact it began in 1337 and did not end until 1453, although no formal armistice was ever signed. It is sometimes too easily written off as a squabble between families – the Plantagenets and, later, Lancasters of England and the Valois of France – over sovereignty and real estate. The causes of the war lie deeper than that.

In the middle of the twelfth century, about half of France paid allegiance to Henry II, the English king, thanks to his inheritance of Normandy, Maine and Anjou, and to his shrewd marriage with Eleanor of Aquitaine, which brought him large tracts of south-west France. Two hundred years later, England still had possessions in the west of France, although they had been reduced, and its land in the north had long since gone. By the time that Edward III was crowned in 1327, England was still a small country whose population of some five million was dwarfed by that of France. The Black Death, which struck both countries three times in the next half century, decimated the populace and by Edward's death in 1377, his country could boast only five cities with populations of more than 6,000 people: London, York, Bristol, Plymouth and Coventry.

Nevertheless, by the standard of the Middle Ages, England was a prosperous and orderly kingdom. After the Papacy, the English throne was the oldest political institution in western Europe and the country's economy, based on agriculture, tin and coal mining, and a growing wool and textile trade, was improving as exports flourished. After the turbulent and tragic reign of his father, Edward II, the nation looked forward to a period of stability and prosperity.

The problem was that the throne lay under constant threat. To the north, Scotland remained unconquered; a fiercely independent kingdom which had recently humiliated Edward II at Bannockburn and threatened constantly to sweep across the border to York. To the west, Ireland and Wales, although subdued in theory, required vigilance and expensive garrisoning. To the south lay France, where the English Crown still possessed Aquitaine, a vital source of its wealth, for the revenue from Bordeaux equalled and sometimes exceeded what the king could extract from the royal estates in England. But this jewel in the English crown was an irritant pearl to the French king. He and his forebears had long since absorbed England's other continental possessions and the homage paid to Edward by the wealthy winemasters of Bordeaux infuriated him. Accordingly, Aquitaine's borders were continually being eroded and France was in intermittent and often active alliance with the Scottish crown. The French court remained a welcoming place also for occasional Irish rebels and Welsh insurgents.

The young Edward, then, faced a familiar threat: one of encirclement. On his domestic borders lay hostile and active Celtic enemies. Across the Channel the urbane French, while maintaining diplomatic courtesies and open channels of communication, were always fomenting unrest and undoubtedly planning to re-take English possessions on the Biscay coastal strip and even, perhaps, to invade England. King Philip VI of France ruled over a by no means united kingdom. The great duchies of Normandy and Burgundy remained loose cannon crashing disruptively across the political decks of France for decades. But the king now represented some 20 million French-speaking subjects and their growing nationalism was looking for expression.

Edward of England was aware of this but was in no position to fight on two fronts. He decided, therefore, to use the little time he had left to him to 'shut the postern gate' in the north before turning to the south. He accordingly moved his capital to York and went to war against the Scots. The young English king quickly showed that he had inherited the martial skills – courage, supreme self-confidence and care in planning which had distinguished his grandfather Edward I and which were so sadly lacking in his father, Edward II.

In that Scottish campaign he developed a strategy which, in fundamentals, can be said to have characterised the approach of many great British generals who followed him – from his great grandson Henry V through Wellington to Montgomery. The main strategy was to force his opponents to give open battle on carefully chosen terrain unfavourable to them, and then to fight such battles in a defensive posture, concentrating overwhelming firepower and drawing the enemy within its arc.

In numerous engagements Edward refined this technique until, on 13 July 1333, when he was a mere twenty years old, he lured the Scots into battle at Halidon Hill and decisively beat them. He sent his horses to the rear and took up his position on a 500-foot hill, placing dismounted knights in the middle and archers on both wings. The Scots attacked into a hail of arrows and they broke and fled. The *Eulogium* written at Malmesbury records that the Scots were 'beaten by the English archers'. Another record states that in the battle the arrows appeared 'as thik as motes on the sonne beme'. More was to be heard about arrow storms.

Edward had shut his northern postern very effectively. The Scottish border bastion of Berwick fell shortly after the battle and for the first time in twenty years England was cleared of invaders. The young Scottish king fled to France with some of his bishops and relations between Edward and Philip immediately worsened, although some genuine attempts were made to negotiate a lasting peace between the two countries. Aquitaine remained the obvious problem, as did the French king's envy of England's profitable sea-borne trade.

But the underlying cause of conflict was the insecurity of the English crown; ironic, this, considering that Edward III, who reigned for 50 years – a prodigious span, given the volatile conditions of the time – is usually considered to have been one of the most self-confident of all English monarchs. This mighty Plantagenet broke many moulds. He was given to sudden rages but for most of the time he was sensitive and sensible. Unusually for a medieval king, he loved and had good relationships with his wife and all of his ten children who survived infancy. He was, of course, a great warrior, but he was also a master money-raiser, not above hocking the crown jewels to help his war effort (inventories show that the Great Crown was regularly at the pawnbrokers during fifteen years from 1340). For all his shrewd politicking, however, Edward knew that he was encircled and this made him restive and aggressive.

Nevertheless, there was no rush towards Armageddon. In his preparations for war with France, Edward took great pains to carry Parliament and the nation along with him. Constitutional assent was sought and gained for every step along the road to war and the struggle, when it came, had the general support of the realm's most powerful nobles and magnates. The signal for war came in 1336 when the French moved their fleet, ostensibly assembled for a crusade, from Marseilles into the English Channel. Then Philip confiscated Gascony and Edward responded by assuming the royal arms of France. The French raided Portsmouth and Southampton in 1338 and Dover and Folkestone the following year. The cold war had become hot.

The English king's grandfather, Edward I, had bequeathed him a professional, paid army, based on contracts of service. The system had fallen into some disrepair under the lacklustre control of Edward II, but Edward III had refined it during his early years. By 1341, written contracts were well established. An individual knight or captain contracted to supply a number of men for so many days at a set rate of pay. Boroughs and shires were expected to fulfil ancient obligations to provide manpower, and able-bodied men were paraded locally and selected for service by Commissioners of Array.

The army had its disreputable element in the form of the criminals who served as a means of winning pardon for robbery, murder and rape, but, on the whole, selection worked well and it was a reasonably professional army with which Edward entered the Hundred Years War. The hard core was formed by the nobles and armoured men-at-arms but they were outnumbered by the archers. The minority of these were mounted, on light horses which gave them great mobility, although they fought on foot. The majority were foot archers, of peasant stock, wearing little or no armour and carrying their giant longbows, made usually of yew but sometimes of elm or ash.

The opening engagement of the war, strangely, was a naval battle, set up by Edward, who had no vestige of sailing skills and who was often seasick. He fought it, however, as a land battle and, presciently, it was his archers who gave him a decisive victory. Edward, with much the smaller fleet, attacked the French off Sluys in June 1340, the year in which he formally laid claim to the throne of France. He organised his force as he was later to do on land: a squadron of men-at-arms took the centre, with squadrons of longbowmen on each side and a fourth squadron in reserve. The French, 'like a line of castles', waited at their moorings as the English curled round them, the archers firing devastating volleys into the crowded ships from the flanks until the men-at-arms were able to grapple and board. Edward used bolts, stones and lime and sent divers to bore holes in the French vessels until they were overcome. Both French admirals were executed – an unusual and unpleasant opening to the war – and it was said that the killings were so great that, 'if fish could speak, they would surely speak French'.

That victory ended a real threat of French invasion and Edward immediately turned to mounting his own landings on the Flanders coast. There is no reliable record of the size of the army he gathered for the purpose, but it is clear that it was the largest host ever to leave English shores until that time. Brittany was the main theatre in the next part of the war and the British expeditionary force fared well in initial encounters, at Morlaix and elsewhere. There was much marching and counter-marching, skirmishes, investment of towns and even flags of truce. The main and by far the most influential encounter, however, took place in 1346, when Edward was at last faced with a substantial French army, led by Philip IV himself.

Edward had taken Caen in Normandy, where 105 Normans were painfully killed when they unwisely exposed their bottoms insultingly to the English longbowmen. He moved northwards, tracked now by a large French force, and succeeded in crossing the Somme only by dint of sending archers to wade, chest-deep, across a little-known causeway to clear a passage for his wagons and men-at-arms. But Philip was hard on his heels and Edward was eventually brought to bay at Crécy-en-Ponthieu. Here ensued what Winston Churchill was to call one of the greatest feats of arms in English history.

Until about ten years ago, the site of the battle was difficult to find. Only a small plaque, erected on a roadside bank by 'the Friends of Old French Windmills', announced diffidently that on this site stood a windmill which (and almost by the way) had been used as a command post by the English King Edward III during the battle of Crécy in 1346. It was a poor memorial – not least to the brave Frenchmen who died that day. Now, however, probably as a result of the promise of English tourists flooding through the Channel Tunnel, the local authority has re-created Edward's command post as a 30-foot-high timber viewing platform, showing the French and English dispositions, and set opposite reproductions of the two kings' coats of arms. It is all a little vulgar but functional for all that.

The hill seems to have changed remarkably little since the chroniclers first described the battle. Contours have softened, perhaps, and the field itself is now cultivated where, in 1346, it was probably gorseland. But the view from the tower confirms that Edward had an eye for a defensive position. If he had to turn and fight, this was the place for it.

He deployed his force along the ridge, facing south-east and downhill. To his right was the village of Crécy, towards which the hill fell away almost precipitously. To his left lay the hamlet of Wadicourt, set on the edge of woodland, sufficiently thick to protect his flank there. And at his rear, across the lane which then, as now, ran from Crécy to Wadicourt, bristled Crécy Farm Wood, safe enough to house his wagons and baggage. The French had to mount the slope ahead of them into the setting sun, across a front some 2,000 yards (1,800 metres) wide.

Crécy is one of the most written-about battles in English history. Yet we are still unsure about the numbers on each side. Certainly, the English were vastly outnumbered. Robert Hardy, actor, archer and scholar of the period, has written one of the most detailed accounts in his impeccably researched book *Longbow*. He estimates that Edward had between 12,000 and 13,000 men to defend the ridge, of whom about 8,000 were longbowmen, many of them from Wales and Chester. Philip's army probably numbered between 20,000 and 25,000, though some historians claim up to 40,000. The cavalry alone almost certainly matched the English total force.

They glistened and gleamed across the other side of the valley as Philip unfurled the dreaded Oriflamme, the great red pennant which announced that no quarter was to be given.

It was late in the day, and the French king had planned to camp for the night, deploy his forces and attack early next day. But the sight of such a derisorily small force opposing them, drawn up in three puny divisions or 'battles' along the top of the ridge, was too much for the French. They attacked – and as they did so the heavens opened. As the thunder rolled and the rain poured down, threatening the bowstrings of crossbowmen and archers alike, the battle was suspended before it began. Legend has it that the longbowmen had slipped their strings and wound them beneath their shirts and helmets before the clouds broke. Maybe, although their linen bowstrings would not have been stretched by rain – unlike the crossbowmen's thick, twisted strings, which could well have absorbed moisture. Either way, it was the crossbowmen who were the first into action as the skies cleared and the evening sun sent steam rising from cloth and armour.

So began the first major battle of The Hundred Years War and the first classic encounter between longbow and crossbow. The crossbowmen numbered about 6,000, probably more. They were Genoese mercenaries, whose countless successes in European wars with their heavy, steel-tipped bolts, had made them the most feared artillerymen in the world. Like their noble employers, they despised the longbow: a crude weapon, fit only for gentlemen at the hunt and for peasants in war. They knew nothing of the size of the English bows, nor of the stern apprenticeship they had served in the Scottish wars. The shock, when it came, was profound.

As the clouds dispersed, the Genoese gave a great shout, advanced up the hill to within bowshot of the English, and fired their bolts. Whether the rain had affected their strings is not clear. What is known is that the longbowmen, set on the wings of the English army and in little pointed salients or *herces* between the men-at-arms, loosed such an arrow storm in reply that the crossbowmen were decimated. As they stooped to re-load, the arrows hissed toward them, 'so thick that it seemed like snow'.

The Genoese fell back in disarray and, as they did so, the French noble cavalry rode them down contemptuously. The French chronicler Jean Froissart writes that the French king cried: 'Kill all this rabble, kill them. They are getting in our way.' But the cavalry met the same fate. As they neared the defenders' lines, the archers fired at point-blank range, with no elevation, and the bodkin-headed arrows penetrated even plate armour at that distance. Horses plunged and reared in agony and still the arrows came. In all, the cavalry charged fifteen or sixteen times up the hill, into the sun.

Many reached the lines and were met in fierce hand-to-hand fighting by the English nobles and men-at-arms, but the defenders held. The only break in the line came when, between charges, the archers darted among the bodies, retrieving arrows. In all, Hardy estimates that about half a million arrows were fired at the French that day. And they were not cheap. Edward had paid a halfpenny each for them.

It was a complete and overwhelming victory, all the more galling for the French because it had been achieved mainly by peasants of low birth. Even King Philip had been wounded in the face by an English arrow and had been forced to leave the field long before the battle petered out by moonlight. The flower of French chivalry had been brought down by the peasants' weapon. Among the dead was the blind King of Bohemia, who had ridden in one charge with his reins tied to those of knights on each side. They were found still harnessed together in death.

After the battle an elated Edward gave much of the credit to his 16-year-old son, Edward the Black Prince, who had led the right flank division and taken the brunt of many of the charges. The king also founded a new order of chivalry for his knights, the Garter, to celebrate the victory. But it was the longbowmen's battle. From the beginning they had out-ranged the crossbowmen and easily out-matched them in firepower. Their discipline had been impeccable. Although comparatively unarmoured themselves and protected only by a few holes dug before them, they had not flinched at the sight of the thundering war-horses bearing down on them. They had kept on firing coolly and decisively. Most of the French casualties had been caused by arrows. More was to come.

While the cat was away in France, the mice in Scotland seized their opportunity to force open the postern gate. Two months after Crécy, the Scots invaded under King David Bruce and they met a hastily assembled English army at Neville's Cross, near Durham. Untypically, this time the English attacked, but, as at Crécy and Sluys, the archers – not every longbowman was in France – were on the flanks. Their arrows broke up the Scottish light troops and poured into the massed ranks of the spearmen, allowing the English men-at-arms to go forward and win the day. King David was captured and imprisoned in Windsor Castle. This time the postern gate was firmly locked and bolted. Shortly afterwards Edward besieged Calais, which fell after a year, giving him a deep-water base on the French coast.

So began a period of prosperity for the English state. The booty taken from Caen, Crécy, Calais and a hundred sacked towns poured into England. The contemporary chronicler Walsingham refers to the vast amount of stuff sent home by the English soldiers, to the extent that almost every woman in England had received something: 'clothes, furs, bed covers, cutlery, tablecloths and linen, wooden and silver bowls'. The archers were allowed their share, and so thatched mud huts as well as timbered manors received part of the pickings.

Both the prosperity and the war was interrupted by the Black Death, which made its first (but not its last) visit to both countries at the end of 1348. In August it took Edward's young and much loved daughter Joan at Bordeaux, on her way to be betrothed to King Peter of Castile, and by the time it had swept through the country, approximately one third of the population had died. For a time it completely destroyed the stability of the nation, but there were hidden benefits. Shortage of labour forced wages to rise for the first time in decades and gave a stimulus to improvements in working methods, forcing, *inter alia*, the replacement of the back-breaking sickle by the scythe and the introduction of the butter churn. In Gascony, hostilities began again.

This time it was the Prince of Wales, now an experienced general of 26, who occupied centre-stage – although it was the longbowmen, once again, who supplied the chorus. In 1355, the young man set off from Bordeaux on an ambitious *chevauchée*, or mounted raid. Through the late summer of that year, the marauders penetrated deep into south-west France, pillaging, sacking, burning and looting, living partly off the land and stacking their wagons with valuables. Edward used the excuse of demonstrating against those territories which gainsaid his father's claim to the French crown. But it was piracy on land; 'war' waged to the standards of the day. Carcassonne was put to the torch before the column, sated, turned for home and winter quarters. This strategy was draining the French and, more importantly, humiliating them.

Young Edward tried it again in the following summer. Fresh archers and more bows arrived through the winter and this time the raiders struck into the heart of France, deep into the valleys of the Cher and the Loire. Edward was hoping to link up with a *chevauchée* led by his brother, John of Gaunt, from the north. But it was not to be. King John of France, stung by the insouciant way these English columns were plundering his country, had raised a large army, before which Prince John prudently retreated. The French King continued south and, in September, by brilliant forced marching, he had placed his army between the Black Prince and his base in Bordeaux. At a point about four miles south of Poitiers, the young man was cornered and had to fight.

Once again the French outnumbered the English, by about 16,000 to 7,000, but this time the French eschewed the use of crossbowmen and, remembering Crécy, the *chevaliers* dismounted, shortened their lances and moved forward ponderously on foot. Nevertheless, it was the French cavalry in the van who charged first – into that familiar arrow storm, this time directed from hedges at the side of the field and from marshes safe from the cavalry. Again the charge was bloodily broken, but the second division, on foot, came on, helmeted heads down, into the sleet of arrows. A vicious mêlée ensued but the English line held.

The French second division saw the havoc created by the archers and melted from the field. It was left to King John himself, at the head of his reserve 'battle' to throw everything into the fight. By now the archers had few arrows left, but, like scavenger fish in the shark's mouth, they darted in front of the advancing armoured host, retrieving their shafts from the dead and dying. The two lines met with a deafening clang, with the horse archers mounting and charging into the mêlée and the foot bowmen, fanning out to the sides to shoot into the French flanks. It was a master-stroke on the part of the Black Prince, however, which won the day. He sent a detachment of cavalry from his threadbare reserve to take the French in the rear. They were few but the psychological effect was catalytic. The French army was shattered and fled, routed, back to Poitiers, pursued by the English cavalry.

In many ways, it was a more complete victory than Crécy. The French had lost 2,000 men-at-arms dead, 2,000 prisoners and uncounted common soldiery dead or captured. The French king and his 14-year-old son were captured for ransom and the booty was great. Some archers themselves took five or six prisoners each and a group took from the field the French king's own silver salt cellar, later redeemed by the Black Prince.

In 1360, a weary French king, still a prisoner, sealed the Treaty of Brétigny, ceding Edward III vast lands in Poitou, Armagnac, Gascony, Rouergue and Calais, in return for Edward dropping his claim to the French throne. It seemed to set the seal on and justify Edward's long campaigns. But it was not the end. King John died, still in captivity, and the shrewd Charles V succeeded him. When the war flared into life again in 1369 there began a long period of sieges and marches, with the French refusing pitched battle but retreating, harrying and scorching the earth before the English armies.

The decades that followed represented an extraordinary era, with long stretches of bitter, if indecisive hostilities, broken by scrupulously observed periods of truce, like half-time in football matches. England's aggression gradually sank as the cost of the wars mounted and Edward slipped into decline. His bright morning star, the Black Prince, fell ill and pre-deceased him and the great king himself finally died in 1377. He had certainly saved his country from invasion and his conquests had increased his empire in France and replenished the nation's coffers. But England was growing tired. Her archers were now universally respected and feared and her armies commanded the field. Yet France remained sullenly undefeated. The Black Death made return visits in 1361-2 and 1369 and social unrest, fuelled undoubtedly by the return home of yeomen archers accustomed to a degree of independence in the field, culminated in the Peasants' Revolt of 1381. Once again, local actions and politics began to erode the boundaries of the English crown's French possessions. The Black Prince's young son, Richard II, presided over a surly, dissatisfied nation, used to success and unhappy with weak leadership.

The break came when Henry of Lancaster, son of John of Gaunt and grandson of Edward III, seized the throne in 1399. His reign of only fourteen years was marked by his ill health and continuous revolt in Wales, in which his eldest son, Henry, won his spurs. France itself underwent periods of unrest as Charles V lapsed into insanity and the great dukes battled for supremacy. An uneasy truce in the Hundred Years War was just beginning to break down again with French raids on the English coast, when Henry V succeeded on his father's death in 1413. It was another watershed.

The young king was probably only 27 when he came to the throne (his birth date was never precisely recorded because no-one expected him to be king). He inherited a country which lacked unity, was experiencing fiscal problems and yearned for a strong monarch. The call was answered. Young though he was, Henry had been blooded militarily by long years on campaign in the Welsh marches and, latterly, had been well inaugurated by his father into the arcane ways of political administration. Sniffing the air like a Plantagenet, he looked to the south – to France. The road he took was to lead to a field outside a little village called Agincourt and to the apogee of the English longbowman.

THE ARCHER

On the eve of his great battle, this is an appropriate moment to take a closer look at the longbowman himself. His name doesn't really matter because we will conjure him up now as a composite figure. But let's call him William Gladewyne, because an archer of that name was with King Henry on St Crispin's Day. You will note that it is spelt with a 'y' and two 'e's, though William is not too fussy about that because, like most of his mates, he can't read or write.

He stands before us now, slipping the loop of his bowstring over the horn nock at the end of the bow. He has to stretch just a little because, although at 5 foot 8 inches he is tall for his time, his longbow is taller – about 6 feet. But look closer ... there is something rather strange about him. Look at his legs. He's wearing no breeches, except a fragment of tattered hose that hangs down beneath his jacket. It's not a particularly pretty sight, although he seems unconcerned. In fact, like many of the king's soldiers, he has dysentery, although he calls it 'the flux'. This is the result of months spent under the city walls of Harfleur, followed by nearly three weeks of forced marching across country. The journey to Calais was only supposed to take eight days but they've been dodging the French. It has rained most of the way and there has been little to eat, except for handfuls of berries and a hedgehog or two. He doesn't know what he wants more: a roast chicken or new hose. Anyway, the French have caught up with them now and bar the road to Calais. Tomorrow they must stand and fight.

That closer look has revealed something else. William is ever so slightly misshapen. His left forearm is distinctly thicker than his right and, as he stands, he skews his body trunk round to the left a little. (Archers' skeletons recovered from the wreck of the Tudor ship *Mary Rose* revealed these characteristic legacies of lives spent pulling longbows.)

Not that he is a bad-looking man. Despite his recent deprivations, he is broad and stockily built and there is about his leather-textured face the countryman's air of self-confidence and alertness. His beard is stubbly and grey-flecked and he is about 30 years of age. If the French, the pox or the plague don't get him, he can expect to live about another twenty years, but no more than that.

On his head is a *querbole*, a hardened leather conical helmet with iron rim and vertical crosspieces. His tunic is heavy and quilted and reaches below that semi-naked bottom. His boots are of leather but they are scuffed and down at heel. The tunic is gathered in by a heavy belt from which hangs a large dagger and a wooden mallet. On the ground is a quiver containing arrows and more are stuck into the ground in front of him.

Having completed the stringing of his bow, William selects one of the arrows from the group stuck in the grass and, in one smooth movement, nocks it to the string, tilts the arrow until it has an elevation of about 35 to 40 degrees, pulls it and the string back until his right thumb brushes his cheekbone and the steel of the arrowhead touches his left-hand knuckles – and lets fly. His stance is balanced, the greater part of the pull being taken by arm and shoulder muscle, with the left arm extended, but not locked, and the right elbow fully flexed. To take the arrow back he has developed a pull of about 180 pounds (81 kilograms), but he has been doing it dozens of times a day for the last twenty years and shows no sign of strain. Hardly waiting to see the arrow clear, he bends and repeats the process, so that the second arrow is well on its way before the first strikes the trunk of a tree some 200 paces away. Then again and again until he has sent winging twelve shafts in a minute, to group around the first in the trunk of the tree.

William smiles, turns to the north and gives to the air a triumphant two-fingered V sign. He has heard that the French king has threatened to cut off the bow fingers of every English archer left alive after the battle tomorrow. And this is what he thinks of that. His action has lived on long after him ('V Sign: a gesture symbolising vulgar derision' – The Concise Oxford Dictionary).

He has been shooting with the longbow all his life – mainly for the pot. In fact, as a boy he was in trouble many times for poaching. Most game is out of bounds; even rabbits, which were brought over by the Norman invaders, are protected. Apart, then, from the odd, illegal pheasant or young buck, he honed his skills on shooting pigeons, hedgehogs and the like, although some of his mates from the south boast about shooting dolphins off the coast. William is from Cheshire, where everyone says that the best bowmen come from. Usually, only the Welsh disagree.

William still has some difficulty conversing with soldiers from the south and the far north, although, on the whole, they communicate well enough. It was not so when his great-grandfather fought at Crécy, 70 years before. Then, north and south could not understand each other and only Midland folk could understand both. The nobles, of course, spoke French, but, as John Trevisa, an early historian from the west, helpfully wrote:

'the country language is apayred and som useth straunge wlafferynge, chiteryne, harrygne and garrynge grisbayting'.

Gladewyne and his forefathers have always been encouraged to practise with the longbow – unlike in France, where peasants are forbidden to possess arms and the law is enforced. In England, that attitude died out (if it ever really existed) in the 12th century. After Crécy and Poitiers, Edward III had even gone so far as to ban 'foot ball, bandy ball and other such vain plays' and ordered that archery become the main recreation of Englishmen.

Like most of the peasant contingent of the army, William is a tenant, in debt to his lord of the manor, and is in France as part of the fighting contingent provided by his master. But apart from the flux – he's not complaining. On the whole, life on campaign is better than being at home. There, he has a narrow strip of land for his own use but owes most of his labour and a goodly part of his produce to his lord. Now his wife carries on with the work. Back home he is not much more than a ploughman, making about seven shillings a year. Here he is an artilleryman, paid sixpence (half a shilling) a *day. And* his share of booty from Harfleur means that he has been able to send some fine linen and woollen cloth back home.

It is not easy to equate that sixpence a day wage to 1990s income. Probably it is equivalent to about £20,000 or 30,000 US dollars a year. But William now has a firm and respected place in the military hierarchy. On this campaign, Dukes are earning 13 shillings and fourpence per day – two-thirds of the old pound. Earls are making six shillings and sixpence, barons four shillings, knights two shillings, esquires and men-at-arms one and six-pence and a shilling. Then come the archers; they are earning three times as much as lancemen.

There have been many signs of respect, other than the pay. Just before Poitiers, during the winter resting at Bordeaux, an archer named William Jauderel was forced, for some reason, to return home. It is probable that he wasn't a rank-and-file bowmen: more likely a member of the Prince of Wales's élite guard of archers. But it was the Black Prince himself who sealed his leave pass:

'Know all that we, the Prince of Wales, have given leave on the day of the date of this instrument to William Jauderel, one of our archers, to go to England. In witness of this we have caused our seal to be placed on this bill. Given at Bordeaux, 16th December in the year of grace 1355.'

This document remains in the possession of the Joddrell family, William's descendants. Its survival for more than 600 years is all the more remarkable because it is written on paper, not parchment.

Another example of the royal respect for the archers originates from roughly the same period. At Crécy, Edward III was so impressed by the per-formance of a band of archers from the small town of Llantrisant in South Wales that he granted the town its first charter. Eleven years later, after Poitiers, the Black Prince made the Llantrisant archers – still serving, still shooting valiantly – freemen of their town. In addition, he granted them 260 acres just outside the town to be used in perpetuity by them and their descendants for the grazing of cattle. By the early 1990s those descendants – having beaten off 600 years of attempts to buy, compulsorily purchase or otherwise sequester their inheritance – were still grazing the land. Appro-priately, the people of Llantrisant are called 'The Black Archers' to this day.

William's standing, however, has been hard earned. Traditionally, the archers, whether longbowmen or crossbowmen, were treated with lordly contempt *(vide* King Philip's cry of 'kill the rabble!' at Crécy) In the early 12th century, the death of Geoffrey de Mandeville at Burwell Castle in Cambridgeshire during the Stephen–Matilda conflict was caused, it was written, by his being hit in the head by an arrow from the bow of a 'very low class archer'. The medieval chronicler Girard de Viane referred to the bow as 'that weapon of a dastard'. Part of the contempt, of course, was based on fear and on the bowman's very effectiveness, especially from a distance. Men of noble birth could be killed by low-class archers before getting close enough to raise their swords in defence. For a time, the Pope even banned the use of crossbows in 'Christian wars'. It was perfectly all right, of course, to use this barbaric weapon against unbelievers.

So kings and noblemen were well aware of the capabilities of the bow. They knew how to shoot with them because they used them for hunting. But on the whole the bow was seen as the weapon of the lowly, peasants, mercenaries and citizen militias. This prejudice is amusingly captured in paintings of the period. One would never know from these colourful and dramatic recordings of great battles that it was the archers who were the decisive factors. A few longbowmen are shown (see illustrations) daintily drawing their strings on the fringe of the mêlée, while mighty hosts of nobles and men-at-arms lay about them with sword and mace.

The bowman is rarely, if ever, mentioned in early medieval literature in a favourable manner. It is not until about 1400 – significantly, after Crécy and Poitiers – that he gains star billing. Then he emerges, flitting between the oaks of Sherwood Forest, in *Robin Hood and the Monk*, one of the first of the tales of that mythical figure. Did he exist? Early glimpses have been caught in glades from Yorkshire to Cornwall, from the time of Arthur until Edward III. We shall never know. But he was undoubtedly the first literary archer hero. Even then, however, the social mores of the time couldn't quite accept him as a yeoman. He was a Saxon nobleman, forced into outlawry. To the Tudors, he was Robin, Earl of Huntingdon.

But William Gladewyne, on the eve of Agincourt, is undoubtedly no nobleman. He is what we see: a highly-skilled, peasant soldier, an ordinary man of his time – who with his longbow, is about to do extraordinary things once more.

THE WEAPON

The English longbow was one of the most simple weapons ever used in warfare. Yet it caused great carnage. A rather oblique but none the less profound compliment is paid to it by Donald Featherstone in his book, *Weapons and Equipment of the Victorian Soldier*. Lauding the introduction to the British Army of the Martini-Henry rifle in 1871, Featherstone writes:

'Its easy operation and quick reloading gave rise to the claim that it was the earliest general issue of a shoulder-arm that could compete successfully with the longbow of the Hundred Years War, so far as range, rapidity of firing and robustness were concerned – every earlier firearm had been in some degree inferior to the master weapon of Crécy, Poitiers and Agincourt.'

Wooden bows, we know, were in use in many parts of the world in prehistoric times. Longbows of a sort, although probably not as long as the great English medieval war bow, were almost certainly used by the German tribes to repulse the Romans on the Rhine in AD 354, and the Vikings, those great close-quarters fighters, also considered the wooden bow to be an essential weapon in their armoury. In the Middle and Near East, the lack of timber created the short, composite bow, with horn and sinew bequeathing great power – the precursor, in fact, of the strong and accurate plastic bows which today have superseded the longbow in archery societies throughout the globe.

The Saxons who invaded Britain in the 5th century certainly seem to have been armed with wooden bows and it is unlikely that the Britons they fought, strong hunters all, were not themselves similarly armed. It is the last successful invasion of Britain in 1066, however, which has given rise to the view that bows and arrows had more or less died out as weapons of war in England during Saxon times.

Harold Godwinson had seized the English throne and in 1066 he faced two invasions. The first was made by Harald Hardrada, the King of Norway, who, aided by Harold Godwinson's brother, Tostig, landed in the north-east. Godwinson immediately marched to meet him and defeated him comprehensively at Stamford Bridge in a battle that would have won him undying praise had it not been followed immediately by Hastings. There is inadequate evidence of archers being used at Stamford Bridge, but plenty to show that they were influential at Hastings. The Normans, of course, were direct descendants of the Vikings, who had long valued the bow. It is not surprising, then, that William of Normandy should have a strong contingent of archers in the force with which he attacked Harold at Battle, near Hastings. They were deployed skilfully by the Norman to open the battle and were used throughout as a cohesive group, being brought forward again at the climax. Harold's death has long been attributed to receiving a Norman arrow in the eye.

There is little evidence, however, of the Saxons using archers in this, the first battle in medieval European history in which the bow can be shown to have played a significant role. The Bayeux Tapestry depicts 28 Norman archers and only one Saxon and he a small, rather badly dressed figure. The truth is probably that Harold included bowmen in his heroic march to the north but that they dwindled away in the rush back to Hastings. If so, they could not have figured largely in the King's strategy.

But this does not mean that the bow was not used for warfare at all in the Britain that was then emerging from the Dark Ages. The Welsh tribes of the west had long since won a reputation as doughty fighters which had kept their mountains and valleys out of bounds to most Saxons. Their main weapon was a bow – short and rough, but effective. In the late 12th century an account of their prowess was written which stamps the Welsh as being the true founding fathers of those later great archer armies.

In 1188, a young cleric, Gerald of Wales, made a journey through Wales. He had spent his boyhood in Manorbier Castle in the south and he had affection for the place and the people. He recorded his travels in a journal, *Itinerarium Cambriae*, and sang the praises of the Welsh bowmen. At the capture of Abergavenny Castle, he records, Welsh archers put arrows through an oak doorway which was as thick across as a man's palm.

'William de Braose also testifies that one of his men-at-arms was struck by an arrow which went through his thigh, high up, where it was protected outside and inside the leg by iron armour, and then through the skirt of his leather tunic. Next it penetrated that part of the saddle which is called the alva or seat; and finally it lodged in his horse, driving in so deep that it killed the animal ... The bows they use are not made of horn, nor of sapwood, nor yet of yew. The Welsh carve their bows out of the elm trees in the forest. They are nothing much to look at, not even rubbed smooth, but left in a rough and unpolished state. Still, they are firm and strong. You could not shoot far with them; but they are powerful enough to inflict serious wounds in a close fight.'

It looks, then, very much as though the Welsh war bow was short and rather primitive. We know that by the time of the Hundred Years War the bow in Britain had developed into a much more refined weapon, longer, thicker and needing both strength and skill to use it effectively in battle. Dominic Mancini, a contemporary visitor to Britain, wrote of the English longbowman:

'Their bows are thicker and longer than those used by other nations, just as their arms are stronger – so that it seems they have hands and arms of iron and, as result, their bows had as great a range as crossbows.'

In fact, as we know, the English war bow was out-ranging the European crossbow by the middle of the 14th century. Infuriatingly, however, not one longbow has survived in England from this time. There have been wooden bows of various lengths found in northern Europe dating back as far as the Roman Iron Age, but despite the hundreds of thousands – perhaps millions – that must have been made in England before and during medieval times, nothing has been found dating back to Crécy or even Agincourt. The reasons are clear. Longbows were easily degradable artefacts which could be and were replaced comparatively easily. They were common tools of everyday life, used daily and not treasured as, for instance, a good sword might be. And, of course, unlike a steel sword or a lance, they could not survive the ages.

Nothing, then, from the Hundred Years War has survived. But the recovery of the Tudor warship, *Mary Rose* from the sea bed off the Isle of Wight, has given valuable clues about the size and shape of the longbow of that time. The ship dates from 1545 and it was known that she was carrying archers when she capsized. More than 130 bow staves were found on board, preserved by mud and silt so that they are in remarkably good condition. They range from about 100 pounds (45 kilograms) to about 185 pounds (84 kilograms) draw weight, that is when the bow is stretched to about 30 inches (76 centimetres) along the arrow. Expert opinion agrees that these staves could have changed very little from those used 130 years before at Agincourt, and even 70 years before that, at Crécy.

We know how the medieval war bow was made. The best were cut from yew imported from the continent, although the great demand for bows during the wars forced the use of less suitable English yew. In extremis, wych elm and even ash were used, but yew was always preferred. Yews in Britain today always seem to grow in churchyards. One explanation which has stubbornly survived the generations is that the yews were planted there in medieval times deliberately, so as to be close to the archery butts which were usually sited near the church. But there is no reason why bow-making should have been near practice site or church. It is far more likely that yews were planted there to prevent cows, for whom yew leaves are poisonous, from getting among the graves. Either way, we know that Henry V, before his great campaign of 1415, sent his principal bowyer round the country to buy bow staves but specifically forbade him to take yew from church land.

The heavier, stronger bow staves would be cut from the bole of the tree and the weaker ones from the branches. It was important to season the wood for three or even four years, during which the log or branch was usually roughly reduced to a stave. When sufficiently seasoned – although it is highly likely that the demands of war would sometimes hurry the process – the staves would be fashioned by the bowyer, using tools which have hardly changed to this day: drawknife, spokeshave, scraper, knife and sandpaper. Today, wooden longbows are usually made in two pieces, of paired billets which are carefully butted together in a 'W' double fishtail joint and glued. At Crécy, Poitiers and Agincourt, however, it is likely that the bows were of one piece, the 'self' bow. Certainly all the bows recovered from the *Mary Rose* were in this form.

The secret of the yew wood's suitability for bow staves, of course, lies in its strength and elasticity. This derives from the combination of hard-wood and sapwood which, for good bowmaking, must be positioned in the middle, or hand-grip portion, of the stave. The longbow is really a D-sec-tioned wooden spring, with the sapwood on the outside, away from the archer, providing the elasticity and the hardwood the strength. The bowyer would taper the stave towards the ends and then either notch the wood at the tip to take the string, or glue on a carved horn 'nock'. By the time of the English bowman's ascendancy, his bow had grown to a length of between 5 feet 9 inches and 6 feet, depending on the height of the archer. The ideal was a bow about four inches taller than its user.

The strings were usually of hemp or linen, the latter particularly use-ful if, as at Crécy, the bowmen were caught in the rain, for linen strings do not weaken or stretch when wet. The arrows? A mixture of woods, but ash was favoured because of its straightness and weight; the flights were made from feathers of the grey goose – alas, long since disappeared from English village ponds – glued to the rear of the shaft and often reinforced with a thread of fine silk bound tightly through the flights. By Agincourt, the steel arrowheads would have been mainly bodkin shaped, the old broad, barbed head being no longer able to penetrate the new plate armour.

As in modern warfare, the military technology of the Hundred Years War represents a series of leap-frogs, with defensive armour being improved to combat sharper, tougher weapons and the aggressor, in turn, introduc-ing second generation arms of even higher efficiency. So chain mail, ade-quate against a sword blow but vulnerable to the English arrow, had given way by Agincourt to plate armour which was set on the body in curves and at angles to deflect the bowman's shafts.

By 1415, in fact, the balance between bow and armour was probably about even. The heavier bodkin headed arrow, two or more inches long, could certainly penetrate plate armour, but only at shortish range – say less than 100 yards – and even then it could be deflected. But the armoured knight remained vulnerable at those joints of his body which could only be covered by chain mail. And it remained difficult to protect a war-horse. Even at the pinnacle of the success of the great English war bow, however, the seeds of its decline were being sown. Two developments – one major, one far less so – were in evidence which would eventually remove it as a weapon of war.

Cannon had been in use for some time. Edward III had trundled at least two of them with him across Normandy to Crécy, and their boom, it was said, had frightened the Genoese crossbowmen. This was their only contribution to that battle. It was the ash shafts of the bowmen that were the real frighteners on that day. Cannon were also in evidence at Agincourt, but, again, played no effective part. Nevertheless the writing was on the wall and, in the long term, gunpowder would see off the longbow.

For the time being, the crossbow remained the main threat. Still unwieldy, although the introduction of the winch had helped, it remained accurate but with a range and rate-of-fire which the big longbow could better. At about the time of Agincourt, however, steel replaced wood as the bow part of the crossbow, prodigiously increasing its range and giving it greater armour penetration. Whether the new steel crossbows were seen on St Crispin's Day at Agincourt is not known. Crossbowmen were certainly there but there is no doubt that the day was to belong to the English longbow.

THE BATTLE

In his magisterial *The Face of Battle*, military historian John Keegan sets the scene for the battle of Agincourt, fought between the British and the French on 25 October 1415. He does so in words which illustrate the way in which the encounter has caught the imagination of millions over the years:

'Agincourt is one of the most instantly and vividly visualised of all epic passages in English history, and one of the most satisfactory to contemplate. It is a victory of the weak over the strong, of the common soldier over the mounted knight, of resolution over bombast, of the desperate, cornered and far from home, over the proprietorial and cocksure. Visually, it is a pre-Raphaelite, perhaps better a Medici Gallery print battle – a composition of strong verticals and horizontals and a conflict of rich dark reds and Lincoln greens against fishscale greys and arctic blues. It is a school outing to the Old Vic, Shakespeare is fun, *son-et-lumière*, blank verse, Laurence Olivier in armour battle; it is an episode to quicken the interest of any schoolboy ever bored by a history lesson, a set-piece demonstration of English moral superiority and a cherished ingredient of a fading national myth. It is also a story of slaughter-yard behaviour and of outright atrocity.'

This evocation is colourful, even lush. But then it was a literally colourful – even perhaps a Technicoloured – age, at least for the privileged. The late medieval world was still only marginally literate and it compensated by being intensely visual, delighting in architecture, painting, silverware and costume. Jousting was at its height, with richly caparisoned knights tilting in the lists for the favour of a lady. The food served to the merchants and nobles in the manors of England and France sounds surrealistically rich to the modern ear: gilded swans, peacocks in their plumage, miniature pastries filled with cod's liver or beef marrow, eels in thick, spicy purée, lampreys with hot sauce, sturgeon, jellies – usually all magnificently and indigestibly served together.

Before that hard march had begun, even William Gladewyne had eaten well in France. King Henry had seen that his army besieging Harfleur was well provisioned. Beef, mutton, salted pork, oats, beans, peas, cheese, dried fish, wheat bread and ale had all been imported from England. But as the summer and the siege continued, the food began to run low, the weather changed for the worse and the Technicolour began to fade.

After his succession, Henry had lost no time in re-opening hostilities with France. The times were propitious. France was a divided kingdom, with King Charles VI often lapsing into fits of insanity and the Dauphin, the other princes and the great dukes vying for power. Henry immediately revived his house's claim to the throne of France and claimed also the lands ceded to his great-grandfather Edward III at the Treaty of Brétigny, most of which had been frittered away to the French in the intervening years. His claims predictably rejected, he gathered together an army 10,000 strong, made up of 2,000 knights and men-at-arms, 8,000 archers and – a sign of the new times – a handful of gunners with ordnance from London and Bristol.

This was no headstrong youngster. Like his great-grandfather, he had been careful to carry English public opinion along with him and, when he sailed, it was with the support of nobles, Parliament and a nation longing for half-forgotten glory. The trouble was that Henry had left it rather late in the year.

He sailed for France on 11 August 1415 and immediately invested Harfleur. But the prize did not fall quickly into his lap. The garrison defended stoutly and, although King Charles showed no real sign of coming to its aid, the besieging English suffered badly from sallies from the defenders, disease, and heat which eventually brought rain. Dysentery became endemic in the tented army and the desertion figures mounted – probably stimulated by strict rules which Henry had laid down against looting and pillaging the surrounding towns and villages.

It was not until 22 September that Harfleur fell and so presented the English King with a dilemma. What next? Autumn was imminent, the weather was foul and his army was now sadly reduced by sickness and desertion. Should he retire to England, sit out the winter in Harfleur or press on to Paris? Henry took plenty of counsel but he could not bring himself, weak as his force was, either to retire behind Harfleur's walls or limp back home. He decided on a defiant compromise. He would not deliberately attack the French, but would show his contempt for them by marching the 160 miles through their country – trailing his coat – to English-held Calais. He would make a *chevauchée*, like his great-uncle and great-grandfather before him. Henry did not wish to fight, but he would if he had to.

So William Gladewyne and his brothers set off with their young king through the wind and rain of a devastated countryside, retracing to some extent the march of Edward III 70 years before. This time, however, there was little food and the ravages of dysentery dogged every step. So, too, after the first few days, did the French.

The English army had left camp with about eight days' rations. This represented tough marching for 160 miles, so much of the force must have been mounted. Certainly we know that the intention was to travel light and quickly, for the baggage train was small by the standards of the day. But the flux, the waterlogged terrain and the need to cow fortified towns in their path slowed down the pace and the food soon ran low. By the time the little army had reached the Somme, about 60 miles from Calais, it was living on dried beef, the odd hedgehog, nuts and berries. And, at the Somme, Henry heard that the French were waiting on the other side. History was repeating itself.

By cutting across a large bend in the river, the English were able to make a crossing, although French horsemen quietly observed them doing so. Later, French heralds arrived and, in the manner of the day, politely inquired which way the English king was heading, for their master wished to give him battle ... at his convenience, so to speak. Henry replied that he was marching straight to Calais and if anyone disturbed him '... it shall not be without their utmost peril. We seek them not, nor for fear of them shall we move slower or quicker.'

Brave words, but many an English heart sank next day when, after marching past Péronne, the invaders crossed a track which had been beaten flat by a French host 'as if it had gone before us in many thousands'. Indeed it had. Henry's *chevauchée* had had the effect of uniting Charles's disparate kingdom. From all parts of the realm had come nobles with their retinues, incensed by the invasion and the insult offered to their king and country. The host had taken time to assemble, but by the time it had caught up with the English after their crossing of the little river Ternoise, it formed a vast gathering, gleaming and shimmering in the evening sunlight, pennants waving, lances glinting.

As always, there is no hard evidence of the exact size of Charles's army. Estimates of between 25,000 and 40,000 have been given and there may well have been more. Henry's force was smaller, pitifully smaller. Disease, desertion and the privations of the march had reduced its number to about 6,000, consisting of some 5,000 archers and 1,000 men-at-arms. The comparison, however, was not only one of size. The French host was formed mainly of nobles and men-at-arms, who had travelled across country, it is true, but at their leisure, well sustained by good food, wine and shelter. They were fresh and fired by the virtuous courage of motherland defenders.

The English, on the other hand, were tired, hungry and bedraggled. One historian described them as 'a crumpled and ragged squad, with harness out of joint and jacks all tattered'. Nor, perhaps, was their courage all that jingoistic chroniclers would have us believe. Sir Walter Hungerford eyed the French and confessed to his king that he wished for 10,000 more of the best English archers, to which Henry replied: 'Thou speakest as a fool, for I would not have one more even if I could ... this people is God's people.'

The French king had placed his army astraddle the road to Calais, across a meadow between the woods of Tramecourt and the little village of Azincourt. As with Crécy, the site has changed comparatively little in the intervening 580 years. It was farmland then, heavily ploughed on the day, and it remains under cultivation today. The Calais road still runs north, hugging the trees of Tramecourt, where they close towards the little wood which fringes Azincourt village. From the air, the meadow seems in fact like a giant fire-break, only about 900 yards (822 metres) across at this point. It was here that the main fighting took place. It was not the ideal place for King Charles to bring the English to battle. The corridor nature of the site prevented any sophisticated manoeuvrings, but more to the point it also negated to a large extent the French vast superiority in numbers.

Not that that would have given the English much heart as a wet dawn broke on the morning of 25 October. They stood silently and hungrily to arms in the rain as their enemy lit their fires, breakfasted and called cheerily to one another. The French were in no hurry. The prey was within their reach and they would take it at their leisure. They were blocking the road to Calais and the English could not escape. They were vastly outnumbered and, anyway, comprised an inadequate little army of peasants, of archers, whom the French called 'men without worth and without birth'. Within a couple of hours these invaders would all have lost their lives or, at least, their bow fingers. The *chevaliers* could afford to finish their breakfast, don their armour with care and attack when it suited them.

So the two armies faced each other for four hours across about 1,000 yards of heavily ploughed land. The English were drawn up in a line about four deep. The dismounted nobles and men-at-arms waited in three battles or blocks, separated by the far more numerous bowmen, who also formed the flanks. The archers were thrown slightly forward in pointed, wedge-shaped formations. The baggage was to the rear and was only lightly protected. Henry could afford no reserve and had thrown every man into the line. It was a desperate thing to do but he had no choice; he had to form a line to avoid being surrounded.

In contrast, the Frenchmen facing them were arrayed in three great lines, one battle behind the other, stretching from wood to wood. The first block numbered about 8,000 heavily armoured nobles and knights, all on foot and including no less than twelve princes of the blood. They were flanked, as best they could form between trees and men, by 1,000 heavy cavalry. Four thousand crossbowmen who had been intended to form a first line of skirmishers had been shouldered aside by the nobles, eager for glory, and they formed a disorganised muddle between the first and second blocks, postponing for ever the chance to match improved crossbow against the longbow at its peak. The second battle consisted of some 14,000 lesser noblemen and mercenaries, also heavily armoured and on foot. The third block, about half a mile behind the other two, comprised an indeterminate number – but certainly more than 10,000 – of cavalry and foot soldiers.

When first Henry had heard of the size of the French army that was shadowing him and of the number of cavalry in its ranks, he had ordered his archers to cut large stakes, sharpened at both ends, to act as protection against a cavalry charge. For two days his exhausted troops had carried these on the march, cursing their weight and their awkwardness. At first light he had commanded his bowmen to hammer the stakes into the ground, breast high, facing the enemy, so defining the archers' wedges in the English line. Now, after the English had waited so long for the attack which never seemed to come, he ordered his bowmen to pull up their stakes and ... march toward the enemy.

It was an audacious and, it must be said, a seemingly foolish thing to do. No, not seemingly. It *was* a foolish thing to do. While it was in a defensive position, Henry's little army stood at least a chance. Its longbowmen, behind protection – however crude – could brace themselves and slip into their definitive artillery mode, giving full support to the hard core of infantry lance and sword men. On the march, however, carrying heavy stakes, they must be at the mercy of an armoured cavalry attack. They would hardly have time to nock arrow to string before they were engulfed.

Henry, however, was tired of waiting. He had noted the languid preparations of the French knights and the state of the heavily ploughed land between the two armies. He decided to take a chance and provoke an attack. Accordingly, the English line ponderously moved forward, keeping its dressing as best it could in the mud under the command of old white-haired Sir Thomas Erpingham, the marshal of the army. The French watched with what must have been amazement. Then, when within long-shot of the enemy – about 250–275 yards – the English halted and, quickly, the archers drove in their stakes and ran behind them. On command, their bows were bent and the first flight of arrows sped towards the French lines.

It is unlikely that that first salvo caused much damage, given the recent exertions of the bowmen, the long range and the strongly armoured nature of the French front line. But it had the required result. There was a clang of visors and the flank horsemen lowered their lances and charged.

The French war-horses were strong – big hunters rather than the carthorses of popular belief – but they carried a very heavy load: probably about 250 pounds (113 kilograms) (man 150 pounds, armour 60 pounds, often more, and saddle and trappings 40 pounds). And they were being urged to gallop across furrows of newly ploughed land which the rain had turned to mud. They came, then, not that quickly, into a devastating arrow storm.

William Gladewyne and his mates, hunger forgotten but with adrenalin pumping and, no doubt, their hearts in their mouths, stood and shot as coolly and as quickly as only they knew how: ten to twelve arrows a minute, between 25,000 and 30,000 arrows in thirty seconds. The first flight may have been comparatively ineffective, more a nuisance, but as the range narrowed and the bowmen lowered their elevation, the arrows took terrible toll, penetrating the quilted war coats of the horses and finding the chain mail gaps in the knights' armour. Horses plunged and reared, throwing their riders into the mud to be trampled by hooves or simply left to wallow helplessly under the weight of their battle trappings. The cavalry charge, designed to put the archers to flight and leave the English men-at-arms at the mercy of the vastly more numerous French infantry, had failed completely. Wide-eyed, riderless horses, some with arrows protruding from their quilts like pin-cushions, plunged back towards the French lines, encumbering the French knights who had begun their own advance. The French crossbowmen had filled the gaps left on the flanks by the departure of the horsemen. They stepped forward and loosed a desultory discharge of their bolts, before melting away from the arrows.

Heads down, visors lowered, as at Poitiers, the great phalanx of French men-at-arms trudged forward through the mud. As they neared the English line they diverged into three sections, avoiding the archers and heading for the narrow lines of English nobility, who stood impassively under their banners between the wedges of the bowmen. It was, clearly, beneath the French nobles' dignity to attack peasants. It was equally clearly a great mistake. They made an unmissable target for William and his fellows, now left between their timber stakes to shoot as fast as they could pull their longbows. Arrows now penetrated plate armour and marksmanship entered the contest as shafts hissed into unprotected armpits as sword arms were raised to strike.

The two lines, one 30 men deep, the other four, met with a crash of steel and the English line gave 'a spear's length'. It was the key point of the battle. Unmolested, the bowmen shot into the flanks and, drawing knife and mallet, slipped in and out of the fray to fight hand to hand. The line held. Now the very size of the French army began to count against it. As the vast mass of nobles pressed forward from the rear, so they prevented the front line from wielding its weapons, and the dead bodies themselves began to form a low wall from behind which the English could fight. The living fell on the dead and were themselves crushed. It was, as Keegan says, a slaughter-yard.

Seeing that the first line had not overwhelmed the English, the second block of French infantry began its advance, climbing over horses and dead men to thrust forward against the rear of their comrades, eager to enter the mêlée. This served to hold the French front even more firmly in place to suffer further butchery from the English line which was much freer to swing sword and axe. And still the arrows came, from the flanks and from the wedges superficially protected by the stakes. And still the bowmen nipped in and out of the lines, thrusting, stabbing and retrieving their arrows to shoot again. The fighting at the front was intense and King Henry himself sustained a fearful blow on his helmet (still to be seen in Westminster Abbey) in hand-to-hand combat with the Duc d'Alençon.

Somehow, in the midst of the carnage, the English had time to take prisoners and escort them to the baggage train in the rear. One contemporary French chronicler wryly commented: 'some, even of the more noble, surrendered themselves more than ten times'. Slowly, the French second line eased its attacks and then broke and fled. Shortly after midday it seemed to the exhausted and amazed English that they were left in possession of the field. But not quite.

The huge French third battle had not been involved and could clearly be seen, attempting to get into some vestige of formation. And then a note of farce crept into the day. Soon after midday, the French Duke of Brabant arrived on the scene. He had been forced to attend a family christening in the north and had galloped as fast as possible to join his king, terrified that he would be too late to win honour and spoils. He arrived with his retinue to observe what seemed to be a pause in the battle. The English were still there and a French line appeared to be preparing to attack. Having left the christening without armour, the Duke borrowed that of his chamberlain, cut a hole in his trumpeter's cloth of arms, put it over his head as a surcoat and, with a cry, charged into battle. It was heroic but absurd. He was cut down almost immediately.

The Duke's intervention, however, played a part in prompting the most unsavoury episode in a day otherwise marked by courage and chivalry on both sides. As Brabant and his retinue charged against a background of what appeared to be a re-grouping for attack by the French third line, Henry heard a disturbance to his rear, where the prisoners, *en parole* and unhelmeted, were lightly guarded. There a small force, led by local noblemen, had attacked the baggage train. They had been easily repulsed but, to Henry, it appeared that the day was far from won and that, indeed, there was a danger that he could become surrounded. He immediately ordered all the prisoners to be killed. Now this was not only against the laws of chivalry but such an act represented a great loss of ransom to the English nobility and archers alike – not that the latter had any opportunity to protest. The nobles did, however, quite fiercely, and refused to do the grisly work. So the king ordered up 200 of his archer guard to carry out the killings. They had begun to do so when Henry realised that no further attacks were developing, the French third line was leaving the field and that the day was his. He called off the executions, although not before some of his noble captives had been killed.

The battle had lasted three hours. Ten thousand Frenchmen had been killed, including half the nobility of France. Another 2,000 had been taken prisoner. Incredibly, the English losses numbered less than 200 men. Rarely had a battle been won so decisively against such huge odds. It was a complete and overwhelming victory for the ragtaggle, half-starving English army and their young king. It was also the greatest testimony to the power of the English longbowman.

THE AFTERMATH

If the field of Crécy today seems to posses the cheerful vulgarity of a theme park, that of Agincourt has an air of poignancy. More open, though flatter, than Crécy, the site seems windblown and empty, despite the crops which now grow where sword split helm and peasant arrows brought down the finest in the land. A little copse of trees near Tramecourt marks grave pits where 6,000 Frenchmen are buried. A crucifix keeps lonely vigil. It is a sad place, reminding the visitor that the charnel-house has no lasting glory.

Henry V had *his* glory all right. After Agincourt, his fame as a warrior king echoed all round the Christian world. On his return to London, virgins in white lined London Bridge and sang a song of victory, while others blew gold leaves on to his head. There was a procession to Westminster, a pageant was performed and sparrows were released into the air. The procession included the bones of the Duke of York and the Earl of Suffolk, both of whom had been slain in the battle. Their bodies had been boiled in France, so that the bones could be taken home to England and their deaths honoured. The church bells rang throughout the land and rarely can a battle have been more widely publicised and celebrated.

Yet Agincourt was not the last English success, nor even the high-water mark of the English advance in France. There was no surrender by the French following their defeat and Henry resumed his campaign, regaining more of the Norman and Angevin territories before he imposed a peace treaty at Troyes in 1420. This gave him Charles VI's daughter, Katherine, in marriage and the right of succession to the French throne on Charles's death. The dispossessed Dauphin, however, had his adherents in the east and south of France and the war continued, stimulated anew by Henry's untimely death in 1422.

Henry's brother John, acting as regent for the infant Henry VI, led the English armies now and at Cravant in 1423, and at Verneuil in 1424 the archers were again instrumental in providing English victories. After that, however, English fortunes waned, although there was never a victory won so decisively on either side as those of Crécy, Poitiers and Agincourt. The year 1429 is generally seen as the final turning point of the wearisome business. It was the year which saw the emergence of Joan of Arc, the saving of Orleans and the French victory at Patay. It is significant that the French won the day there because they were able to disperse the English archers before they were set in position in numbers on the flanks. By now the French had their own archers, although they were never as important to the French as the longbowmen were to England. Guns were important for sieges, but they were not significant factors in open battle until Castillon in 1453, the final battle of the Hundred Years War.

The great conflict died without a concluding peace treaty – more with a whimper of exhaustion than a great final cry of victory from either side. Certainly, the English eventually gave up all their territory in France, although it was not until 1805 that the British royal family formally relinquished its claim to the throne of France. So the English lost their empire. But they had removed the threat of French invasion and waxed rich on a century of booty from the war. It was a kind of dishonourable draw; a stalemate, after 116 years of conflict and carnage.

Were Crécy, Poitiers and Agincourt meaningless, then? Did the longbowmen of England produce their unlikely victories only for them to end as footnotes to a medieval power struggle? In purely military terms and, given that most wars are never worth the deaths and anguish they cause, the answer must probably be yes. But William Gladewyne and his brothers deserve to be regarded as catalytic players in a more profound scenario.

The longbowman's prowess on the field of battle broke him out of his feudal background. He became highly paid by the standards of the time and, more importantly, a hitherto unheard of democracy emerged in those Plantagenet armies. The archer remained humble – sometimes still a bondman, although Henry V declared that he wanted his archers to be freemen. But it was possible, by feat of arms, for him to make his way. Robert Salle was a bondman when conscripted in 1335. Thirty years later he was a knight and commander of a Calais fort. The bowman was allowed not only to kill but to take prisoner the nobleman to whose throat he presented the dagger. In one battle, John Ballard, archer, captured the Archdeacon of Paris. He later sold him for £50 on the prisoner black market in London, sufficient to set himself up for life.

The English commanders were proud of the feats of their longbowmen. They encouraged them to practise every day, gave them leave (*vide* William Jauderel) and no doubt were quite happy for them to play to the hilt the part of the old sweat in the ale- houses at home. Certainly, the archers had the wages to do so. Both Edward III and Henry V were shrewd propagandists. Both sent back to Parliament detailed reports of their success in the field and Edward took great care to publish dispatches which he ordered to be read from church pulpits throughout the land. The bowmen became famous – and not only at home. Writing as early as Crécy, the French nobleman Jean le Bel commented that the English troops were prepared to fight even when they were not paid their wages. They were emerging as a new breed of fighting man.

Yet the English kings and nobles were also ambivalent about the archers. On the one hand, they rewarded, praised and publicised their performance in battle. On the other, they became afraid of the proletarian power which they were unleashing. These men could, it was feared, become a threat to society. Accordingly, although the common folk were urged to practise archery, they were discouraged from hunting with bows (although they continued to do so). In 1390 artificers, labourers, butchers, shoemakers, tailors and 'other low persons' were ordered not to hunt in parks on holy days when Christians were at church. The reason given was 'fear of banding together for the purpose of insurrection'.

There was also a feeling that too much money was falling into the wrong hands – not least, no doubt, as a result of the booty emanating from France. This prompted a law in 1363 about what people should wear and eat. Under the statute, grooms and servants were to wear cloth costing not more than 13 shillings and 4 pence for a whole suit and their wives and children the same. Silk and gold, silver and enamel embroidery were forbidden. Carters, ploughmen and herdsmen were forbidden even cloth, being restricted to blanket or homespun wool. They were to 'eat and drink in the same manner that pertains to them, and not excessively'.

These fears were not groundless and the English aristocracy received its biggest shock in 1381, with the Peasants' Revolt, led by Wat Tyler. He led an uprising in Kent which gathered force and marched on London. The rebels burned Southwark Prison, plundered Lambeth Palace, burst into the Tower and killed the Archbishop of Canterbury. Eventually, they were met by the young King Richard II, the Black Prince's son, at Smithfield, where the Lord Mayor of London, Sir William Walworth, killed Tyler. The latter is alleged to have been an ex-archer and a veteran of the wars in France. Many other bowmen were in the ranks of his peasant army and it is said that, for the confrontation with the King and the nobles at Smithfield, the mob slipped into separate 'battles', reminiscent of the English configurations at Crécy and Poitiers and that Tyler's followers came 'each with his bow ready to shoot'.

The revolt disintegrated but a lesson had been learned. The bowmen had achieved too much, they had been too vital and large a part of the successes against the French – successes which had been celebrated throughout the land – for them all to slip back into feudalism. From the Dark Ages, the archers had emerged as the first real proletarian army. Peasants had won battles and influenced campaigns in the past. Wallace's men at Stirling Bridge in 1297 and the Flemish townspeople at Courtrai in 1302 spring to mind. But the bowmen had a consistent success over 70 to 80 years, winning an early form of independence for their class which never really disappeared.

The craft of bowmaking itself became respectable and bowyers, fletchers and bowstring-makers stood alongside the other craft guilds. At Norwich in 1449 the fletchers and bowyers bore the lights around the body of

Christ at festival time and eighteen years later, at Beverley, it was the fletchers who were given the honour of presenting the pageant in the local play cycle. The longbow had come a long way from being 'that weapon of a dastard'.

The archer could also fairly be credited with playing a crucial, if unwitting, background role in changing the cultural life of England. His great victories stimulated a new feeling of nationalism. This was the time when English architecture moved from the flamboyant and very continental Gothic of the 14th century to the definitively English Perpendicular style, epitomised by Gloucester Abbey. The humiliation of France hastened the demise of French as the language of England, so that by the end of the 14th century it had virtually passed out of use as the vernacular of government and the ruling class. In the early 1350s the Mayor and Aldermen of London ordered that proceedings in the sheriff's courts should be conducted in English. Six years later – after Poitiers – the Chancellor opened Parliament using English for the first time and it was ruled that English should become the language used in all courts throughout the realm.

At last an English literature began to be established, although only a minority could read. Laurence Minot was a northern poet whose patriotism reflected the mood of the times and influenced Chaucer, who burgeoned initially under the patronage of Edward III's Queen Philippa. Langland, whose first version of *Piers Plowman* dates from 1362, wrote in the West Midlands dialect, and the unknown author of *Sir Gawayne and the Grene Knight* was a Lancashire man. From these great wars the English were emerging as a nation with a common language.

Paradoxically, the French also eventually took benefit from the successes of William Gladewyne and company. The traditional disunity of medieval France meant that, although a French king often had the support of a Francophile Pope, the strength of the great dukes – particularly of Normandy and Burgundy – resulted in national rule from Paris being spasmodic and often ineffective. Gradually, however, the English strategy of devastating the French countryside brought about an internal immigration of French peasants into the fortified towns, which, in turn, became the engines of French nationalism. Agincourt was the last straw and, although it took time, after that great battle the English became aware that they were fighting a more united nation.

Continental warfare changed in many ways. In the 1440s the French set up their companies of free archers. These were levied by parishes, one man from every 80 hearths. In the mid 15th century there were some 8,000 free archers and by the time of Louis XI there were 16,000. The best men were recruited and were given valuable exemption in tax (this in a country which, until recent years, had banned the carrying of weapons by peasants!). It was part of the development of more professional forces in France and of the standing national armies which transformed the nature of war. By 1470 Burgundy, like France, possessed a standing army in which archers played a key role, despite the presence of cannon.

At this time the chronicler Waurin wrote: 'The most important thing in the world in battle is the archers, but they must be in thousands, for in small numbers they do not prevail.' He was emphasising the fundamental point about the great English successes in the Hundred Years War. The longbowmen were skilled specialists who held the key to success, but they had to be sited on the flanks or with some basic protection – as batteries of artillery, in fact – and then deployed with trust and skill by their commanders. Given that, they could bestride the medieval battlefield.

So – what of William Gladewyne? We can presume with reasonable confidence that he survived Agincourt, given that so few of King Henry's archers were killed or injured there. It is to be hoped that he also survived the French lances and diseases of the rest of the campaign to return to the ale-houses of a young, burgeoning England to boast of his feats.

We can take away one last picture of him from his great battle. It is dusk and Henry V has long since called in the heralds to ask them the name of the nearest habitation, so that he can name the battle. 'Azincourt', they said. 'Agincourt it shall be, replied the King. Camp fires are flickering on the grim field and the English are eating, at last.

One figure is picking his way carefully among the dead. He examines each prostrate figure carefully. Looting? No – or, if he is, he is very particular about what he takes. Eventually he bends down and produces his knife, carefully cutting away leather straps which hold plate armour. At last he has what he wants and with a cry of relief he pulls on to his poor, sore, chapped shanks a pair of fine French hose.

William Gladewyne, the first Tommy Atkins, has found dignity at last.

3
THE SKIRMISHERS
The Riflemen of Saratoga

T he concept of skirmishers was not new in battle by the last quarter of the 18th century. The need to throw out a screen of fast moving, lightly equipped infantry, in loose order and in advance of the main force, had been felt since the Roman eagles first crossed the Alps. A commander needed to test his enemy; to feel him out – sometimes even to draw him into battle precipitately – before the main conflict began. Henry V used his artillery, his bowmen, for this purpose to open proceedings at Agincourt. The revolutionary, pre-Napoleonic armies of France overran Europe behind a swarm of ragged skirmishers. And there was no general better than Bonaparte himself at deploying these curtain raisers.

Skirmishers, however, did not win battles, let alone wars. Comparatively lightly armed and lacking heavy equipment, they tended to melt away as a discrete force once battle had been joined. Traditionally, they were not trained or suited to the heavy, shoulder-to-shoulder mêlée and their job was done once the enemy had been drawn into battle. They were provocateurs, the *banderillos* preparing the bull for the entry of the *matadors*.

This was the role played to perfection by the American riflemen against the British at the Battle of Saratoga in 1777, the third year of the War of American Independence. But these backwoodsmen did not slip away after the opening skirmishes and they added an additional, battle-winning factor to the usual techniques displayed by these specialist foot soldiers: that of accurate marksmanship. If one adds the term 'sharpshooter' to that of skirmisher, it is difficult to offer any practitioners of this dangerous role who stand out more effectively in military history than the frontier riflemen who fought for Washington in 'the glorious cause'. Their success was such that they became mythologised. Many schoolboys today visualise the Revolutionary War, as it is known in America, as being won entirely by buckskin-shirted frontiersmen who stayed in the forests, quietly picking off the Redcoats who marched obligingly towards them in the open, elbow-to-elbow, scrupulously keeping line so that they made easy targets. In fact, most battles were fought by Washington in the classic European style: a direct confrontation by two armies, using artillery and the bayonet charge as key elements. After all, Washington had been an officer in the British army. That is how he had been trained to fight and he even employed a German baron to show his raw American troops how to drill in the accepted way.

But Saratoga was rather different. There, as the forests of Upstate New York were being turned into a rusty Technicolour by the autumn of 1777, Washington's riflemen played a key role in defeating and capturing the British army of General John Burgoyne. These frontiersmen skirmished, of course, and were in their element among the trees and brush of the forest. But they stayed to outshoot the British continually throughout the battle, bringing down the most able English general and proving how deadly the rifle could be.

The war was far from over but it had been made quite clear to a watching world that Britain could not win it, however long she campaigned. Two days after the news of the British defeat reached Paris, France formally recognised the United States of America, as, later, did Spain and Holland. A great nation had been born.

NO TAXATION WITHOUT REPRESENTATION!

Throughout the 18th century, America had consistently grown in attraction as a Utopia across the ocean: a land where dissent was tolerated and opportunities existed for men and women who were prepared to work hard and take risks. It was a beguiling prospect for drop-outs, but also for Europeans of spirit who were tired of taxes, kings, aristocratic wars and established religions. Nor was the New World an illusion. To the immigrants who, in increasing numbers during the century, staggered off the hell-hole ships, the new colonies were a revelation. Once the immediate squalor of the receiving harbours was left behind, the country was, literally, beautiful. Near the coast, plantations and tilled fields lapped the edges of white-painted, orderly towns. Farther west – and, sooner or later, all immigrants moved west – the forests were sun-dappled, full of game and threaded with fish-stocked creeks and rivers. Once cleared, the land was usually fertile and, if a man listened to his neighbours and worked hard, harvests were adequate and, often, bountiful.

What is more, unlike the situation in crowded and feudal Europe, a man was positively helped to buy land. The British Act of Burgess, passed in 1701 'for the better strengthening of the frontiers', empowered the colonial authorities to issue grants of from 10,000 to 30,000 acres of western land to companies or societies that would settle 'one Christian, war-like man' for every 500 acres granted. The Act had practically no immediate effect but it did set an important precedent. Land was to be used as an inducement for frontier settlement.

Liberal landowners such as Lord Fairfax in Virginia and, farther north, Lord Baltimore and the Penn family, all applied the principle to the vast tracts which had been granted to them by the Crown. In 1732, Baltimore offered land parcels of 200 acres each, with the payment of both the £20 per 100 acres purchase price and the fees ('quidrent') deferred for three years to enable settlers to get started. Farther west, on the wilderness side of the Blue Ridge Mountains, land was cheaper and before 1740 a price of £3 per 100 acres was the norm. That reference in the Act of Burgess to 'war-like men', however, betrayed one discordant element in the Promised Land. The Indians in the eastern coastal territories had long ago either moved out or been assimilated. To the west, however, rose the great barrier spine of the Appalachian Mountains and beyond that lay a vast and little-known country claimed by the French but inhabited by bear, deer, beaver, otter – and Indians. Settlers who ventured to this wild frontier were on their own. They cleared their land, built their cabin, planted their corn, went hunting in the forest and lived as best they could with the itinerant Iroquois, Shawnees, Cherokees and other tribes on whose hunting grounds they intruded. Many Indians were friendly, many were not, and the farmer had to harvest his crops and bring up his family with his rifle and tomahawk by his side at all times. He had to be, perforce, a war-like man.

The French presence was distant. Although the French king claimed all the immense and uncharted territory which reached out from the Appalachians to the Rockies and which was known as Louisiana, his main interest lay in the profitable fur trade, most of it based in the French possessions in Canada. He made no attempt to colonise formally elsewhere. As a result, there were only a handful of trading posts, stretching in a tenuous line from New Orleans to Quebec, to fly the yellow Bourbon lilies in the wilderness south of the Great Lakes.

Nevertheless, the French looked with growing anxiety at the increasing number of settlers who began filtering through the mountains from Pennsylvania, Virginia and the Carolinas. They could tolerate the British if they stayed on the eastern seaboard but not if they thrust westwards and began cutting the lucrative north-south fur trade route. The French felt they had to protect that route by driving a wedge south, deep into the wilderness. They found ready allies in the Indians along the Ohio river who also feared losing their hunting grounds to the British settlers. At least the French left them their land and, by buying their skins, contributed to their lifestyle. Armed, then, with French muskets and newly honed Canadian tomahawks, the Shawnee war parties slipped down the ancient warrior paths to the south and began raiding the frontier settlements. It was a bloody, intermittent conflict which was to last for the next 130 years, the last battles being fought far to the west to where the ever-moving frontier had pushed the Indians.

In faraway London, the British Board of Trade, with an insouciant disregard for local claims – a characteristic which was to grow stronger – granted a group of Virginians 500,000 acres of rich land in the disputed Ohio valley, provided that they built a fort there and settled a hundred families. The Virginians attempted to build the fort on the Ohio, the French threw out the contractors and shots were exchanged. Before the year was out, Britain and France were at war again.

The conflict became known in America as the French and Indian War and, to the British, as the Seven Years War. It was fought in Europe as well as North America and it culminated in a decisive British victory at Quebec and the collapse of French power in Canada. It established the British as the world's leading military nation and a strong imperialistic power. It also sowed the seeds of dissent between the settlers in the British colonies of the American seaboard and the British government in London.

In 1763 the Peace of Paris tidied up the land apportionments following the defeat of the French and, in the same year, the British government decided to keep a standing army in America. It was an unusual thing for it to do. Such forces were expensive to maintain (the East India Company provided what troops were necessary at that time in India) and the public was antipathetic to funding standing armies in faraway places.

The news met with strong opposition in the thirteen colonies. Much of the brunt of the fighting with the French had been borne by the British Army, but the colonists had made a strong contribution. They felt ill-rewarded to be told that an army would now stay in place. It was there, they felt, to cow them, not to protect the frontier. And the displeasure heightened when London announced that a new Stamp Tax would be imposed to help pay for the North American Army. Riots occurred, stamps were destroyed, Parliament was petitioned and eventually the Stamp Tax was repealed. But the gulf of misunderstandings between government and colonies widened and discontent flared again in 1767 when London attempted to impose import duties on tea, glass and other articles. The duty on the other articles was grudgingly dropped but that on tea remained, as a token of the British Parliament's right to tax its colonists. The Americans refused to buy supplies of English tea and in Boston a band of men disguised as Indians boarded the tea ships and threw their cargoes into the harbour.

So the revolt escalated. To London – and government and opposition were united in this – it seemed quite reasonable for colonists to be taxed to bear part of the cost of protecting and governing them. But the colonists had come of age. They had played their part in the past war and they had left Britain in the first place to escape heavy-handed authority. They wanted no more of it. There was the additional, emotive point that no Parliamentary representation was allowed to the Americans. The cry went up 'No taxation without representation!' and the two sides marched inexorably towards collision. It came in April 1775 when troops opened fire on a group of Americans in Lexington and, in the fight which followed at nearby Concord, the British lost 303 men and the Americans 93. The War of American Independence had begun.

It was a reluctant war on both sides. The thirteen rebellious states were themselves fiercely defensive of their individual independence and they certainly did not march to the beat of the same drum. Nor was there serious talk of a complete break with Britain at this time. Nevertheless, a Continental Congress was formed and, at its second meeting, in Philadelphia, it appointed as commander-in-chief of the American forces, George Washington, a respected Virginian farmer, landowner and soldier.

The British reluctance to make this an all-out war was reflected in the appointment of General Howe to command the British forces. Howe was a soldier of proven ability, if of somewhat lethargic and uncommunicative demeanour. He knew the North American terrain quite well and rather liked the colonists. He viewed the insurrection as a local revolt which could be put down quickly and firmly, after which life in the colonies could be resumed as before. The military action was to be more a matter of chastising unruly children who deserved some form of admonishment before being sent back to the classroom.

The first real action of the war, in fact, took place on the eve of the second Congress meeting and before Howe's appointment, while he was still serving as second in command to General Gage in Boston. This Massachusetts city, with its strong tradition of Puritan dissent, had been the cradle of the revolution. It was not surprising, then, that the first real battle should be fought there. The Battle of Bunker's Hill was won by the British but at great cost. They lost more than half their force. There was no going back after this scale of bloodshed.

General Washington was in no position to offer serious resistance. He was attempting to raise and train a completely new army. While he was doing so, a volunteer force marched on the British stronghold in Canada. The audacious little army seized Montreal and attacked Quebec. Rebuffed, the Americans laid siege to the city but were ravaged by disease and bad weather. Montreal was re-taken and, of the American commanders, General Montgomery was killed, Allen was captured and Benedict Arnold was wounded. The frozen remnant of the rebel army was forced to withdraw.

But the Canadian expedition was a side-show. The truth is that a formal states' army hardly existed in those first few months of the war. Bunker's Hill and the Canadian invasion were fought, on the rebels' side, by enthusiasts in the first, honeymoon flush of revolution. Preparing for a long haul campaign against the most feared army in the world was a very different matter, as General Washington well knew. The recruits whom the states sent to him fell into two categories, the 'Continentals', the core of the army, who usually signed on for one year's service after which they returned to their homes, and the Militia, the part-time soldiers of each state who could be called out in emergency, usually to defend their local territory. This gave recruits in both categories a distinctly detached and short-term view of soldiering. Discipline was weak, particularly with recruits from the democratic New England states. At Cambridge (according to Charles Knowles Bolton's *The Private Soldier under Washington*, Kennikat Press, Washington, 1902) one captain of horse was seen on the parade ground shaving one of his troopers. Many officers depended for their commissions on their ability to raise companies and to persuade men to serve under them – the test was of popularity and not of military skill or experience. Nathaniel Greene, one of Washington's favourite generals, complained sadly, 'The men are much better than the officers.'

In those early months, Washington himself oversaw virtually every element of training, personally seeing to camp sanitation (to him, earth closets were 'the necessaries') as well as attempting to instil elements of military skill into his un-uniformed, ill-equipped, grumbling force. He was never quite sure of the size of his army, so frequent were the desertions and so unreliable the flow of reinforcements. At one stage, along the Delaware in December 1776, retreating yet again from Howe, he had but 3,000 troops under his immediate command, with about half of them due to go home at the end of the month when their term of enlistment ran out.

Against him was arrayed an army of professionals, which had built to about 32,000 in number in the first six months of the war. It was an army experienced in European warfare and included 8,000 Hessian mercenaries hired from Germany. Both they and the English line soldiers were hard-bitten veterans, trained to respond unthinkingly to orders, however loud the cannon. Led by experienced officers and NCOs, they were cool under fire and impressive to witness in action. They were schooled to keep their line in battle; to wheel and re-form, load and discharge their muskets quickly, in devastating, sequential volleys by file, and then go in with the bayonet to finish the enemy. At that time, they were simply the best.

It was very much, then, a fight of professionals versus amateurs. After Bunker's Hill, Washington brought up his raw forces to surround Boston and, when rebel batteries were installed on Dorchester Heights, Howe felt it wiser to slip away by sea to New York and await his reinforcements. Then the war lapsed into a series of plodding British attacks, with Washington defending as well as he could, but usually managing to retreat and keeping his army together to fight another day. Somehow, the rebel army survived. In fact, the odds were not all stacked against the Americans. Although the British were usually the larger force in the field and were better fed and equipped, they were nearly always encumbered by unwieldy baggage trains, and Washington's more lightly equipped, faster-moving men were more familiar with the terrain. The rebels were thrown off Rhode Island and out of New York City, but Howe failed to bring them to a battle in which his superior forces could win a decisive victory.

So the war marked time for a while during the winter of 1777. The colonists now knew that there could be no reconciliation with the mother country and, on 4 July 1776, they had declared their independence. This enabled them formally to seek foreign alliances for, without them, it was clearly going to be impossible to secure the comprehensive victory in battle which would convince Britain to quit. Yet, for all their longing to see the British humiliated in the field, the major European powers remained firmly on the fence. They would not recognise the rebels until they had shown, with a great victory, that they could survive – a classic case of what later generations would call Catch 22.

It was against this background of seeming stalemate that a charismatic English general sailed for London to sell to the British government his 'Grand Strategy' for winning the war.

THE GRAND STRATEGY

Lieutenant General John Burgoyne was one of those Englishmen whom many Americans – and many Englishman, for that matter – cannot help disliking. A portrait by Sir Joshua Reynolds (see illustrations), painted when Burgoyne was a young colonel serving in Portugal, captures his good looks:

a patrician profile, with straight nose and firm chin, one hand jauntily on hip, the other on his sword, his slightly bulbous eyes stare into the future with supreme self- confidence. Arrogant, witty, debonair and a gambler who possessed a facile pen, he was popular with his troops. They called him 'Gentleman Johnny'. Jealous contemporaries thought him an *arriviste* who had been incredibly lucky. As a penniless captain of Dragoons, he had eloped with the Earl of Derby's sister and been forced to resign his commission. His charm had won his way back into the favour of his influential brother-in-law and a return to the army. He had never looked back. Successful campaigns in Europe, a seat in the House of Commons and his confident urbanity had earned him the favour of the King. He had sailed to Boston with Howe and one other major-general, Henry Clinton, and taken part in the Battle of Bunker's Hill. Ambitious and a political schemer, he had little respect for the rebel army and felt it should be crushed as quickly as possible. He was now back in London to promote a military initiative which he believed would shorten the war – and, more importantly, bring him honour and glory.

The idea was not new, nor even of Burgoyne's creation. In fact, it was an obvious strategy, whose very simplicity has obfuscated its authorship. The only feasible inland invasion route into America from Canada lay along the north–south waterway offered by the Richelieu river, Lakes Champlain and George and then, via a 20-mile portage, the Hudson river, which debouched into the Atlantic at New York. It presented a perfect opportunity for an invading British force to split off the hard-line states of New England, the cradle of the revolution, from the perhaps not quite so enthusiastic rebels in the south. A tentative plan for British troops to march northwards up the Hudson from New York had earlier been discussed and shelved. Now Burgoyne, pleading the need to see to constituency affairs, had taken leave to come home to press his version. It was a propitious time. Lord North's government and the King himself were fretting at Howe's seeming lethargy and the equal caution displayed by the Canadian governor-general, Sir Guy Carlton, to whom Burgoyne was nominally second in command.

Burgoyne's plan was approved. Fundamentally, it proposed an invasion force leaving Montreal in the late spring and using the lakes (subduing the rebel-held Fort Ticonderoga on the way) to reach the Hudson and, by boat and river road, press on and take Albany, some 100 miles up the Hudson from New York. A subsidiary force would make passage down the Mohawk river from the west to create a diversion. The question of what was planned to happen after Albany has remained a matter of debate for more than two centuries.

There is clear evidence that Burgoyne's plan called for him meeting up with Howe's main army at Albany. This would involve Howe leaving his New York base and mounting an organised expedition up-river. But Howe was dedicated to an attack on Philadelphia, the rebels' capital, and he was later to deny vehemently that he received orders to support Burgoyne with his main army. The role played by Lord Germain, the Secretary of State for the Colonies, in London, is an obscure but culpable one. As the politician with overall responsibility for the direction of the war, it was for him to issue firm orders and allocate responsibilities. Nevertheless, communications were difficult in those days of six weeks' Atlantic passages, and Germain had the right to expect a degree of co-operative goodwill from his generals. In the event, it fell far short of what was needed. Howe saw Burgoyne as a threat to his own position and was not at all enthusiastic about changing his own plans to accommodate him. Burgoyne was not overly worried about whether Howe met him at Albany or not. He himself foresaw no problems in reaching there and then he could decide whether to push on to New York or winter in Albany. Howe could join him, anyway, after he had captured Philadelphia. After all, they were both only opposed by 'undisciplined rabble'. In such small jealousies and arrogance are great military disasters conceived.

In April 1777, Gentleman Johnny assembled his invading army at St John's, on the Richelieu river in Canada. It totalled just under 9,000 men, comprising 3,274 British regulars, 3,000 Hessians, 473 artillerymen and an assortment of Canadians, loyal Americans (called Tories by both sides) and Indians. The seven German regiments had been hired from the Duke of Brunswick and were commanded by Lieutenant-General Friedrich von Riedesel, an experienced cavalry officer who had fought at Minden and who, in fact, had seen more action than Burgoyne. The British government had been forced to hire mercenaries for North America because Britain's small population could only muster a standing army of 50,000 men, most of whom were already committed to America, the other colonies and to protecting the homeland.

Burgoyne could not have asked for better men. His transport was another matter. Although he had ordered his troops to leave behind their blanket coats and leggings and the officers to strip down their personal baggage to the minimum (an order which he personally ignored), he took with him 138 pieces of artillery, carried on an assortment of hastily built and requisitioned carriages and carts or on the backs of horses and mules. The commissariat and women camp-followers, including many officers' wives, swelled the column. Burgoyne wanted more than 1,000 carts to carry his artillery and provisions. He got 500. It was not a happy omen.

Arrogant and personally self-indulgent he may have been (he took the wife of one of his officers as his mistress and lived with her on the march), Burgoyne was no fool. He had learned enough about conditions in North America to realise that scouting and skirmishing were to be of unusual importance on this campaign. To a large extent he relied upon his Huron and Algonquin Indians to be his eyes, but, admiring the marksmanship and speed of movement of the American skirmishers (it seems that not all of the enemy army were 'rabble'), he had commissioned young Captain Alexander Fraser, nephew of his favourite senior officer, Brigadier-General Simon Fraser, to pick from the infantry the best marksmen to act as light infantry or rangers.

The problems of logistics had delayed him severely and Burgoyne knew that it would be fatal to be caught on the march by the North American winter, but the army sailed at last on 12 June. It was an impressive armada: the birch bark canoes of the Indians in the lead, followed by the pinnaces of the generals, two frigates, six brigs and sloops, 28 gunboats, a bomb ketch and 500 troop-carrying *bateaux*. The large ships, of course, would have to be left behind at the portage between the lakes and the river, but they would play their part in intimidating the defenders of Fort Ticonderoga.

Perhaps it was the size and grandeur of his fleet or merely his innate pomposity, but Burgoyne could not resist issuing a proclamation to the rebels. He had embarked, he said, on a crusade to restore 'the general privileges of mankind', and he urged Americans to join him in 'the glorious task' of restoring the blessings of legal government. To those who did not, he warned, he would 'give stretch to the Indian Forces under my direction to wreak devastation, famine and concomitant horror upon the miscreants'.

It was only twenty years since Britain and her American colonists had hurled abuse at the French for their use of the Indians during the Seven Years War. The horror of those barbaric attacks on farms and homesteads were still remembered. There was already the beginning of a renewal, under British encouragement, of Indian attacks along the long frontier. Now here was a British general promising to unleash the barbarians upon the tranquil interiors of the States of New York and Vermont! In London it brought strong criticism and some ridicule of Burgoyne in the House of Commons and, more importantly, had repercussions of immense value to Washington in his never-ending campaign to raise more recruits.

Burgoyne's threat was almost certainly hollow. The day after his proclamation he addressed his 400 Indians and forbade them to indulge in bloodshed if no resistance were encountered. Aged men, women, children and prisoners should be spared and no scalps should be taken from the wounded. He wished his Indian brothers to fight as civilised soldiers, not savages. The red men grunted, drank the white general's whiskey, gave him a ceremonial war dance and went smiling to sharpen their scalping knives.

The Grand Strategy could not have had a more impressive launching. Within three weeks of leaving his Canadian base, Burgoyne had captured Fort Ticonderoga. The news, when it arrived in London, sent George III capering into his Queen's bedroom crying 'I have taken Ticonderoga!' But it sent a thrill of horror through the rebel states. Washington, still facing Howe near New York, had been assured that the fort was impregnable and that it closed the route from the north. To hear that it had been abandoned with hardly a shot fired in its defence seemed incomprehensible – even though the garrison had escaped.

The truth is that Washington had been misled. The fort's importance was not in doubt. It was set in a strategic position, commanding the narrows where Lakes Champlain and George converged. Any force moving south had to take it. The bastion therefore had been well fortified and had recently received a garrison of 3,000 men. The problem was that the defenders were ill-equipped to resist a siege – many were bare-footed and, more importantly, the fort could be dominated if cannon could be hauled to the summit of a nearby hill. This the energetic British had done and the garrison commander, Colonel Arthur St Clair, realised that resistance was hopeless. His main aim now was to preserve his force intact. To lose it would be to leave New York State and New England wide open to the enemy. Under cover of darkness he slipped away south, sending some of his cannon, the sick and 600 soldiers by boat and the majority of his force on foot via the forest road.

The pursuit began at once. Brigadier Fraser and his light infantry – 'light' although each man carried sixty pounds on his back – went after the main body and Burgoyne, quickly blasting away the boom across the lake narrows, sailed after the boat party. In a prodigious feat of forest marching through the night, Fraser overtook the sanguine American rear-guard and, with last-minute reinforcements from the Hessians, defeated it in a brisk engagement at Hubbardton, in Vermont. Burgoyne caught up with the surprised boat party and destroyed their boats, captured their guns and forced them to flee to Fort Edward on the Hudson river. Exultantly, the British general re-united his forces at Skenesboro (modern-day Whitehall) to await the arrival of cannon, carts and provisions.

Burgoyne then pushed on overland, but with difficulty. The road was narrow and passed through thick forest and swamp where a log causeway had sunk into the morass. The size of the baggage train and its inadequate transport now were a great hindrance. Further problems emerged. Burgoyne's Indians had proved unreliable and had had to be replaced by 400 Ottawas from the west. Then Carleton in Canada refused to release troops to garrison Ticonderoga, on the grounds that his authority did not extend south of the border. Consequently, Burgoyne was forced to release 900 men to protect this vital post in his rear. Work teams had to be found to remove felled trees and heavy boulders which the rebels had carefully placed across the track. Forty bridges had also been destroyed. All the while, rebel skirmishers sniped from the forest and there were frequent brushes between them and the scouting Indians.

During one of these encounters a young girl named Jane McCrea was killed. She had been visiting a house near Fort Edward where lived a recently immigrant Scots widow, a relative of Brigadier Fraser's. In yet another coincidence, Miss McCrea was betrothed to a young Tory in Fraser's command, who was looking forward to meeting her fleetingly on the march south. With horror he recognised the scalp brought into the camp by one of the Ottawas as the long hair of his fiancée. The true story has never been defined. What is clear is that the girl had been tomahawked and the body stripped, mutilated and rolled in leaves. It was a propaganda gift to the rebels which they were to use to the full. It also shocked Burgoyne and he called for the Indians to give up the culprit for execution. They refused and he had to be content with ordering that all Indian raids in future be accompanied by a British officer. When eventually the army emerged from the forest to take possession of an abandoned and burned Fort Edward on the banks of the Hudson, the Ottawas, offended by the restriction and daunted anyway by their encounters with the American skirmishers in the woods, slipped away home. The army was now without its eyes.

It was at this point that Burgoyne received a letter at last from Howe. Written in New York some two weeks before, it coolly informed him that the Commander-in-Chief's 'intention is for Pennsylvania'. There was to be no move north to meet or assist Burgoyne, unless Washington turned towards him, in which case 'be assured I shall soon be after him to relieve you'. Sir Henry Clinton was left in command at New York and would 'act as occurrences may direct'. This was the first definite intimation received by Burgoyne that Howe would not sail and march up the Hudson to meet him at Albany. Even so, Burgoyne was not unduly perturbed. He was not averse to collecting all the glory that was available. He replied confidently, saying that he expected to be in Albany by 23 August at the latest.

Burgoyne now turned his attention to the question of provisions. He was on the east bank of the Hudson and must cross to advance on Albany. Once across the Hudson, however, he would have virtually severed his supply line to Canada, so great were the difficulties in transporting equipment. It was now, characteristically, that the gambler took over. He decided to cross, take with him what supplies he could and live off the land. He knew that the enemy was grouping somewhere in front of him, that he must bring him to battle soon to clear the way to Albany and then New York. Burgoyne had not the slightest doubt about the outcome. True, perhaps he had rather under-estimated the difficulties of taking an army and its baggage train through this infernal country. But fighting was a different matter. Presented with battle, the rebels would do what they had done at Ticonderoga and what they always did sooner or later – break and run.

The British army crossed the broad, green Hudson by a bridge of boats below the Miller Falls. Thunderstorms made the crossing difficult but, between the storms, the sun lit up the golds, purples and reds of the forest. To the east the mountains of Vermont were still green-tipped and a man couldn't but feel confident. Burgoyne therefore granted Von Riedesel permission to send a strong party into Vermont to obtain new mounts for his dragoons. While he was at it, he could also forage for the army.

A detachment of 750 men was selected. It consisted mainly of Brunswickers but a contingent of Captain Fraser's marksmen and some Canadian loyalists were included. At the last minute, Burgoyne changed their destination to Bennington where, he had heard, there was a large rebel supply depot to be plundered. The countryside around, he had been assured, was loyalist and the party would be welcomed. But it was not. The shock of Ticonderoga and the stories of Indian barbarities had stirred New England and 1,500 Militiamen – part-time soldiers – were waiting at Bennington. The fighting was fierce, but after a series of blunders by the Germans, mixed with bad fortune, the amateurs won the day. More than 200 Germans were killed and 500 captured, against the loss of 30 Americans killed and 40 wounded. The rebels captured four cannon, four ammunition wagons and several hundred muskets.

This was the General's first set-back in the field. It shook him, as did the realisation that, contrary to what he had been told in Canada, he was operating in a country which was not only devilishly difficult to traverse and to fight in, but also universally hostile to his force. He sent a rather plaintive letter to Howe complaining '... I little foresaw that I was to be left to pursue my way through such a tract of country and hosts of foes without any co-operation from New York.' He was also disturbed to hear that the diversionary force which had been dispatched from Canada, via Lake Ontario, to come down the Mohawk and join him above Albany, had been forced to turn back. Then his floating bridge was destroyed by a storm.

Burgoyne now displayed his best qualities. He cast out dismay, presented a confident face to his staff and, with great dispatch, crossed back to the eastern bank, marched further down-river, re-built his bridge and crossed again just above Saratoga (present-day Schuylerville). Then he destroyed his bridge behind him. He was there, he said, to stay and to fight.

CONFRONTATION AT SARATOGA

The American army which was gathering some twenty miles away to give Burgoyne his fight comprised a combination of continentals and Militiamen, all serving under a new and comparatively untried general. Horatio Gates was 50 in the year of Saratoga but he looked older. His short-sightedness forced him to wear spectacles which gave him a bookish, elderly air. He was an Englishman, born humbly of parents in domestic service and this had given him a chip which rarely left his shoulder. By one of those coincidences which seem to characterise the American Revolutionary War, Gates and Burgoyne had been commissioned into the same English regiment, on the same day, 32 years before. They were, then, old acquaintances, although hardly old friends. Burgoyne's path had been smoothed by privilege. Gates had been forced to work hard and scheme not a little to make his way.

Having served with distinction in North America in the Seven Years War and the Indian Wars, as well as in Martinique, Gates had returned to England to seek promotion. He did not progress beyond major and, in disgust, he resigned his commission and emigrated to West Virginia in 1772, where he prospered as a farmer and was appointed a lieutenant colonel in the local militia. His disappointment in England had soured him of the old country and he became an ardent American nationalist and a friend of Washington's. It was no surprise, then, that when war broke out Gates was appointed a brigadier general and made Adjutant to the Forces. He did well in this staff appointment and he also devotedly cultivated friends in high political places. When, therefore, the aristocratic and unpopular General Philip Schuyler lost his command of the Northern army after Ticonderoga, it was Gates who succeeded him.

Sufficient reinforcements had come forward to enable Gates to stand and fight on the Hudson and, thanks to the discredited Schuyler, who had ably harassed and delayed Burgoyne's march south, Gates found that he had time to select the best site to fight the battle. He moved forward and found the ideal position, four miles north of Stillwater. Here a steep and thickly wooded bluff called Bemis Heights looked down over the Hudson and commanded its passage and the road to Albany. Gates dug a line of fortifications which stretched from the river almost a mile to the north-west, curling round to the south to protect his flank and rear. The logs and earthworks were spiked with cannon and, although unfinished, they formed a most formidable fortress, completely blocking the only route south. The defensive posture suited Gates's cautious temperament very well. Burgoyne was the invader; let him therefore come to him. The earthworks looked out on to forest and scrub, broken only by ravines, a few creeks and the odd 15-acre clearing hacked out by farmers. Narrow tracks connected the clearings. The great irony of it all was that this magnificent defensive position would never have a shot fired at it. The untidy but vital Battle of Saratoga was destined to be fought in the wilderness and clearings away from the defences.

On 15 September the Royal army set out from Saratoga along the river road with drums beating and fifes playing. Desertions, sickness, battle losses and the need to protect his rear had left Burgoyne with only about 8,000 men able to take the field, the main force of infantry being split between the British and the Germans. But morale was high and the thought of bringing the rebels to battle at last gave spring to the step. The infuriating problem was that the desertion of the Indians meant that Burgoyne had no idea of the enemy's position. Fraser's scouts were good soldiers but not skilled enough in woodcraft to be the army's eyes. In the forest, they blundered rather. On full alert, then, the army camped on the heights above the river at Dovecot (the modern Coveville).

Gates had no problem in following the enemy's advance, for he had the best scouts in the world. It is estimated that, by the time the battle commenced, the American army was more than 10,000 strong, 7,500 of whom were continental troops. But Militiamen kept flocking to the colours from the surrounding area throughout the month which elapsed between the opening shots and Burgoyne's surrender – thanks, no doubt, to poor Jane McCrea and the victory at Bennington. Among both the continentals and the Militiamen were a strong minority of Americans who came from the long western frontier which stretched from Canada in the north to the Southern Carolinas. Gates's scouts were among their number, of course, because these men were skilled woodsmen who could virtually disappear in the forest. They shared the Indians' ability to travel lightly, quickly and quietly, but unlike the Indians they were deadly shots. And, as Burgoyne had discovered, the Indians were frightened of these men and had no wish to fight them.

In the literature of the war, the riflemen are referred to by a bewildering number of names: back countrymen, longwoodsmen, frontiersmen, mountainmen, over-mountainmen, shirt-tail men, rangers, longhunters and even light infantry. The nomenclature is usually inter-changeable, except that light infantry is too generic and longhunter too specific. Longhunters were men who, like Daniel Boone and the mountainmen, would make long journeys into the wild – sometimes staying away from their families for a year or more – to trap, hunt and explore. Some of these men were present in the American army, but most of the riflemen were subsistence farmers, living on the edge of civilisation.

The two fundamentals they all had in common were their experience in fighting Indians and their use of the long, so-called Kentucky rifle, rather than the musket. They were the only troops on either side to possess this distinctive weapon, which was never, of course, army issue. Gates went into battle with about 500 so-called riflemen, who were his scouts and skirmishers. They typified and were the élite of the frontiersmen who played a decisive role, not only at Saratoga, but throughout the War of Independence. For the first time in this narrative, then, they must come into close focus.

THE RIFLEMAN

'These Americans had riflemen – they could hit a man anywhere they liked at two hundred paces distance. We came to dread them far more than the regular continentals.' Memoirs of Prevost, an English Captain, 1802.

When, on 14 June 1775, the Continental Congress realised that it was facing war, it called out the militia in New England but then turned to the frontier to raise its first, new troops. Today's American army is therefore seeded in the draft which went out on that day for 'Six companies of expert riflemen to be immediately raised in Pennsylvania, two in Maryland, two in Virginia, to be employed as light infantrymen.' At first glance, it seems strange that the first call for troops ever to be made by central government in what is now the USA should be directed at the territories farthest away, for riflemen were only to be found on the frontiers of those states. Why did Congress send hundreds of miles into the wilderness, when there were plenty of young bloods willing to enlist in the seaboard towns? Why did members of Congress, men of the east, where there were many muskets but few rifles, stipulate riflemen?

The answer, of course, is that these frontiersmen were the nearest the thirteen states had to skilled fighters. The Militia was everywhere in being: farmers, shopkeepers, professional men; all giving of their spare time to train in the rudiments of soldiering and most of them, as was the way in the colonies, used to firearms. But none of these good men actually lived by their weapons and depended for their lives on them. The riflemen of the frontier did – and that is why they used rifles, rather than muskets. A rifle had twice (sometimes three times) the range of a musket and it was infinitely more accurate when used in the frontier way. The difference between hitting or missing a bear or an Indian at 200 yards could mean life or death to the frontiersman. The earnest Congressmen, meeting in Philadelphia in their powdered wigs and elegant hose, knew this.

So, too, did General Washington, who was appointed C-in-C two days after that first draft was issued. It is inconceivable that the politicians would not have consulted him on this matter. He knew the frontier. He had lived with these men when he had first ventured west of the Alleghenies as a young surveyor 25 years before; he had marched with them on Braddock's fatal expedition against the Indians. When jealousies among the states were creating a sense of disunity in the embryonic army, Washington wrote to the President of Congress asking for 10,000 hunting shirts to be provided. 'I know nothing', he wrote, 'in a prospective view more trivial, yet which, if put in practice, would have a happier tendency to unite the men and abolish those provincial distractions that lead to jealousy ...' Hunting shirts were a practical symbol of liberty. They were 'American'.

The recruiting call was met with alacrity by the outlying counties. Frederick County was asked to provide one of the two companies from Virginia and the local Patriots Committee unanimously turned to Daniel Morgan to raise the company and lead it. Morgan's role was destined to be as important, in its way, as that of Burgoyne or Gates, although his origins could not have been more humble.

Born of poor Welsh farming immigrants, probably in New Jersey in 1733, Morgan left home after a bitter argument with his father and trudged westward through Pennsylvania before working his way down the Great Wagon Road to the south. By 17 he could hardly read or write but he was massive, over 6 feet tall and weighing more than 200 pounds. He drank and fought and found work as a wagoner, carrying for the British during the Seven Years War. He got into an altercation with a British officer who hit Morgan with the flat of his sword. The young giant knocked the officer to the ground and was immediately arrested. He received 500 lashes for the crime – often a death sentence. But he survived and, until the day he died, claimed that he had been short-changed by the British in that he had only counted 499 strokes. Morgan recovered and later the officer had the grace to apologise to him. Despite (or because of) this, Morgan was granted a commission in the army and, as an ensign, he was ambushed by Indians in 1758. A musket ball entered through the back of his neck, passing through his mouth and knocking out the teeth in his left jaw. Losing blood and hardly able to remain conscious, he somehow stayed on his horse while pursued by an Indian who, on foot, kept pace with him, waiting for him to fall so that he could scalp him. But Morgan hung on dizzily and, as Winchester finally appeared, the Indian dropped behind, throwing his tomahawk after Morgan in disgust.

By 1775, Daniel Morgan had fought in all the Indian wars of the Virginian frontier of the past twenty years, had brawled, gambled but finally become a respectable married man. He remained one of the best shots in the country and was universally admired, so there were no shortage of recruits as he rode round the county. He was most selective however. All applicants had to submit to a test of marksmanship. A board one foot square was propped against a tree at a distance of 150 yards and a man's nose drawn on it. Only those who hit the nose were considered. Eventually Morgan selected 96 recruits, 28 more than stipulated, and set out with them to march the 600 miles to Cambridge, just north of Boston, to join Washington, with whom Morgan had served in the Braddock expedition. That march was completed in 21 days, the men travelling light – 'a band of young giants, blankets on backs, a supply of corn in their pouches' – and averaging 28 miles a day. No one dropped out. They joined Washington's raw army, to find that they and their fellow riflemen were the talk of the town. Dr James Tatcher, surgeon's mate at the hospital at Cambridge, noted in August 1775:

'Several companies of riflemen, amounting, it is said, to more than 1,400, have arrived here from distances of from 500 to 700 miles. They are remarkably stout and hardy men remarkable for the accuracy of their aiming: striking a mark with great certainty at 200 yards distance. At a review, a company of them, while in quick advance, fired their balls into objects of 7ins diameter at a distance of 250 yards.' (Military Journal During the American Revolutionary War, 2nd ed., 1827)

A loyalist clergyman in Maryland thought it his duty to send a warning home about these men. He wrote to the Earl of Dartmouth on 20 December 1775:

'Rifles, infinitely better than those imported, are made daily in many places in Pennsylvania. The Americans [are] the best marksmen in the

THE MARINES

Above: This Anglo-Saxon grave marker, found on Lindisfarne in the ninth century, shows warriors with raised axes and swords. It almost certainly depicts the first Viking raid on the island on 8 June 793. (English Heritage)

Below: The beauty of the Viking longship is illustrated in the Oseberg ship on display at Bygdoy, near Oslo. This 1,000 year old example, however, was likely to have been a ceremonial vessel, like a royal yacht.(Photo by L. Smestad. Oslo University Museum of National Antiquities)

THE ARTILLERYMEN

Left: The first real encounter between longbow and crossbow. This painting of the Battle of Crécy in 1346 from Froissart's *Chronicles* shows how cumbersome the crossbows were. They were out-shot by the longbowmen. (Bibliothèque Nationale de France, Paris)

Left: The Battle of Poitiers, 1356, from Froissart's *Chronicles*, hints at the devast-ation caused by the English bowmen. Few are shown in this painting, but, on the day, they far out-numbered the men-at-arms. (Bibliothèque Nationale de France, Paris)

Above: This fine statue of Arthur de Richemont, Constable of France, outside the Town Hall in Vannes, shows how armour was subtly developed to deflect the bowmen's shafts. De Richemont fought at Agincourt, although the sculptor probably depicted him here in later life.

Left: This poigant memorial to the 6,000 Frenchmen who were killed at Agincourt was erected in a little copse at Tramecourt, fringing the battlefield. It marks the site where the French were buried.

THE SKIRMISHERS

Left: General Horatio Gates had joined the British Army on the same day and in the same unit as the opponent he defeated at Saratoga, 'Gentleman Johnny' Burgoyne. But Saratoga was his high point and he never won another victory.

Above: The arrogance and self-confidence of General John Burgoyne shines through this portrait by Sir Joshua Reynolds which now hangs in the Frick Collection, New York. It was painted when Burgoyne was a Colonel and had distinguished himself in Portugal. (The Frick Collection, New York)

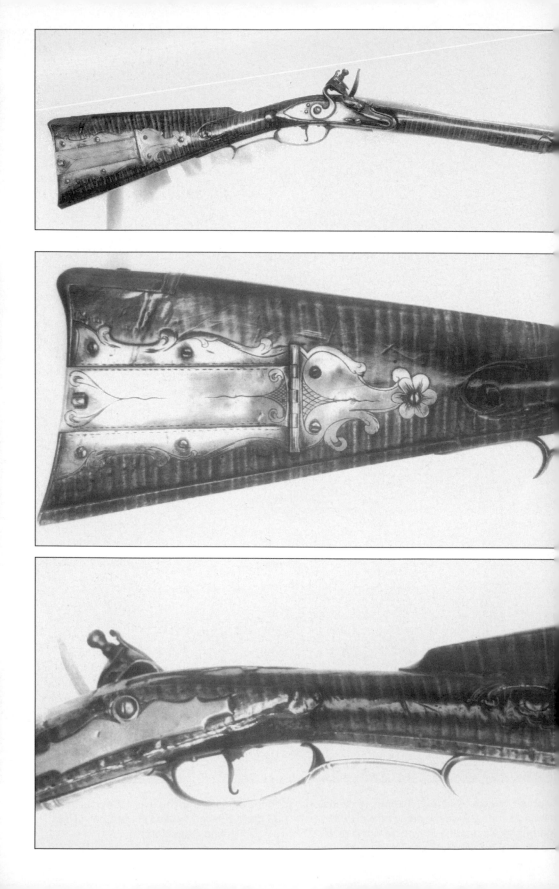

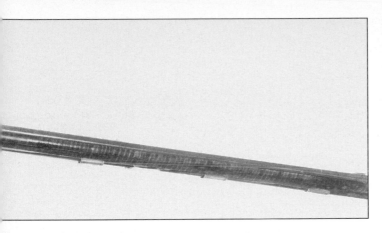

Left: The weapon that swung the Battle of Saratoga and, therefore, the American War of Indepedence. This typical late eighteenth century rifle was made by Jacob Dickert, a German immigrant, in Lancaster County, PA. Its overall length is 62 inches and it fired a ball .52 inches in calibre. (Dr James Whisker)

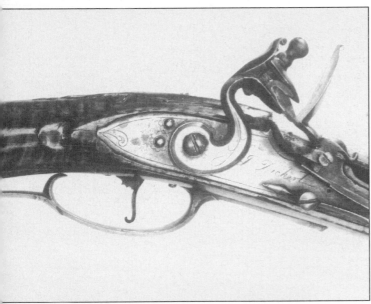

Left: The Dickert rifle stock. The central strip in the finely worked brass plate in the butt swings back to reveal a box used for carrying the greased patches in which bullets were wrapped before firing. (Dr James Whisker)

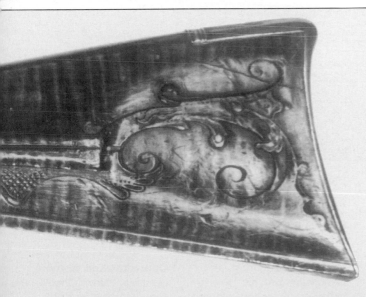

Left: Like most so-called Kentucky rifles, the Dickert was made in Pennsylvania, where German and Swiss immigrants refined the rifle to meet specific needs. The front sight was made larger than the rear so that it could be seen in the forest gloom and the trigger guard was modified so that it did not catch on forest branches. (Dr James Whisker)

Above: From the woods on the skyline the British Redcoats advanced towards the American gun emplacements across this clearing – then a grainfield – at Bemis Heights. It was 7 October 1777, and the beginning of the second and decisive Battle of Saratoga.

THE SPEARMEN
Opposite page, top: Lieutenant Teignmouth Melvill, who was given the task of escaping from Isandlwana with his battalion's Queen's Colours.

He was killed and, with Lieutenant Coghill, became the first man to be posthumuosly awarded the Victoria Cross.

Opposite page, bottom: Lieutenant Nevill Coghill, who came to the rescue of

Lieutenant Melvill when the latter was attempting to cross the Buffalo River with their battalion's colours. Like Melvill, he was posthumously awarded the Victoria Cross (Ian Knight)

Above: Officers of the 1/24th Regiment, photographed in 1878, the year before most of them perished at the Battle of Isandlwana. Sitting in the centre are (left to right) Sir Bartle Frere (second left), High Commissioner for South Africa; Lieutenant-General Sir Arthur Cunyngham, the then Army C-in-C; and Colonel R. T. Glyn, who accompanied Chelmsford and so missed the massacre. (Ian Knight)

Right: Isandlwana today. This is the nek, looking north, and was where the remnants of the 24th Regiment made their last stand, having been forced back by the *impis* who attacked from the right of the picture. The white stone cairns cover the bones of British soldiers killed.

THE PRIVATEERS

Above: *U55*, very similar to Amberger's *U58*. These Project 25 Ms cruiser (ocean-going) boats were efficient and reasonably safe work horses which bore much of the brunt of the great 1917 U-boat offensive. (Gus Britton)

Below: Kapitänleutnant Lothar von Arnauld de la Perière (second left), supreme U-boat ace of both World Wars. He sank 194 merchant ships, grossing 453,716 tons - and survived the war. (Imperial War Museum)

Above: The crew of de la Perière's *U35* bathing under a rigged shower on deck. This boat created a record when, during a three week cruise in 1916, she sank 54 merchant-men, grossing 91,000 tons. But she mainly operated in the Mediterranean, where anti-submarine activities were less than in the Atlantic. (Imperial War Museum)

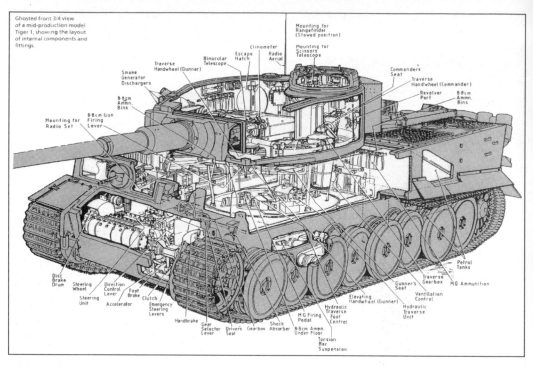

Ghosted front 3/4 view of a mid-production model Tiger 1, showing the layout of internal components and fittings.

THE ARMOURED ONES

Above: The German Tiger 1 tank, not the most widely-produced tank of World War Two, nor even the most successful, but certainly the most charismatic. It was outstandingly well armed and protected and became the most feared of the German tanks.

Below: This middle-production Tiger 1 was captured intact in April 1943 in Tunisia and was shipped to the UK for close inspection. (Peter Gudgin)

Above: Colonel (later Major-General) Ernest Swinton, who has most claim to the title 'Father of the Tank'. He wrote a memorandum to the British General Staff on the need for 'a machine-gun destroyer' and then raised and commanded the first 'Tank Detachment'. (Bovington Tank Museum)

Above: 'Mother', the prototype for all Mark 1 British tanks, three of which went into action at the end of the Battle of the Somme in September 1916, the first time the tank had been used in battle. (Bovington Tank Museum)

Below: German tank commanders are briefed at the roadside during their breathless sweep through France in the summer of 1940. (Imperial War Museum)

world and thousands support their families by the same, particularly riflemen on the frontier. In marching through woods, one thousand of these
riflemen would cut to pieces 10,000 of our best troops.' (Niles, Principles
and Acts of the Revolution)

The wild men of the frontier found that impressing – and shocking –
the honest tradesmen of Cambridge relieved the boredom of camp life.
They held shooting matches. Some shot lying on their back, some on their
side, some after sprinting 30 yards and firing without pause. Several held
the clapboard target between their knees as others shot. They also fought
most of the time.

Morgan, who had been instantly appointed to head three rifle companies on his arrival, was as bored as the rest and, when he heard rumours
of the Canadian invasion, he asked to join the column. He and his men
were selected and they set off under Benedict Arnold on the long journey
north. The expedition ended ultimately in failure and Morgan was taken
prisoner. But he had covered himself in glory in the attack on Quebec and,
after Arnold's wound, he had assumed command. While in captivity the
British offered him a colonelcy in their own army but Morgan refused with
dignity. He and the 22 of his Virginians who were all that remained of his
original company were later exchanged and sent back to Virginia.

Morgan's exploits had made him famous and he was promoted to be
Colonel of the 11th Virginian Regiment. But Washington had other plans
for him. He asked him to raise a special corps of riflemen, a select, specially
chosen group of sharpshooters who were to be 'exempted from the common duties of the line'. But Morgan had time only to gather about 500 of
these – he repeated his marksmanship tests and was criticised for taking his
time about recruiting – before, on the orders of Congress, Washington
reluctantly sent him and his corps to Gates at Saratoga. He arrived in time
to take part in the move north to Bemis Heights, but Gates was disappointed that the big man had brought only 374 men who could fight. The
rest were sick. Nevertheless, the general, who also had served with Morgan
on the Braddock campaign and respected him, gave him five newly formed
light infantry companies to swell his command.

On the eve of Saratoga, then, Gates had a fair number of experienced
riflemen to scout and skirmish for him. This is an appropriate time, therefore, to take a close look at one of them. Private Isaac Miller comes easily
to hand from old muster rolls. He is serving in Captain Gabriel Long's company of 'Detached Riflemen' commanded by Colonel Daniel Morgan. We
know that Miller fought at Saratoga and that he survived the battle because
he features in the pay roll for August, September and October of 1777 (he

lived to pick up a total of 20 dollars pay in October for those three months, equivalent to £15 at that time).

He moves easily as we see him now, carefully approaching the American camp through the woods, carrying his long rifle at the trail and unthinkingly putting his feet down on the dry leaves quite flatly, as the Indians do. He is a tall, rawboned man, like most of the riflemen, but he moves quickly and quietly, slipping from tree to tree, his head moving all the time looking about him. He is perfectly balanced so that he can freeze behind a trunk if he sees or hears anything untoward. He is dressed in a manner which immediately distinguishes him as a rifleman.

A wide-brimmed, low-crowned, floppy hat is pulled down over his eyes and he wears a long hunting shirt of dun-coloured linsey-woolsey, caped at the shoulders and fringed there and at the sleeves. In the summer, he sometimes wears buckskin but this is cold and uncomfortable now that autumn is coming on. The shirt is drawn in at the waist by a wide leather belt, from which hangs a tomahawk and a scalping knife. Scalping? Oh yes. Isaac Miller has scalped many a man; it is normal practice on the frontier and not confined to the Indians. He had amused himself last night in camp by showing a group of New England recruits how it is done. First, the hand grasps the hair and pulls it taught, then the razor sharp end of the knife makes a quite superficial incision about three inches in diameter around the victim's head (he doesn't have to be dead but it helps); then a foot is placed on the neck, the hair is jerked back and the scalp comes off with a popping sound. It is really quite easy. Isaac can't understand why all the Easterners make so much fuss about it.

The shirt hangs quite low (this is why riflemen are often called shirt-tail men) and his legs are tightly enclosed in leggings, fringed and decorated with beads. These are vital to protect his legs from thorns in the forest. On his feet he wears deerskin moccasins, which he has cut from one piece and tied with leather thongs. A large powder horn and a smaller, primer horn hang from his neck, as does a leather hunting pouch. His rifle seems incredibly long but it is roughly the same length as the common musket; it seems longer because the barrel looks much thinner, shooting a smaller calibre ball than the musket, and the gun has a shorter stock. It is, though, a thing of elegant design. Even in the darkness of the forest the rich maple of the stock glows, as does the decorative brass scroll set in it. Isaac Miller carries the rifle with care. It is noticeable in camp that he rarely moves without it. It is his constant companion, his friend and his lifeline.

Like Morgan, Miller is a Virginian, although he did not step forward when the Colonel made his first recruiting drive two years ago, He knew he could pass the marksmanship test right enough, but his cabin and cleared piece of land lie beyond the Blue Ridge Mountains, in Shawnee country, and he felt he could not leave Martha and the children. Now Samuel is 15 and can hit a mark at 250 yards and Nathan is almost as good at 13. For that matter, Martha could take out any Indian – and has. But he feels happier at leaving them now that the boys are older. Martha and he married only seven years ago when they already had three. In the Blue Ridge, preachers don't come by very often. They just had to wait until one did.

Isaac hears the gobble of a wild turkey and stills. Then he sees, 200 yards away, the outline of Abe Murray, his fellow scout and nods across to him. Nothing so far.

If it were possible for a modern Ulsterman to hear Isaac Miller speak, he would feel at home, for Miller's voice has more than a trace of that distinctive accent. The largest ethnic strain in all the frontiersmen is Scottish-Irish and, by 1790, more than 250,000 Northern Irishmen will have emigrated to America, at least three-quarters of them settling within the Appalachian region between Western New York State and Eastern Tennessee. They have brought with them their ballads, a taste for whiskey, Presbyterianism and a fighting spirit. In fact, James Logan, the secretary of Pennsylvania for William Penn and himself an Ulster Quaker, confessed in 1720 that he had been deliberately encouraging Ulster immigrants to settle on the frontier because they would be able defenders of the province against the Indians in view of they way they had 'so bravely defended Londonderry and Enniskillen'.

The original country of Isaac's very distant ancestors is the borderland of England and Scotland, a territory fought over and plundered for more than 700 years. In waves of generational emigration, its people had taken their everyday acceptance of violence with them, first to Northern Ireland and then to America. Of them, the scholar David Hackett Fischer is to write: 'The so-called Scotch-Irish who came to America thus included a double distilled selection of some of the most disorderly inhabitants of a deeply disordered land.' (*Albion's Seed*, Oxford University Press, 1989)

The more sheltered among the people of modern Ulster, however, might perhaps be a little shocked by Isaac's vocabulary. The earthy Scottish and Northern Irish ways of the early 18th century had easily travelled with the immigrants. Isaac, for instance, affectionately refers to his youngest as 'little shits' and, until Victorian prudery changes them in eighty years time, two small streams in Lunenberg County, not far from Isaac's cabin, are called Tickle Cunt Branch and Fucking Creek. More acceptable, perhaps – and more redolent of modern country'n'western times – is Isaac's frequent uše of old Ulster expressions such as 'honey', as a term of endearment, 'let on' for tell, 'fixin" for getting ready and 'cute' for attractive.

For all his scalping and cussing, Isaac is a moral man. When Martha and he were married at last, the Revd Samuel Kercheval, the Anglican clergyman who tied the knot, told him that 94 per cent of the brides he married either had children or were pregnant. But there is no question of abandonment or desertion on the frontier. A man is married for life and Isaac's whole existence is centred around the family. His interests are short term and he makes no elaborate plans to gain money to better his way of life. He supports his family (there are six children so far) with a few acres of corn and vegetables, the meat of his hogs and what he can get by hunting and fishing. They are not self-sufficient: he trades furs, skins and meat for flour, whisky, cloth and other essentials. He is not self-indulgent. Travelling fast, he will exist on 'pinole' – parched corn, pulverised the Indian way – and rum and water. As long as the Shawnees don't come raiding he is happy enough. Of course, there is this present business to clear up. He knows nothing about politics and he doesn't care whether America is part of the British Empire or not. But raising the Indians is a different matter. If the British are doing that then they have to go.

Isaac Miller softly spits and, in the forest half light, glides towards another tree, and then another ...

THE RIFLE

Miller's Kentucky rifle had never seen Kentucky – and neither, for that matter, had most of the riflemen who used the weapon. In 1777, Kentucky was the name still loosely used to describe the vast territory west of the Cumberland Mountains, first explored by Daniel Boone and now incorporating the States of Kentucky and Tennessee. Boone was the definitive longhunter and on his epic, lonely journeys, he lived by his rifle. Boone's fame – he first prospected and then led the party which widened the Indian trail through the Cumberland Gap and which, in turn, opened up the west to the seaboard immigrants – also brought fame to his gun, so Kentucky rifle it became. Much of the glamour attached to the great explorer and Indian hunter rubbed off on to the weapon and high claims have been made for it.

In his seminal work, *The Kentucky Rifle* (the Rifle Association of America, 1928), John G. W. Dillin went so far as to dedicate the book itself to the rifle, in terms usually reserved for the all-American hot dog or George Washington:

'Light in weight; graceful in line; economical in consumption of powder and lead; fatally precise; distinctly American; it sprang into immediate popularity and for 100 years it was a model, often slightly varied but never radically changed. It was a rifle which changed the whole course of world history, made possible the settlement of a continent and ultimately freed our nation of foreign domination.'

In fact the rifle was very much a minority weapon throughout the war. It was used by both sides (ironically, the British army's first rifle regiment was the Royal American Regiment, raised in 1757) but most of the infantry – and certainly all the men of the line – used either the English Brown Bess musket or, on the American side, the French Charleville musket, claimed to be lighter and better designed than the English weapon. Towards the end of the war, Congress even made moves to standardise firearms used by the continental army by replacing the rifle with the musket.

Why, given the claims now made for the rifle and its undoubted effectiveness at key times during the war, was it disliked by the establishment?

The answer lies in the retention by most American generals of the belief that European armies could only be beaten by European methods: direct confrontation in the field, disciplined volley firing, supported by artillery, and then the decisive bayonet charge. The fact that for much of the war American troops were neither trained, equipped, nor psychologically prepared for this kind of warfare did not prevent the entrenched feeling that this was the way it *should* be done. If America were going to be a nation state fit to live alongside the other great states, it had to learn to fight the proper way. Only a stand-up victory would impress the watching European nations. And in any case, was there another way?

Of course there was, and a proposal to wage guerrilla warfare from the back country, leaving the seaboard to the British, was discussed and rejected by Congress. The trouble was that irregular warfare, and the weapon which suited it best, the rifle, did not fit into the pattern of conventional confrontation. The musket could be loaded and fired four or five times a minute, compared with the rifle's twice. The musket fired a heavier ball than the rifle – .69 calibre for the Charleville and .75 for the Bess, compared to the rifle's .48 calibre. The Brown Bess, in particular, had a smashing, shock effect. Clearly, then, the rifle was too slow and lightweight to send out the sort of close-range volleys which won battles. And one could not fit a standard bayonet to a rifle, so the weapon could not be used for the final, great charge which, in the last quarter of the 18th century, was the way to clinch a battle.

There was no rifleman sufficiently highly placed in the army to argue the case for his weapon; no one to point out that the rifle could be deadly, in some cases at up to 300 yards, while the musket was limited to 100 yards;

or that the rifle was twice as accurate as the smooth bore. And who needs a bayonet when you can stop a man before he reaches you? So the rifleman would have to make his case by his achievements.

The so-called Kentucky rifle had been developed specifically as an American frontier weapon, particularly for hunting. The early weapons used by pioneers in the later part of the 17th and early 18th century were found to be wanting. They were of large bore, unwieldy when travelling and clumsy in construction. Early gunsmiths of the new continent competed to find the answer. It came in eastern Pennsylvania, probably in Lancaster, which was called Hickory Town until 1730. This was a centre for German and Swiss immigrants, many of them Tyrolean mountaineers used to the grooved rifles of the *Jägers* (hunters) of their region. Gradually, the new gun evolved.

The rifles were all hand-made so each had its own subtle idiosyncrasies, but by the time of the Revolutionary War the basic pattern was more-or-less established. It was about 57 inches overall, its octagonal barrel being usually about 42 inches long. The size of the trigger guard had been reduced to prevent snagging among the trees of the forest, and the front sight was slightly larger than the rear, so as to be more easily visible. There was a box set in the stock for greased patches, and to save weight the iron ramrod had been replaced by a length of hickory. Weight was important, hence the comparatively small bore. A pound of lead for a .70 calibre gun would make 16 bullets, whereas it would yield 48 bullets of .45 calibre. As a result a trapper away on a month-long journey into the wilderness could carry three times more ammunition. If he placed the ball correctly, he could kill a deer, bear or Indian as easily with a .45 calibre shot as with the larger bullet. The accuracy was bestowed by the rifling, of course, but the American riflemen had their own, unique application which helped to explain their marksmanship. Before ramming the ball down the barrel, it was wrapped in a small piece of greased linen or buckskin which would grip the rifling on expulsion and give much greater accuracy. If the patch were not centred exactly to the bore, the bullet's emergence from the muzzle would be erratic.

It is a salutary thought that the bowmen of Agincourt, 350 years before, could shoot over roughly the same range as the riflemen of Saratoga but deliver five times the number of shafts, albeit without the same accuracy. The clumsy loading procedure, however, could be refined by a skilled riflemen – and Isaac Miller is reckoned to be the quickest in his county. He can load his rifle in just about 23 seconds, given good preparation and an easy hand on the whiskey jug the night before. Watch him now in the woods as he loads and primes.

In a smooth movement, he pulls the larger of the two powder horns to his mouth and pulls out the plug with his teeth. He pours the powder into a measure held in his left hand. The plug is replaced and the horn left to swing as he transfers the measure to the right hand. That movement brings forward the barrel of the rifle which has been cradled by his left arm and he pours the powder down the muzzle. The small tear of greased leather is then placed precisely over the muzzle, the ball centred on it and the whole rammed down the barrel on to the powder below. Now he must prime. He lays his piece across his left arm and pushes forward the frizzen steel to expose the pan, which he fills with powder from the small horn (this powder must be finer to ensure quick and certain ignition). He now pulls back the high, goose-necked hammer as he brings the stock to his cheek. The rifle is heavy but he balances carefully, feet well apart, his left hand quite near the trigger guard and his right elbow stuck out level with the shoulder, to form a compact and stable platform. After a moment of intense concentration he gently squeezes the trigger. The frizzen steel strikes the flint to produce a spark which ignites the fine powder and is transmitted to the main charge through a small channel. There are, then, two explosions: the first, small, one in the pan and, a split second later, the other, at the base of the barrel, which sends the bullet on its way.

Firing erect in this way, without a rest for the long barrel, is called shooting 'off hand' (we now use the phrase to describe a statement or action not prepared or thought-through) and Isaac dislikes it. He much prefers to rest his rifle against a tree branch or boulder while taking aim, or to lie on the ground. To him, firing his rifle is a deliberate and important affair. On the frontier bullets are scarce (he often moulds them himself) and missing the target is unforgivable. In war, however, time is a luxury – though care is not – and he knows riflemen who go into battle carrying six lead balls in their mouth, and their greased patches spread between the fingers of the left hand. Anything to save time. He himself has made a small, flat piece of wood, containing six holes, exactly the diameter of his shot. Into these he inserts the lead balls, already wrapped in their patches. They sit there until he needs them, when he quickly pushes them through and into the muzzle of the rifle.

On the evening of 18 September 1777, in the American camp at Bemis Heights, Isaac Miller has his patent bullet carrier stocked with its full complement. With his scalping knife he has also cut fifty new bullet patches from an old piece of buckskin and greased them carefully. His observation of the British camp during the day has told him that tomorrow will be the day of battle. The Redcoat pickets were nervous and, behind them, there was much parading and shouting of orders. He had so reported to Colonel Morgan, who had just nodded and seemed unconcerned. But the Colonel had gone off to General Gates right away. Yessir, tomorrow will be the day.

THE BATTLE

And so it proved. On the morning of the 19th a thick fog shrouded the hills but it lifted by nine a.m. and Burgoyne began his approach. Deserters from Gates's camp had informed him of the Americans' dispositions and the approximate size of the army confronting him only three miles away. Burgoyne realised that he was outnumbered and that the rebels' position was strong, but he was not in the slightest daunted, only glad that the waiting and the insufferable marching was over.

The British plan was to advance in three columns and then converge with a concentrated attack on the American left, which could be vulnerable to cannon fire from a nearby hill. The column break-down was necessitated anyway by the inadequacy of the tracks through the woods, which would not allow single passage to the full army and its artillery train. The river road was dominated by the American guns and seemed equally impassable to the full force. Accordingly, von Riedesel took just under 3,000 men, mainly his Germans plus artillery support, along the river road; Fraser led the largest force of just over 3,000 men in a sweep through the forest to the west; and Burgoyne himself brought up the centre with 1,700 regulars. At a given signal, the two flanks were to swing in and concentrate with Burgoyne in the attack.

To succeed, Burgoyne had to deploy his artillery so that it could breach the American fortifications, which would then fall to the savage assault of the infantry, attacking in depth. It was a bold, imaginative idea, worthy of Burgoyne the gambler and designed to minimise the British inferiority in numbers. The Americans would be forced to spread their defenders along their line, not knowing where the real attack would come, while Burgoyne could concentrate in depth and, at that point, completely outnumber the Americans. It could well have worked, given the British experience of siege tactics and their fire power, both with cannon and musket. That it did not, owes much to Morgan's riflemen and to Morgan's old commander, Major General Benedict Arnold.

Arnold was probably the most brilliantly intuitive commander on either side throughout the war. Personally brave, he had the gifts of immediately grasping the strong and weak points of dispositions and the articulacy to promote his point of view. Indecision was unknown to him and his men adored him. It was he who had failed only by a whisker to take Quebec in the first year of the war. It was he who had compelled Burgoyne's second force attacking along the Mohawk to turn back ignominiously. Unfortunately, to his courage and tactical shrewdness, Arnold allied vanity, arrogance and disloyalty. Later in the war, incensed by what he felt to be lack of recognition by Congress, he was to betray his force to the British, switch sides, be condemned as a traitor, and eventually die in his bed in England. Now, however, he was in his pride, and commanding Gates's left, including the riflemen.

The cautious Gates and the impetuous Arnold made awkward bedfellows. When Gates learned of the British approach his reaction was to wait behind his defences and let Burgoyne batter himself to defeat on the Bemis Heights fortifications. But Arnold pointed out the danger of allowing the Redcoats to get close enough to site their artillery and to deploy their volley firing and bayonet charge. He argued that the army should go out to meet the British or, at the least, a smaller force should skirmish in the woods and pick them off as they toiled through the trees. Gates was apprehensive of von Riedesel's river advance but he finally agreed that Arnold's division, led by Morgan's skirmishers, should move to probe the British right.

Arnold's exact role in the engagement which followed is hard to define. It is likely that he was ordered by Gates to direct the operation from the rear and, late in the day, he was certainly, and abortively, ordered to return when he dashed into the fray. Equally certainly, Gates himself stayed within his redoubt, where, apart from reconnaissances, he was to remain throughout the battle. Still wary of the German threat from the river, he kept his main force with him throughout the day.

It was Morgan's corps, then, which led the way out at about noon, loping quickly and silently in two irregular lines. In Morgan's command were his Virginian riflemen, including some who had recovered from sickness, and contingents of Dearborn's light infantry. In all, they probably numbered about 600. Their orders were to make contact with the British right wing as it moved through the woods and along the track to Freeman's farmhouse, which stood in a clearing about a mile and a half from the American HQ at Bemis Heights. A main action was not contemplated, Gates's ambition at this stage being merely to harass and delay.

There are conflicting accounts of how the battle began. What seems likely is that at about midday an advance picket of Morgan's skirmishers slipped into the farm clearing from the south side and occupied a log cabin, overspilling behind a rail fence at the side. A larger force of riflemen, backed by Dearborn's light infantry, was moving across the clearing to support them when the pickets opened fire on and dispersed a body of the British 9th Regiment seen emerging from the other side of the clearing. With a whoop, Morgan's men rushed after them, only to meet the main body of the British central column and, from the left, an attack by Brigadier Fraser's infantry supported by cannon. Caught in the open in loose order and completely outnumbered, the riflemen and light infantry fell back in disarray into the woods.

Here, the air was suddenly filled with the call of a wild turkey. It was Morgan who, hurrying forward from the rear, was just in time to see his corps rushing back into cover. Using his turkey call to rally his men at a hill in the forest some 80 feet back from the farm, he hurriedly re-deployed them along the fringe of the clearing from which they opened a deadly fire on the British advancing across the open space. Some of the sharpshooters climbed trees the better to target the English officers.

Soon the British centre column arrived in force, with the advance guard of Fraser's men coming in, too, from the British right. Hearing of Morgan's stand, Gates began dispatching further regiments of infantry piecemeal throughout the afternoon to support him. As a result, the engagement became the major battle which Gates had wished to avoid. The clearing and the surrounding forest was a bedlam of smoke and explosions. The battle swayed throughout the afternoon, with first one side attacking across the clearing and being repulsed and then the other. Neither side broke. This was to be expected of the British troops – fine soldiers like the Grenadiers and senior regiments of the line – but the British were amazed that the 'rebel amateurs', in their shirt coats and leather breeches, kept coming at them across the clearing. With the light infantry and the militia reinforcements, the skirmishers had stayed to fight.

The British were now thoroughly committed and they had brought up their artillery. There was no response from the American cannon, for Gates refused to forward any from his defensive position. But the American small-arms fire was devastating, setting their fringe of the clearing alight with powder flashes, and wreaking havoc, particularly among the officers and the gunners serving the cannon. The British 62nd Regiment lost their colonel and his second in command within minutes, and Lieutenant James Hadden, in charge of cannon on the regiment's left, saw his captain and nineteen of his 22 men killed. Three subalterns of the 20th Regiment, all aged 17 or less, fell side by side. Three British regiments lost half their strength. Morgan's riflemen had charged and counter-charged across the clearing with the rest of the infantry, despite their lack of bayonets, and they had captured a cannon. Morgan himself had his horse shot from under him.

Burgoyne, too, was in the thick of the action and distinguished himself by personal bravery. By 4.30, however, his position was so desperate that he called urgently for von Riedesel to hurry his advance from the river to attack the Americans' right. As the Germans arrived, Gates, realising at last the size of the engagement, committed further infantry. But night was falling and, desperately short of ammunition at last (we can be sure that Isaac Miller used all his leather patches and, at the end, would have had to fire without them), the Americans fell back. Burgoyne was left in possession of the field.

If it was a victory, it was a pyrrhic one. The British had suffered 160 dead, 364 wounded and 42 missing. The Americans had lost 63 with 212 wounded and 38 missing. After the battle, Burgoyne confided to Captain George Pausch, one of von Riedesel's artillery officers who had arrived with the relief party: 'No fruits, honour excepted, were attained by the preceding victory, the enemy working with redoubled ardour to strengthen their left; their right was unattackable already.'

Reviewing that first day in his book, *The Generals of Saratoga* (Yale University Press, 1990), Max M. Mintz has no doubt where the main honours lay. 'The key to the performance', he writes, 'had been Morgan's superlative battalion [*sic*] of riflemen, useful not merely for scouting and sniping but for spearheading a major engagement.'

This was the view taken by General Gates. In his report to Congress, he assigned the glory of the action 'entirely to the valour of the Rifle Regiment and corps of Light Infantry under the command of Colonel Morgan'. While generous to the riflemen, this was less than fair to the other troops of Arnold's division who, later, had fought side-by-side with Morgan's men. Arnold was not mentioned in the dispatch. This made him furious and his anger was further fuelled when Gates transferred the riflemen to be part of his own, headquarters command. Arnold confronted Gates, voices were raised and Arnold formally applied for, and was granted, re-assignment to Philadelphia. Angry though he was, however, the junior general could not bring himself to leave while the army faced the enemy. So he stayed in camp, languishing in his tent and passing snide remarks about the conduct of the army commander to anyone who would listen. Gates studiously ignored him.

The battle was far from over. The British had been prevented from attacking the American lines and had suffered losses they could ill afford, but they showed no sign of retreating. Burgoyne licked his wounds and, buoyancy returned, reflected that if the action had been fought a little nearer the river von Riedesel could have come up more quickly and the day would have been won. His spirits further lifted when, on 21 September, a messenger reached him from Clinton in New York, offering to send a force of 2,000 men

up the Hudson to attack the forts there. Burgoyne sent off a grateful acceptance and decided to dig in and wait for Clinton either to reach him or draw
off sufficient of Gates's force to enable him to attack again.

The British immediately began strengthening their new line. A high
abatis was erected at Freeman's Farm, called Balcarres Redoubt, and another
log and earthwork fortification, Breymann Redoubt, was thrown up on the
extreme right, close to two fortified log cabins. On his left, above the river,
Burgoyne built a fortified camp, the Great Redoubt, where he established
his headquarters. His centre was protected by artillery, a ditch and cleared
fireways, and his total front now stretched for almost two miles. He now
knew that he was fighting troops who were worthy of respect. Somehow
'the rabble' had matured.

The waiting period grew increasingly uncomfortable for the British.
No further word came from Clinton and the days grew colder and the
American skirmishers maintained a constant sniping fire on the invaders'
lines. The nights were now made hideous by the howling of wolves who
were feasting on what was left of the bodies at Freeman's Farm. Burgoyne
sent further messages south warning that his provisions were running low
and that if help were not forthcoming soon he would have to retire to
Canada. Even this option, however, was virtually removed when news filtered through that the Americans had taken Fort George and Skenesboro in
his rear. Burgoyne put his army on half rations and held a council of war
with his staff. His senior officers were divided, but on 6 October Burgoyne
decided that he could wait no longer. The rebel riflemen in the woods had
clamped a tight ring around him and prevented him from sending out for-
aging parties. He must break through or starve. He decided to carry out
what he called a reconnaissance in force against the left of the rebel force,
which he still believed to be vulnerable – if only he could reach it. Accordingly, he set off in bright sunshine on the 7th with some 1,700 men, drawn
from every British and German regiment but one, and supported by two
12-pounders, six 6-pounders and two 6in howitzers. It was clearly meant to
be more than a probe. When he did find that weak spot on the American
left, Burgoyne intended to call up his main force and attack.

Once again it was a relief to be advancing. The sunshine was warm-
ing, but the patchwork quilt of autumn, the golden hickories, yellow and
scarlet oaks and the brilliant red and orange maples, reminded everyone
that the beginning of the cold North American winter was only a matter of
days away and that retreat would then be impossible. The force moved on
cautiously, meeting no opposition until it reached a large field of wheat,
about a mile from Gates's fortification and a little under half a mile forward

of the site of the Freeman Farm battle. Here Burgoyne rested his column while a work force began clearing a way across the field.

They were not unobserved. Gates waited until he was sure that the British advance was not a feint and then said, 'Order on Morgan to begin the game.' Once again the riflemen were in the van, but this time Gates committed a substantial force to do the business. Morgan was ordered to make a wide sweep to a hill on the left and fall upon Burgoyne from above, while Brigadier Enoch Poor, with three regiments, would attack the British left and Brigadier Ebenezer Learned's brigade the centre.

The action began at about 2.30, with Morgan's men, who had been delayed while mopping up parties of Captain Fraser's rangers in the woods, swarming down the hillside and delivering a withering fire upon the British. Within minutes, the whole of Burgoyne's column on a front of about 1,000 yards was involved in fierce fighting against a force which outnumbered it by at least four to one.

On the American right, Poor's infantry confronted the British Grenadiers lined, shoulder to shoulder, on the crest of a slope and supported by cannon firing cruel grape shot at the New York and New Hampshire men as they attacked up the hill. The British volley firing was, as ever, impeccable. But the Americans were too many in number and, perhaps, by now too experienced and too incensed to break. They charged with a yell, the guns were captured and the Grenadiers, the ground strewn with their dead and dying, were forced to fall back, still loading and firing. On the left, Morgan's men curved round the rear of the 24th Regiment, forcing it to change front. But the fire of the riflemen, again, was too accurate and the young Earl of Balcarres ordered his men to fall back. The recoil of both flanks left the Germans exposed in the centre and, after gallant resistance, they too began to disintegrate.

The whole British line was now in retreat – orderly in some parts of the field but little less than a rout elsewhere. On their right, the turkey call was heard again and Balcarres' measured retreat was beginning to break up when Brigadier Simon Fraser arrived with sections of his 24th Regiment and immediately restored order. Fraser himself galloped everywhere to rally the men, recklessly exposing himself and succeeding, for a moment, in establishing a new line of defence. Noticing this, Daniel Morgan took a handful of his best marksmen and pointed out the 'devilish brave fellow on the white horse'. It has never been proved who fired the shot – one story is that a noted Indian fighter, an Irishman named Timothy Murphy, climbed a tree and picked off the brave general. Whoever the marksman, Fraser collapsed with a bullet through the stomach and was carried off the field, mortally wounded. It was one of two turning points in the battle.

The other was the arrival of Benedict Arnold. At Bemis Heights he had fretted and fumed as his old division had gone into action without him. At one point, Gates, pushed to the limit, had turned upon him and said, 'I have nothing for you to do. You have no business here.' As the sound of the battle swept up to the Heights, Arnold could stand it no longer. He borrowed a big brown mare, swallowed a dipperful of rum and rode towards the gunfire, followed by an officer sent by Gates to restrain him.

Arnold arrived as Learned's brigade was attacking the Germans in the British centre. He immediately assumed command and rode furiously into the fray, waving his sword and urging on the cheering Americans as the Germans, their flanks exposed, fell back. Galloping along the whole front, impervious to shot and shell, Arnold cut a frenzied but inspiring figure. By the strength of his personality, he took command of the field; Gates's aide never did catch up with him. The Major General was everywhere, once striking one of Dearborn's officers on the head with his sword by accident. In the centre, many of the British had rallied in the Balcarres Redoubt and were now defending it stubbornly. Finding this impenetrable, Arnold led a force to attack the Hessians entrenched at the Breymann Redoubt, on the British right. Rebuffed on the front, Arnold carried the two cabins which protected the Redoubt's rear and then, collecting twenty of Morgan's riflemen, led them in a charge which turned the defenders' flank and allowed a frontal attack to succeed.

In that last charge, Arnold's luck ran out. A musket shot brought down his horse which rolled on him, breaking again the leg which had been injured at Quebec. But the day was won – as it probably was even before Arnold's intervention. The British fell back on their Great Redoubt and night fell to put an end to the engagement. The British had lost 184 killed, 264 wounded and 183 taken prisoner. Despite their attacks over open ground, the American casualties were surprisingly light: about 30 dead and 100 wounded.

SURRENDER

Like a wounded tiger in the jungle, Burgoyne was still dangerous. Gates was in no hurry to tackle him again, even though the American army had now grown to about 17,000. He allowed the British to retreat farther north, back to Saratoga, and there he surrounded them – and waited. He did so just a trifle nervously, for news had come that General Clinton had carried out his pledge to Burgoyne and captured the American forts on the Hudson below Albany. But it was too little too late and Gates knew that Burgoyne was now trapped, his provisions, ammunition and fuel fast running out.

Reluctantly, in an agony of frustration compounded by the faint hope that Clinton could still penetrate further north, Burgoyne came to the same conclusion. After three consultations with his staff and, with every officer in his command above the rank of captain, Burgoyne decided to surrender. The risk to his career was great. His army was still mainly intact – it numbered a little under 6,000 men – and to deliver it to the rebels without a final fight would be a great blow to the British cause in North America. He would never be forgiven at home. But his men had had enough. He had lost a staggeringly high proportion of his officers, thanks to the marksmanship of the rebel riflemen, the troops were under-fed and wet, and even if he could break through to Albany they would probably starve to death on the march or be besieged there.

In a series of parleys with his old colleague Gates, Burgoyne negotiated what he called 'a convention', which allowed his army to march out of camp with the honours of war and be granted free passage to Great Britain on condition that they did not serve again in North America 'during the present contest'. The ceremony was carried out with dignity. Burgoyne was entertained to dinner by Gates in his tent where they toasted each other's countries. Daniel Morgan was too junior in rank (and perhaps too earthy?) to be at table, but he arrived during the meal to deliver a message to Gates. He was introduced to Burgoyne who, one account has it, grasped Morgan's hand and told him, 'Sir, you command the finest regiment in the world.'

It had been a strange battle, unusual in that it was split into two quite separate encounters, fought over much the same ground with an 18-day break between, and in that despite the severity of the fighting and the marksmanship bequeathed by the rifle, there were no great swathes of casualties, as occurred in the American Civil War or even the South African Boer War. Burgoyne's army was still virtually intact when he surrendered.

A visit to the battlefield today can explain this, at least in part. The site of the battle is roughly nine square miles in extent and the key points – the locations of Freeman's Farm, the Redoubts, the headquarters of both generals, etc. – have been restored with great fidelity by the US National Park Service. Surfaced roads take motorists to the main action points and, for the hardy, pleasant walking tracks link them also. Between them, however, the forest is not so dissimilar to 1777: a little more scrub, perhaps, but still a place of flickering sunlight, low trees and poor visibility. There is nowhere, except the few clearings hacked out by the farmers of the 1770s, to form line or to deploy artillery. It is terrain ideally suited for skirmishers and, most of all for marksmen, shooting behind cover. In the end, it was the Americans' mastery of forest warfare which proved conclusive. The skirmishers – the riflemen of the frontier – drove the Indians out of the woods, so that Burgoyne had to move blind, leaving him vulnerable to attack. They then picked off his officers, closed him down completely in camp, leaving him unable to forage and forcing him to choose between fighting, starving or surrendering. He chose surrender.

Untidy, and lacking in great strategic moves though it was, the Battle of Saratoga remains one of the turning points in modern history. Sir John Creasey included it in his classic *Fifteen Decisive Battles of the World* and wrote: 'Nor can any military event be said to have exercised more important influence on the future fortunes of mankind, than the complete defeat of Burgoyne's expedition in 1777; a defeat which rescued the revolted colonists from certain subjection; and which, by inducing the courts of France and Spain to attack England on their behalf, ensured the independence of the United States.'

Congress did not ratify Gates's 'convention' with Burgoyne. The surrendered army was not sent back to England but languished for the rest of the war in captivity in Virginia. Gentleman Johnny, however, was allowed to go home, where he wriggled out of accepting culpability, wrote a most successful play and sired four children by an actress. The war continued, but the north was no longer a theatre. The entry of France and Spain (and, later, of Holland) on the side of the colonists widened the struggle, and England was forced to restrict its army in America while it resumed its familiar sea and land battles with the great powers of Europe. Washington eventually trapped Cornwallis (Howe had long since been relieved) in 1781 and, two years later, Britain signed a treaty recognising the United States of America.

Saratoga was not the end of the war for the other protagonists. Gates, his ears ringing with the plaudits of Congress, intrigued unsuccessfully against Washington and suffered an ignominious defeat at the Battle of Camden in South Carolina. He never saw action again, retired and, now a widower, married a rich English woman. The men of Morgan's corps again reverted to Washington's command after Saratoga, but disbanded as a unit when their term of service expired. Morgan himself became a brigadier general and, with the help of Virginian riflemen, won a decisive victory against the British at the Battle of Cowpens in January 1781. This time he was in command. He retired shortly afterwards and went back to Virginia where he became a miller and a respected elder statesman. Like his great frontier contemporary, Daniel Boone, Morgan died peacefully in his bed in suburban Winchester, Virginia; his doctor was astonished by the lash marks still visible on his back. His pretty, white-painted house is set in a quiet, tree-lined street which could be anywhere – Hampstead in London or a suburb of Geneva. There is not even the smallest plaque on the fence to say that here lived and died one of America's greatest frontiersmen.

Isaac Miller slips back into anonymity after Saratoga. His service expired, he almost certainly returned to Martha. But like many of his fellow riflemen he may well have signed up for further service in the war; the money was good and regular. If so, he would have seen plenty of action. Richard B. LaCrosse Junior's definitive work, *The Frontier Rifleman* (Pioneer Press, Tennessee, 1989), lists 65 engagements in the war in which riflemen played a major role. Of these, he claims that 49 were won by the rebels, twelve were lost and sixteen were inconclusive.

There is no doubt about the effectiveness of these master skirmishers. They were good because their upbringing and daily life on the frontier had taught them to use terrain and background to advantage: they could disappear into an undulation in the ground and melt into the forest, helped by the earth colours of their clothing. They moved quickly and softly (the moccasin to them was 'a decent way of goin' barefoot') and, above all, they shot with care and precision.

The lessons they taught about infantry warfare were not completely assimilated, even by the Americans. Immediately after Saratoga, Washington lost Philadelphia and, in a conventional attack, the Battle of Germantown, although he preserved his army once again. It was not until the late 1830s that the rifle was accepted in the American army, but it took Gettysburg in 1863 to drive home the folly of attacking defensive positions manned by determined, well-trained riflemen. The British were still showing themselves vulnerable to expert marksmanship as late as 1899 in the Boer War. Only at Mons, in 1914, did the lessons they should have learned at Saratoga bear fruit.

Saratoga remains the American rifleman's great memorial. He played a distinguished role in the second encounter but he was absolutely the key to the outcome of that vital first engagement. By preventing Burgoyne's force from reaching the rebel lines and, by demonstrating that American troops *could* stand and fight, he swung the battle and proved to be the catalyst in the creation of the world's most powerful nation.

One soldier who watched Burgoyne's ride into the American camp to surrender says that, halfway there, a wild turkey cried in the forest and made Burgoyne swing round in alarm. There are those who still feel it inappropriate that it was the eagle and not the turkey which became the national emblem of the United States of America.

4
THE SPEARMEN
The Zulus of Isandlwana

The name itself, Isandlwana (pronounced Ee-sant-klwaanah), means 'little house' and it refers to the crouching shape of a bare block of sandstone which rises some 500 feet above the Nqutu plateau, about eight miles into KwaZulu from the Buffalo River in south-east Africa. Not large enough to be a mountain and too sheer to be a hill, it dominates the plain, running for about 500 yards NNE to SSW and looking a little like the Sphinx of Egypt.

Ironically, it was the Sphinx which was the cap badge of the old 24th Regiment (now the South Wales Borderers) of the British army, the 2nd Battalion of which was virtually wiped out at Isandlwana on 22 January 1879, by Zulu warriors of King Cetshwayo. It was the most comprehensive defeat ever suffered by a fully armed column of western soldiers at the hands of primitive, spear-carrying warriors.

There are many candidates for the role of the finest aboriginal soldiers in history. The list must include the Sioux and Cheyenne who defeated Custer at Little Big Horn; the Riffs and Toureg of the Sahara who led the French Foreign Legion such a merry dance; and the British-baiting Pathans of the North-West Frontier of India. Perhaps we should add the followers of the Mahdi who killed Gordon at Khartoum and kept the British out of the Sudan for more than a decade. They earned this toast from Kipling: 'An' 'ere's to you, Fuzzy Wuzzy, with your 'ayrick 'head of 'air – You big black boundin' beggar – for you broke a British square!'

But none of them matched the achievements of the Zulus. From a small clan of about 1,500 people in the closing years of the 18th century, inhabiting some 100 square miles in a territory between the Drakensberg Mountains and the Indian Ocean, the Zulus grew within eighty years to become a nation of a quarter of a million, creating the separate, united state of Zululand (now part of KwaZulu-Natal) and occupying more than two-fifths of present day KwaZulu-Natal. They came to dominate south-east Africa, subjugating peoples for hundreds of miles around and building an army which was highly disciplined, skilled in battle tactics and structured into a system which, although different in that it was socially-based, intuitively mirrored that of sophisticated European armies.

The Zulu soldier of the 19th century was loyal to his commanders and comrades, he could run fifteen miles and then fight a battle, and he was often unmarried – and therefore dedicated to military life – until middle age. Carrying only a rawhide shield and a handful of spears (the muzzle-loading muskets carried by some were antiquated and virtually useless), he defeated a British field force of regular soldiers armed with cannon, rockets and the awesome, breech-loading Martini-Henry rifle. His achievement flashed around the world. It incurred savage vengeance from the forces of imperialism. It also, however, brought down the British government of the day and put South Africa on the world's political agenda, where it has remained virtually ever since.

Unlike the other warriors analysed in this book, the Zulus remain very much alive today and the subject of great attention from the world's media. The characteristics which first brought them to the attention of a Victorian public – courage, independence, intelligence and occasional flashes of cruelty – are still in evidence and are the subject of as much debate and careful negotiation as in 1879. The Zulu story is far from over.

SHAKA

Few modern nations can point to one man as their creator. The Bolivians and Colombians, perhaps, with Simon Bolivar; maybe the Germans with Bismarck and, to a lesser extent, the Italians with Garibaldi. Most names are ringed with caveats and they soon run out. But there is no doubt that, in twelve brief years, Shaka took the small and listless Zulu clan and moulded it into a strong nation, great by the standards of black Africa. He was the victor of Isandlwana, although he had died fifty years before the battle took place.

His full name was Shaka kaSenzangakhona, but history knows him simply as Shaka Zulu or the Black Bonaparte. He was born in about 1785, illegitimately, to a strong, feisty maiden called Nandi and an unremarkable chieftain named Senzangakhona, ruler of the small Zulu clan, which was one of a hundred such groups, generically called the Nguni, inhabiting what is now kwaZulu. Numbering about 1,500, their territory measured little more than 100 square miles.

It was a time of inter-tribal bickering and skirmishes, but compared with what was to follow, of comparative pastoral tranquillity. There was enough land for everybody, the grazing was good and, provided that homage was paid to the nearest large tribe, real warfare was rare. The boys tended the herds, the women did the rest of the work and the men hunted, lounged and took snuff. The white man was unknown. The Boer descendants of the Dutch on the Cape had seeded eastwards along the coast a little but they were still some 400 miles distant and 50 years away from beginning their great treks to the north. The English had yet to make their appearance. Life must have seemed tranquil to the Zulus.

It wasn't quite like that for Nandi and her baby son, however. Illegitimacy was frowned upon and she had no real status in Senzangakhona's kraal. Her independence and sharp tongue were of no help to her and, eventually, she and her child were returned to her own tribe, the eLangeni, in disgrace. We know little about Shaka's early days, but it seems that he grew up fatherless and something of an outcast. Eventually, Nandi and he were taken in by a clan which lived directly under the powerful Mthethwa tribe and Shaka served as a herd boy there, still quiet and reserved but growing tall, strong and expert with the light spear, the assegai. He earned local fame when he killed a treed leopard and was taken into the Mthethwa army, serving on campaigns for six years.

By his early twenties, Shaka had become a magnificent warrior. More than 6 feet tall, he was broad shouldered and finely muscled. The early dependence on his mother and his close relationship with her has led some historians to speculate that he was a latent homosexual. Certainly, he never had a known relationship with any other woman and he left no heirs. But, if he was less than heterosexual, he was far from effeminate. His courage and bearing in battle led him to the attention of the Mthethwa king, Dingiswayo, and he soon became a royal favourite.

When Senzangakhona died in 1816, Dingiswayo freed the young Shaka to travel to the Zulu kraals to claim his inheritance. Shaka was by no means first in line; he had not been seen in his father's kraal for twenty years, and, in fact, his elder half-brother Sigujana had assumed the chieftainship. Shaka did not hesitate. Sigujana was killed and so was everyone who had offended Nandi in the past. He then set about turning the Zulus into warriors.

Despite their fierce appearance, the tribesmen of South Africa, loosely called the Bantu by Europeans, were not great fighters. In the early years of the 19th century, warfare among the tribes was formulaic, and usually fairly harmless. The two sides would line up facing each other and shout boasts and insults. There would be an exchange of light throwing spears, usually easily deflected by shields, and the side with the most confidence would charge the other, putting it to flight. Casualties were few and the women and children would often watch the fun from a nearby hillock.

Shaka thought this a waste of time. War meant crushing the opposition and this meant killing. In Dingiswayo's expeditions, he taught his troops to kill and to pursue the scattered ranks of the enemy and to destroy them mercilessly. He revelled in hand-to-hand combat and he led by example. It was, then, a seasoned warrior who came to mould the listless, surly Zulu tribe into a fighting unit. The material was unprepossessing. The Zulus had never been a major tribe and they had been happy to live under the Mthethwa shadow, doing as little as possible to get by. This was feasible under the tolerant Dingiswayo but it was not good enough for Shaka. All the humiliations of his childhood now matched with the burning ambition kindled by his years on campaign. He knew exactly what he wanted: an army – a killing machine, carefully trained to do his bidding – and he began building it from scratch.

Shaka summoned every available man of the clan. It is doubtful if he mustered more than about 400. Few of them had had military experience or were married. Marriage profoundly changed the status of the man concerned and was indicated by the wearing of the *isiCoco*, the fibre ring sewn into the hair and polished into place with beeswax. This mark of maturity was unique to the Zulus. The king immediately divided these lacklustre recruits into the nucleus of four regiments. He placed all the married men into the *amaWombe* regiment. They were allowed to keep their wives but they were moved into a separate kraal, under strict surveillance. The second oldest group were put into the *uJubingqwana*. The rest of the men were regimented as the *umGamule*. This left the herd boys, who were bright and eager. These he christened the *uFasimba*, 'the Haze'. With the boys he was working with virgin material and they quickly responded. They became his favourites – 'Shaka's Own' – and the prototype for many regiments to follow.

In creating these units Shaka had followed regional tribal practice. But he had developed and refined it to the point where he had subsumed the key element of the European regimental system: the building of an *esprit de corps* which sustains morale, builds a bond of comradeship between soldiers and kindles fierce loyalty. This untutored African chieftain had intuitively harnessed the army structure which sophisticated western commanders had taken years to develop. Intense rivalry and often fighting developed between the various regiments and Shaka encouraged this with delight.

The light throwing spears were sent away to be broken up and their blades melted down and made into heavier, short stabbing assegais. Shields were made larger, so that all the weapons could be carried in one hand behind them and the enemy could not see how well armed the warriors were until it was too late. Shaka also trained his soldiers to carry the shields on edge to the enemy so that, at a distance, the army would seem to be smaller than it was. Looking at the early movements of his recruits, Shaka was disgusted at how clumsy they were, so he made his men throw away their protective leather sandals and march in bare feet. When this drew complaints he made the grumblers dance on thorns.

Shaka was relentless in his training. Day after day on the beaten earth of the kraal, he taught the regiments how to use the short stabbing spear in close combat, showing also how the longer shield could be deployed as an aggressive weapon. In one flowing movement, he demonstrated how the shield could be hooked under that of an opponent, turning his left arm away and upwards, leaving the ribs open to a killing stab with the new, shorter spear. The name for the spear, *assegai*, was soon replaced by *iklwa*, a phonetic representation of the sucking sound made when the blade was twisted and pulled out after the stab.

Once the embryonic regiments had been taught how to drill and fight as a unit, Shaka took them on to the plains to demonstrate the heart of his tactics in battle – a manoeuvre which was uniquely his own and which was to win him and the Zulu race fame and great success. It was based on the four-regiment structure and used in battle to simulate the fierce African buffalo. The entire force was trained to approach an enemy as one block, marching tightly together. Then, at a given command, the block would break up. The centre regiment, the 'chest' of the buffalo, would immediately engage the enemy in close combat. As it did so two other units would break away very quickly on both flanks and race around the enemy until both 'horns' met in their rear in complete encirclement. The fourth unit, the 'loins', would remain behind the chest as a strong reserve, often sitting with their backs to the fighting so as not to pre-empt the order to engage. It was basically simple but the secret lay in the timing of the movements and their execution at great speed.

These manoeuvres and the drills went on every day for the first year of Shaka's kingship. Dingiswayo left him alone to mould his tribe – he knew, after all, that Shaka's work would provide a new and welcome contingent to join the Mthethwa army and he was content. Shaka imposed fierce discipline on his followers and took care to protect himself. In addition to the Royal Barber, there was a Receiver of the Royal Spittle and even a Wiper of the Royal Anus to ensure that the king's dirt was not smuggled out of the kraal to be used in witchcraft against him. Any transgression, however minor, was punishable by death. Fear and respect walked hand in hand in Shaka's kraals.

When he was ready, Shaka went to war. He had to tread warily. The Zulus paid unquestioning allegiance to Dingiswayo but they lived far enough away for Shaka to operate with a degree of autonomy, as long as he did not build a tribe strong enough to threaten the Mthethwa and kept his fierce little force available to fight in Dingiswayo's service whenever the call came. Predictably, Shaka turned on the eLangeni, the tribe which had rejected and humiliated his mother. Every remembered slight from his childhood was punished with impalement and the kraals were burned to the ground. What was left of the eLangeni was absorbed into the Zulu tribe, the men joining Shaka's force and being drilled to use his weapons and his tactics. Then Shaka attacked another neighbouring tribe, the Butelezi, and, in a battle against evenly matched forces, triumphantly demonstrated his buffalo tactics for the first time. The killing was comprehensive and there were few Butelezi warriors left to swell Shaka's army. But he took the maidens who survived and put them into his *umDlunkulu,* his seraglio or harem.

All chieftains maintained many wives and, accordingly, sired many children. But not Shaka. Although he enthusiastically built his harem until, in his prime, it is said to have numbered 800 women, he never married and there was no issue. The king always proclaimed that he would never have a child because, one day, it could become a threat to him. This was perfectly true and, once royal children reached puberty, patricide was a not uncommon danger to tribal chieftains at that time. Nevertheless, given Shaka's energy and the size of his seraglio, it is hard to believe that one at least of Shaka's dalliances with his women over the years – if any ever occurred – would not have led to childbirth. But there is no such evidence and this adds credulity to the charge of homosexuality, or at least impotence. It can also be argued that Shaka regarded the sexual act in itself as physically weakening. Certainly he deferred the joys of marriage for his three junior regiments, insisting that they should not plait the *isiCoco* into their hair until they were approaching middle age. Only on rare, fixed occasions were they allowed to indulge in sexual foreplay. This enforced celibacy was a cruel denial. Modern Zulu apologists for the more eccentric acts of Shaka's reign argue that the policy was the king's far-sighted answer to the severe droughts and famines which occasionally struck the Nguni peoples; that it was, in fact, a deliberate act of population control. It is possible. But Shaka was building his army at this stage and using young herd boys as the first rung in the martial ladder. It is unlikely that he would have deliberately cut off a source of supply for future recruits. It is more probable that he held back the granting of the *isiCoco* as a reward for good service. And he would not have been unaware of the keener fighting edge which the tension of enforced celibacy gave his warriors.

Small in numbers though they were, the newly disciplined Zulus quickly made an impression. Dingiswayo called them up to reinforce an ambitious attack he was planning against a large tribe, the Ndwandwe. Before the attack could be launched, Dingiswayo fell into the hands of the enemy and was beheaded. Shaka and his Zulus arrived only just in time to fight an orderly rear-guard action against the Ndwandwe as the Mthethwa fled in disarray. In the uneasy peace which prevailed afterwards, Shaka redoubled his efforts to increase his trained cadre and, when the Ndwandwe struck again, he opposed them with his own Zulus and cleverly split the horde facing him by decoying half of it away in pursuit of Zulu cattle and fighting the rest from a shrewdly selected defensive position at the top of a conical hill. Just as at Agincourt with the French, the attackers had insufficient room in which to use their numerical superiority and the *iklwa* was employed at close quarters to terrifying effect by the Zulus.

Shaka lost his cattle and he was forced to retreat. But he did so in good order and his Zulus, outnumbered by more than two to one, had inflicted a huge number of casualties on the Ndwandwe. In 1819 the Ndwandwe invaded again. This time the Zulu ranks had been swollen by ready volunteers from neighbouring small clans who had all been inculcated with the Zulu drill and tactics, armed with the *iklwa* and either been swallowed into Shaka's original four regiments or formed into new units – still observing the age structure. Shaka was still outnumbered, but he retreated tantalisingly, denied the invaders food from the land and then attacked and defeated them comprehensively at a river crossing. A series of further brilliant campaigns followed. Shaka crushed the major clans between the Pongolo and Thukela rivers, before crossing into what is now Natal, dislodging the powerful tribes who lived there and sending them over the Drakensberg mountains or south-east towards the white man's frontier.

By 1824, Shaka's original army of 400 had grown to more than 15,000 and the outcast had become a real king. The people under his sway espoused allegiance to king and country, rather than to clan or chief – and all of them, no matter what their clan or tribal origin, now called themselves Zulus. Through his process of rapid conquest and absorption, Shaka had wielded together hundreds of tribes into a single kingdom which stretched from the Portuguese border at Delagoa Bay in the north to Pondoland in the south and from the Drakensbergs to the Indian Ocean. His insistence on young men joining his regiments meant that he had broken down the local affiliations of Zulu manhood by making them completely dependent upon the monarch for food, shelter and advancement. The army not only 'washed their spears' on behalf of the king in his many raids and wars, but also tended his cattle and reaped his crops. The system was highly centralised and control was extended to the edges of the kingdom through a network of chieftains and *indunas*, or tribute collectors, who represented the king.

The maintenance of Shaka's frightening authority depended upon two factors: the king's ability to keep his warriors happy with new conquests and the booty they produced, and his use of instant execution to quell dissent. As Shaka's reign progressed, the first requirement began to become more difficult to meet as the *impis* or divisions ranged ever farther afield. But his firm grasp never relaxed. The dreadful 'sniffing out' of traitors and wrongdoers – real or imagined – by witch-doctors was a constant feature of life in the royal kraal and, towards the end of his reign, when the great warrior had become fat and reluctant to travel with his *impis*, executions were ordered with a capricious flick of the royal wrist.

Despite Shaka's absolutist grip on the reins of power, it all had to end. The constant killings, the ever more distant campaigning and the enforced celibacy gradually created a groundswell of unrest. On 23 September 1828, Shaka's younger half-brother Dingane plucked up his courage and plunged his *iklwa* into the king's side while he was received a visiting delegation. The big man fell and everyone – including the assassin – fled in fear, leaving his body in a pool of blood.

It had been a remarkable era. Within little more than a decade, the Zulus had achieved dominance of the land, had become a warrior nation and put an end to the age of Nguni pastoral tranquillity, with its many tribes and clans and grazing for all. Shaka's depredations had coincided with other events to send tribes fleeing into the hinterland of what is now the Orange Free State to embark on a series of terrible slayings – still remembered as the *mfecane*, 'the crushing' – which blighted native life for years.

But Shaka's reign had also seen the coming of a far greater threat to the black man. At his death it was only a cloud on the horizon no bigger than a man's hand – a white man's hand.

THE WHITE MAN

Natal was named by the great Portuguese sailor and explorer Vasco da Gama. As his little ship butted on its northerly course off the coast of Africa, he caught glimpses of green hills and crashing surf on the port side. It was Christmas Day 1497, so he named the coast *Terra Natalis*. For more than 300 years, this green, undulating land, protected along its inland border either by the Drakensberg range or by buffer tribes and, from the sea, by shoals, reefs and cruel surf, lay beyond the reach of the white men who were gradually colonising the Cape colony. Then the ripples created by Shaka's conquests lapped at the colony's borders and interest was aroused in the great king who lived far to the north-east. Ivory was the commercial imperative behind the curiosity. Eventually, in 1823, a small band of English entrepreneurs and adventurers mounted an expedition and, during stormy weather, they were swept over a bar and into a bay, about a thousand miles around the coast from Cape Town. The bay was sheltered, the land was green and watered, so the party founded their settlement there and called it Port Natal.

They were, of course, in Shaka's kingdom. Gradually communications were opened with kwaBulawayo, Shaka's kraal, 120 miles to the north. The king could easily have exterminated the small settlement but he was intrigued and amused by the white men, with their ridiculous garments, their firearms (no threat to him – he shrewdly pointed out that his warriors would be upon them before they could reload their muskets) and the fascinating gewgaws they offered as gifts. So the settlement was allowed to remain and Shaka traded ivory with the small party and summoned their leaders to him whenever the whim took him.

On Shaka's death in 1828, his assassin Dingane eventually ascended the throne – gingerly and after first prudently getting rid of his two co-conspirators in the murder. The new king lacked the qualities of his half-brother but he continued Shaka's policy of tolerating the tiny settlement at Port Natal, for he wanted their trade goods and always hoped that he would be able to acquire their guns. Neither side trusted the other but it was not from Port Natal that Dingane's eventual demise came but from the west, down through the stony passes of the Drakensbergs.

The possession by the British of the Cape in 1805, as part of the fall-out of the Napoleonic wars, had not really affected the Dutch inhabitants there. Farmers, not traders, they moved a little further inland, away from authority, keeping to themselves, living their lives within ever-growing family circles, and using local black labour on their farms. Land was plentiful and, as generation succeeded generation, the young men just staked out fresh land to farm, ever eastwards. They never questioned their right to land; it was God's gift to the Boers and, as far as anyone could see, it was infinite. Boer farms were measured in thousands of acres, not hundreds, and the people who owned them were as stubborn and idiosyncratic a race as ever picked up Bible and musket.

The British adopted a *laissez faire* attitude to their Boer subjects. The farmers were more or less self-sufficient and the two races jogged along together uneventfully throughout the early years of the 19th century. Then the problems began. British settlers began to arrive in the Cape and move eastwards. The Boers, faced in the east by the Great Fish River across which lived hostile Kaffirs, found that, at last, the land in the Cape territory was beginning to run out. Their attitude to their native labourers and servants was also beginning to disturb the British colonial authorities. Britain had formally abolished slavery in 1807 and it was therefore an offence to practise it in a British colony. The Boers denied that their relationship with their black employees was that of master and slave, but the difference was not always easy to define. The need to protect the settlers from raids by the border Kaffirs meant the stationing of soldiers which, in turn, meant that taxes became a hard reality instead of a nominal formality. It all became too much for the prickly, independent Boer burghers. In 1835, they began their Great Trek to the north-east to escape from irksome British authority and find new lands in the wilderness.

The great migration was a remarkable act of courage and determination. Whole families packed their belongings into white canvas-covered wagons, harnessed their oxen teams and, with the men on horseback, the boys walking with the cattle and the women in the wagons, they set off into the unknown. It was not a disciplined, united exodus; more a gradual movement, gathering impetus over two years. Across the Orange River went the wagons and the herds, on to the high veldt. They skirted the Basutos but clashed with the Matabele and, finally, defeated them with their controlled fire power. Then the trails divided, some settlers staying to found the Orange Free State, others pressing on north-eastwards to what became the Transvaal, and a third stream turning east and south, man-handling their wagons down through the Drakensberg passes into Natal.

In November 1837, this wagon train halted in the foothills above the Natal plain, while their leader, Piet Retief, and six men rode on to King Dingane's kraal to negotiate terms for settling within his kingdom. Dingane had watched the progress of the Boers with growing apprehension for he feared that they were coming to take his land. But he received the Boer emissaries with courtesy and, after five days of ceremonies and discussion, promised 'vacant lands' within Natal to Retief and his party if they would first recover 300 head of cattle stolen by a Blatokla chief. Retief agreed and, within three months, had tracked down and recovered the cattle.

With 68 mounted riflemen, he drove the cattle triumphantly into Dingane's kraal early in February, putting on a dazzling display of horsemanship and marksmanship for the king and his court. The show had the effect of terrifying Dingane and confirming his fears that these white men were a powerful threat who must be crushed before they gained a foothold in his kingdom. Accordingly, he signed a document (which, of course, he could not read) granting Retief huge tracts of land in Natal and then invited the 69 Boers to witness a ceremonial dance to celebrate the agreement. Retief and his comrades, relaxed and exultant at having successfully completed the negotiation, piled their rifles and sat down to drink beer. At the height of the dancing, Dingane suddenly leapt to his feet and shrieked 'Kill the Wizards'. The Boers were dragged outside to the execution hill nearby and all rectally impaled before having their brains dashed out with clubs. Retief was forced to watch before being killed himself at the last. Dingane then immediately sent three regiments to attack the Boer encampment in the foothills. At dawn, the Zulus decimated the laagers, killing 282 people, mostly women and children.

This act of treachery was designed, of course, to ensure that no more Boers would dare to enter Natal. It was not directed towards the handful of British and native settlers at Port Natal, but if it delivered a warning to them, all well and good. The British took the point and came to the conclusion that their years of privileged existence in Zululand were over. They raised a force to attack Dingane but were severely defeated and the remaining Europeans at Port Natal took to the sea as Zulu *impis* raced in and sacked and burned the settlement. On the high veld, however, the Boers were planning revenge.

In December 1838, ten months after the massacre, Andries Pretorius led a Commando of 464 well-armed men in wagons into Zululand. They encamped on the banks of the Ncome River, laagered their wagons into a ring and waited. On the 16th, at dawn, 12,000 Zulus attacked – and were slaughtered. Pretorius had chosen his site with care, on a high point where a subsidiary of the Ncome flowed in to form a 'V'. As the Zulus were channelled into the funnel formed by the river banks, the muskets mowed them down. Some 3,000 warriors were killed and the Boers named the site Blood River. It was a victory of shot over spear and a humiliation for Dingane.

The jubilant voortrekkers pushed on and put the royal kraal to the torch, the king retreating before them. The settlers' wagons poured through the Drakensberg passes, the Boers built their own capital, Pietermaritzburg, some 50 miles inland from Port Natal, and announced a new republic. The British, watching from faraway Cape Town, decided to let sleeping dogs lie and allow the new flag to be raised over Port Natal, re-named Durban after the settlers there had crept back. But the new Natalia was short-lived.

Determined in war, the Boers were incompetent administrators, continually riven by dissent, and they could find no way of handling either the many clans who now flooded back to the lands from which they had been driven by Shaka or the growth in British immigrants. In 1842, the British moved in to protect their nationals in Durban and annexed Natal. In disgust, the Boers began to trek back to the north-west, the way they had come five eventful years before.

Before they left, however, they had launched one last, decisive attack upon their arch-enemy. Dingane was never able to claim the support of his people as Shaka had done, and when he ordered the execution of his amiable half-brother Mpande, about 17,000 Zulus fled with the sentenced man into Natal. The Boers seized the opportunity, declared Mpande king of Zululand and, with a Commando and an *impi* of Mpande's men, attacked Dingane and drove him into exile, where he was killed by a neighbouring chief. Mpande was installed as undisputed ruler, cheerfully recognised the British as his neighbours in Natal and a uniquely peaceful, 32-year reign ensued for the Zulus.

But not entirely. As Mpande moved into middle and then old age, the question of succession began to destroy the equilibrium of the state. A contest to become heir evolved around the king's eldest son, Cetshwayo, born to his first wife, and his second eldest, Mbuyazi, son of Mpande's favourite wife. The long-smouldering explosion occurred in 1856 when Cetshwayo and about 20,000 warriors attacked his half-brother's forces on the banks of the Thukela River. Outnumbered by at least two to one, Mbuyazi stood no chance. He and five other sons of Mpande were killed and his followers massacred and the king was forced to acknowledge Cetshwayo as his heir. He did so with great reluctance – Mbuyazi had always been his favourite – and for the rest of his reign his authority was diminished. Mpande, the half-brother of Shaka, died in 1872. He was the only one of the many progeny of king Senzangakhona to die on his sleeping-mat.

Although the long years of Mpande's reign had been comparatively uneventful for his country, this was not the case in the rest of South Africa. The two Boer states of the Orange River Territory and the Transvaal were badly administered, with ill-defined borders and recurring problems with their economies and neighbouring black tribes. The pot was stirred when, in 1867, diamonds were found near the borders of both states and the Cape and thousands of prospectors poured in. They attracted capital and demanded black labour, which was often paid with guns, so adding to tribal militancy when squabbles broke out over land. Most of the new immigrants were British and the Colonial Office's traditional exasperated disinterest in South Africa was forced to change. The success of turning the vast states of Canada into one confederation, prompted the thought in London that this could be the solution, too, for the hotchpotch of colonies, independent Boer states and African kingdoms which formed South Africa. Under the British flag, an infrastructure could be put in place which would open up this huge territory to commercial and economic development and eradicate racial tension.

Theophilus Shepstone, the vastly experienced Native Agent in Natal, who had cultivated the Zulus and toiled for the past 30 years in the arcane garden of native affairs – and with some success – was sent to the Transvaal to begin the process by winning over the Boers there. He did little winning over but ran up the British flag at Pretoria in 1877 anyway, unaided but not hindered by the sullen Boers. Shortly afterwards, Sir Bartle Frere arrived in Cape Town as High Commissioner for Southern Africa, with instructions to see the confederation through. He quickly found that he had another Kaffir War, the ninth, on his hands on the Cape borders, and he sent his newly arrived Army C-in-C, Lieutenant-General the Hon Sir Frederick Thesiger, to quell it. It seemed to Frere that black unrest was everywhere: not only on the Cape borders but in the north and in the Transvaal. In fact, famine caused by years of over-grazing and a widespread drought, the displacement of tribes and the spreading of firearms from the diamond fields had all coalesced to bring about the general air of unrest. But to Frere the solution was simplistically clear – and lay in Zululand.

The High Commissioner had immediately grasped that confrontation with the Zulu state was an essential prerequisite for confederation. Zululand was completely independent, it blocked routes to the sea, it was clearly disputatious (Cetshwayo was engaged in a long-running land ownership argument with the Transvaalers) and, most importantly, it possessed a standing army which could sweep across undefended borders and invade Natal at any time. Support for his anxiety, unexpectedly, came from Shepstone. The former Native Agent and friend of the Zulus was now completely immersed in Transvaal's intractable problems. Chief among these was the border dispute with the Zulus. He found, to his annoyance, that Cetshwayo would not bend to the wishes of his old mentor, and Shepstone's vanity, already wounded by his daily skirmishes with resentful Boers in Pretoria, was irreparably damaged. The old man now became a firm enemy of the Zulus and fed Frere with exaggerated stories of their intransigence and cruelty. These were backed by similarly distorted reports from missionaries in Zululand, who had failed to win concessions from Cetshwayo. Frere

126

became convinced that the Zulu king lay behind all the unrest and would have to be taught a lesson.

But events back home had moved on. Disraeli's government was now facing a new threat in the far more politically sensitive country of Afghanistan and wished to have no new native war in Southern Africa. Frere, nevertheless, was completely committed. He received a set-back when an independent commission appointed to look into the Transvaal-Zululand border dispute – the findings of which Cetshwayo had readily agreed to accept – reported favourably for the Zulus, but the excuse he was looking for came gratuitously in July 1878.

Two of the wives of a Zulu *induna* named Sihayo, a favourite of Cetshwayo, who lived near the Natal border at Rorke's Drift, were unfaithful to him and, pregnant, they fled with their lovers into Natal. In Zulu society adultery was a crime punishable by death, and, while Sihayo was absent, four of his relatives, with a party of about 70 warriors, crossed into Natal, found the women and dragged them back into Zululand, where they were executed. Later, in another incident, two white surveyors who had mistakenly crossed into Zulu territory were jostled and accused of being spies before being released. These incidents, minor in themselves, gave Frere the *casus belli* which he sought. He immediately demanded that Cetshwayo hand over the three men for trial, pay a summary and very heavy fine of cattle and virtually disband his army.

The king was now in a predicament. The offenders were men of standing and had acted within Zulu law, although 'invading' Natal was agreed to have been a mistake. Opinion ran high among Cetshwayo's advisers that he should not surrender them. Nor could the king contemplate the complete social upheaval which the disbandment of the army would entail. Bewildered by this sudden aggression from the erstwhile friendly English, the king desperately tried to compromise, offering to pay the fine if the men could be spared. Frere refused, of course, and issued an ultimatum, promising war if his demands were not met within thirty days. Cetshwayo pleaded – truthfully – that the rivers were in flood, that he could not possibly gather the cattle in time to meet the deadline and that he had no wish to quarrel with the English. Frere was unmoved. He had long since commissioned Thesiger to prepare his plans for invasion. The die was cast.

THE WARRIORS

The war which was about to begin in January 1879 was a classic of its kind: symbolic of and, indeed, a kind of culmination of a century or more of such colonial clashes between European – usually British – professional troops armed with the most modern tools of war, and aboriginal warriors carrying primitive weapons. What makes it particularly interesting is that the main protagonists in the war were, arguably, the best of their types in the world at that time. On both sides, the line soldiers were courageous, well trained and experienced. The Zulus were well led, the British less so, but the latter's great defeat at Isandlwana resulted quite as much from the skilled deployment of the Zulus as from a series of mistakes by the army commanders.

It was a battle won, however, by line soldiers rather then generals and it is appropriate therefore to analyse the main combatants involved. In the end, the war proved to be a quite unequal contest; the overwhelming fire-power of the Victorian British army saw to that. But for one remarkable day, the tables were turned.

The men who turned them are represented for us now by Uguku, a warrior of the *umCijo* regiment. He very much existed. He fought at Isandlwana in the centre of the attack and, later, was to tell his story of the battle and have it included in Francis Colenso and E. Durnford's *History of the Zulu War and its Origins*, published in London in 1880. Alas, he tells little of himself in his narrative but we can build a picture of him now on the basis of what is known about the Zulu army of the time, plus a touch, perhaps, of poetic licence to make him representative of the Zulu warriors who fought at Isandlwana.

We see Uguku, in January 1879, at oNdini, the king's 'great place' in the Mahlabathini plain. Many of the age regiments are here for it is the time of the *umKhosi*, the annual first fruits ceremony when, during three days of ceremonies, the king and his army are ritually cleansed and strengthened. It is a useful coincidence for Cetshwayo that this ritual has coincided with the massing of the British troops on his frontier, for it means that his army is virtually already mobilised.

The young warrior (he is about 23 years old) is not himself ready for battle immediately. He is formally dressed for the ceremony – and a magnificent figure he presents. The bushy parts of a collection of cows' tails are attached, garter-like, just below his knees and elbows and they swing and sway as he moves. More hang down across his chest and back, suspended from a necklace. Uguku is not yet married, so he does not have the right to wear the *isiCoco*, but a padded head-band of leopard skin forms the basis of a head-dress from which flaps of monkey skin hang down on each side of his face. Two long black tail feathers of the *sakabuli* bird are stuck into the head-band and rise proudly above each ear. He would dearly love to wear the beautiful blue crane feathers, but these are restricted to more senior regiments.

His regiment, the *umCijo*, is for young warriors who do not yet wear the *isiCoco*. Not that Uguku feels at all inferior. Although his regiment is comparatively new, having been raised by Mpande in 1867 and not, therefore, possessing the battle honours of the veterans like the *amaWombe*, which date back to Shaka, nevertheless it has performed well in brushes with the Swazis in the north and Uguku is proud to carry his black shield. He looks forward eagerly, however, to the day when he can introduce white patches on to it to show seniority. He looks forward even more to the wearing of the *isiCoco* – for Uguku is in love and desperately wishes to marry.

He has met his maiden at the only practice of *ukuHlongonga* he has so far been allowed to attend. This is the favour granted rarely by the king to his celibate warriors, when they may indulge in limited sexual activity with members of a female regiment. The Zulu moral code inveighs strictly against illegitimacy. Children are much loved and carefully tended as babies and trained to take their assigned roles within the community as they grow older. Parenthood, therefore, evokes responsibility and dedication and one-parent families are as rare in the kraals as white faces. Not much has changed since Shaka's day. The occasional pre-*isiCoco* relaxation allowed to his young warriors by the king, therefore, are strictly regulated and amount to little more than foreplay and mutual masturbation.

It has been enough, however, for Uguku to wish to marry his Sibongili. Uguku has grown up in the traditional Zulu way. Throughout his boyhood years he has tended cattle, staying out on the plains from sunrise to sunset, defending the beasts from marauding predators and playing stick fights with his peers. On reaching puberty, his ear-lobes have been pierced and he has formally been admitted to his *intanga*, or age group, with whom he has been taught hut-building, field-cooking and basic martial skills. At 20, he has been admitted to his regiment but he has not yet washed his spear in battle. This is a great problem in Cetshwayo's reign – as it had been during Mpande's time. The cooler, more passive policies of both monarchs have meant that warriors have fewer opportunities to gain the *isiCoco* and advancement in battle. In turn, this has meant that, even if he had permission to marry, Uguku lacks the wherewithal to purchase his bride. He does not know how much *ilobolo* he will have to pay for Sibongili, for he is not yet in a position to begin talks with her father, but she is much prized in her kraal and he fears it will be out of his reach. He badly needs to go to war – even though he is not sure whether fighting the white faces will yield cattle. Do they have any?

Uguku begins to shed his ceremonial trappings. He is hot and the ritual is now over. Off comes the head-dress and the monkey skin sideflaps and he carefully removes the cows' tails which swing around his chest and back. Those around his arms and legs are allowed to remain, but he is now wearing the *umuTsha*, a thin belt of hide around his waist from which strips of dressed hide hang down front and back. He stretches in relief and reveals a fine body, well muscled but as yet featuring no surplus fat. That will come in the future as the beer which Sibongili and his other wives will prepare every day begins to make its mark. What is distinctive about him are the legs. They are so thick and bunched with muscle, particularly in the thigh, that they seem out of proportion to his body, giving him a stocky appearance which belies his 5 feet 11 inches. A life spent continually on his broad, slightly flat feet, tending the herd, running in pursuit of game and engaging in hundreds of mock fights – not to mention hours of dancing – has given him legs which can carry him 40 miles a day if they must.

His diet, based mainly on corn, milk curds and the meat of cows, goats and sheep, is simple and nourishing, although, with cattle as the only means of currency, slaughtering is kept to the limits of strict necessity. As with all his comrades, his two indulgences are sorghum beer and snuff. The latter is taken at moments of relaxation on the march and, paradoxically, before battle. Future historians are to speculate that it might have contained narcotics but, given the ferocity with which Zulus attack, this is unlikely. The other, new indulgence, of course, is Sibongili. Not that he sees her very often. They have met occasionally since *ukuHlongonga* took place, but only to nod and smile. She has written to him, however. The Zulus have no written language in 1879 but a very effective, if limited, method of communication by the use of beads. Uguku has received from Sibongili a string of wooden beads painted white (love and truth), black (night and yearning), green (domestic bliss), yellow (a house and a family). The message is clear enough. Sibongili loves him and will wait for him. All he needs now is his chance to fight. His youth, his strong legs and his fitness place him in the *umCijo* regiment ('the sharp points'). He *must* be in the battle. Uguku lifts his *iklwa* to the skies and softly, so that no one else can hear, breathes the killing cry, '*Usuthu!*'

Superficially, Uguku has nothing in common with the enemy he is fated to meet at Isandlwana. Private James Johnson, of the 1st Battalion of the 24th Regiment of Foot, is heavily moustached and fully uniformed. He is wearing a scarlet jacket (now faded by the African sun to a soft pink), with light green facings on collar and sleeve cuffs; dark blue trousers with a red stripe at the side and tucked into heavy black boots; a once-white pipeclayed belt carrying two ammunition pouches, with a light haversack bumping on his buttock; and a 'foreign service' domed cork helmet, formerly white but now dyed with coffee to a dull khaki to avoid attracting snipers.

Johnson is clearly older. His face is seamed and burned boot-polish brown, and grey hairs peep from beneath the helmet. In fact, Johnson is now 39 and had joined the regiment 20 years ago at its depot at Brecon on the Welsh Borders. Unable to get work, he had been glad to take the Queen's shilling (Jack Frost and unemployment were Queen Victoria's best recruiting sergeants), but he is now very proud of his regiment. It is one of the oldest (founded 1689) in the line and we have met it before, for it fought stoutly under Burgoyne at Saratoga. Johnson has been with his battalion in South Africa since 1875 and has come up with Lord Chelmsford – Thesiger has succeeded his father to the title just before the beginning of the war – from Kingwilliamstown after having defeated the Kaffirs in the latest frontier tussle. Johnson has fought for his Queen in several parts of the Empire and black heathen warriors carry no terrors for him. He knows the officers despise the Bantu and he doesn't think much of them either. He hasn't yet fought the Zulus, but they are bound to be just like the rest.

James Johnson is at Rorke's Drift, on the Natal side of the Buffalo River, waiting with the rest of the column to cross into Zululand and start the war. He doesn't rate the place – just a couple of shacks turned into a mission station and now used as a forward hospital for men with sunstroke and shirker's foot. Life's not too bad. His pay is a shilling a day and he is even managing to send a little of that home because, in the field, there are fewer chances of getting into trouble and incurring pay stoppages. The food is good, too. Its own herd accompanies the army on campaign, so there is usually fresh meat to go with the daily baked bread. And, best of all, there is a gill of rum a day.

From the ford at the Drift, where he is on picket duty, Johnson can look across into Zululand. Nothing to see, though. Just a few cart tracks cutting up the steep bank and disappearing into the waving grass. No Zulus and no sign of life. He is not looking forward to the advance. He is not afraid of Zulus – or of anyone for that matter. He is a British soldier and all the world knows that they are better than anyone. It's the humidity which gets him down. There has been a lot of rain and there is likely to be more by the look of the sky – and that's likely to turn the red, dried-up dongas into raging torrents within minutes. Johnson runs his fingers around his collar. He was serving in India when the army there introduced light, khaki coloured, cotton uniforms for all ranks. But it is still red serge here. Bloody fools. He raises a little spittle and aims it at a column of ants swarming around his boots.

Private Johnson does have certain characteristics in common with Uguku, now relaxing after his exercise, some 60 miles away across the hills and undulating plains of Zululand. Both are fit in their different ways. James Johnson could not jog 40 miles a day in bare feet to save his life. But he can march 25 miles in full battle order and then stand a night's guard duty if he has to. Both men are unthinkingly brave and both are trained to kill. But they part company at Isandlwana. Uguku will attack and live to fight two more battles in the war and then, some years later, die in his kraal with Sibongili and his four other wives at his side. James Johnson will die on the hillside with three *iklwa* wounds staining his faded old red jacket.

THE WEAPONS

Stripped of his regalia, Uguku lopes back to the domed, beehive-shaped hut which is his home in the *amakhanda*, or royal barracks. There are five inch-thick staves stuck into the earth breast-high outside the hut to show the number of warriors housed there and he plucks one before crouching to enter. Carefully placing his head dress and cows' tails on a straw mat, he lays down his small, ceremonial dance shield and takes from the mat an oval-shaped piece of black, rolled cowhide. Unrolling it with care, he smoothes the hide flat on the beaten earth and then, with equal care, slots the staff through the lateral lacing on the back of the hide so that it protrudes about eight inches at each end. Holding it up, he now has his war shield. Not as big as in Shaka's day, it is still long enough to cover his trunk and tough enough, if used correctly, to deflect a cavalryman's lance, although not the white man's bullet, as Uguku well knows.

The main problem in preserving all non-metallic artefacts in Zululand is ants. Nothing can be stored for long and that is one reason why possessions are few and in constant use. Uguku carefully inspects the shield to check for signs of termite depredation and, satisfied, turns to his small arsenal of weapons. The bow is unknown in Zululand because the country lacks trees whose wood is of the required strength and elasticity to produce effective bow staves. The despised bushmen in the north use small bows and arrows dipped in poison, but the Zulu has always relied on team-work and speed of foot in the hunt and, in battle, he prefers close-quarter fighting, where his skill, courage and ferocity give him the edge.

Uguku now lays out his weapons on the shield. There are three clubs of various sizes, six throwing spears and one stabbing *iklwa*. Without hesitation he throws aside two of the shorter, lighter clubs, leaving a long, black, heavy knobkerrie, along the stem of which he lovingly slides his fingers, feeling for imperfections. There are none. The hardwood is as smooth as Sibongili's breast. He smacks the head into his palm with satisfaction. This shall certainly go to war. Now he looks at the throwing spears. He cannot take them all, for he is limited to what he can clutch in the hand which is also holding the shield. The spears are between four and five feet long, with slim blades ranging in length from about five to eight inches. Uguku holds them all in turn, looking along the hafts to detect signs of warping and weighing them carefully in his hand. In the end he jettisons three, not without reluctance.

There is no choice, of course, with the *iklwa*. Nevertheless, he gives this the same scrutiny as the others, except that here, without question, the young man displays an affection not evinced for the other weapons, not even the knobkerrie. The stabbing spear is shorter than the throwing assegais. The haft is about three feet long, ending in a slight 'bulb' at the bottom and tapering to the blade, which is about ten inches from tip to shoulder and about two fingers in width, noticeably thicker in the centre. The tang of the blade has been rammed into the hollowed haft, stuck with resin, bound tightly and covered with wet hide which has contracted after drying. It is a fine weapon, displaying a terrible beauty in its proportions. The blade glitters in the hut's dim light.

Picking up his shield and the chosen weapons, Uguku stoops and leaves the hut for the sunlight outside. After a moment's hesitation, he throws the knobkerrie back into the hut and then, deftly, takes the three throwing spears and the *iklwa* into the hand holding the shield before running, not in the jog which Zulus use to cover vast distances, but in a sprint, as in a charge. In the distance is a solitary tree and Uguku runs towards it, his shield held erect but its edge slightly tilted towards the tree, his right hand free and pumping to give him speed. About thirty yards from the tree he stops and, as if by magic, a throwing spear appears in his right hand. He hurls the spear at the tree where it quivers in the trunk; then throws the next and then the third, until they are all vibrating within a few inches of one another. Suddenly, the *iklwa is* in his hand and he hurls himself at the tree, feinting with the shield and then thrusting with the spear again and again. It is an impressive *tour de force* of savage commitment, the warrior using the shield face and the ends of the shield pole as well as the spear to attack the tree. Eventually, perspiring, Uguku pulls back, looks self-consciously over his shoulder and, seeing that he has been unobserved, allows himself a smile of satisfaction.

At the Drift, James Johnson shoulders his rifle and takes a few paces along the river bank, wondering idly what he would do if a Zulu *impi* suddenly appeared on the far bank and began fording the Drift. Do? Do? Why, kill about 20 of them before they had reached mid-river, that's what he would do. Then, with Ivor Jenkins, his fellow picket, he would fall back in good order on the main guard about 300 yards to the rear and, in all probability, pick up a medal and promotion to corporal.

Johnson smiles faintly at the thought and idly raises his rifle and aims it into the blue distance of Zululand. The weapon is a huge step forward for the British Army. We have already seen, in Donald Featherstone's *Weapons and Equipment of the Victorian Soldier*, how the breech-loading, single-shot Martini-Henry was rated on its introduction in 1871. Having served with it in India and throughout the campaign in the Cape, Johnson now gives it two and a half cheers. It's a man-stopper all right. It fires a black powder, .45 calibre Boxer cartridge with a heavy lead slug so soft that, on impact, it spreads to create the most fearful wound. Loading is just a matter of pushing down the lever behind the trigger guard to open the chamber, thumbing down a fresh round from the top and raising the lever to cock the action. In Johnson's hands, the Martini-Henry is accurate at 1,000 yards and deadly at 600. The trouble is that the 83 grains of black powder behind each slug makes the 10-pound rifle kick viciously and his shoulder is only just recovering from the fighting down south. That big charge also heats the barrel during heavy firing, so Johnson has sewn a cowhide cover around the rifle at the point of balance and then wet it to make it fit tightly. But the rifle is much more accurate and reliable than the old Sniders and Enfields which preceded it.

In Johnson's eyes, however, the most reliable weapon he has is 'the lunger', the long, triangular bayonet which hangs at his belt and which, when fitted to the rifle, gives him a stabbing weapon just under 6 feet long. The Kaffirs in the south had hated it and Johnson is quite sanguine about taking on a Zulu with it. (Surprisingly, he is to prove right. Despite their prowess at close-quarter fighting, the Zulus will come to respect the bayonet and even to fear it.)

Johnson's armoury is completed by the ammunition he carries. On guard, James has four 10-round packets in the leather ammunition pouches on his belt and ten loose rounds in the small canvas pouch slung over his shoulder. In his knapsack back in the bell-tent, he has another two packets. He has a total supply, then, of 70 rounds. But in battle, of course, the regiment has a plentiful supply of ammunition, which is brought to the troops in sturdy wooden boxes, each containing 600 rounds. We shall hear more of these boxes.

Looking out into Zululand, James Johnson notices the harsh outline of a rock-like mountain breaking the skyline in the distance. He does not give it a second thought.

ISANDLWANA

Lord Chelmsford, the British Commander-in-Chief, felt that he would have little trouble with the Zulus. The Bantu he had fought so far – and surely they were all the same fundamentally, weren't they? – had been cunning and slippery but reluctant to stand and fight. The main problem, he reflected, would be to pin down these warriors to a battle in which he could conclusively defeat them. Chasing them across their rolling country, with its rock outcrops and wet and dry river beds, would not be easy.

Accordingly, he decided to invade Zululand from three directions at once, splitting his army into three columns so that the Zulus would be driven back and 'corralled' into a position where they had to give battle. No 1 Column, under Colonel Charles Pearson, would cross the Thukela River, at the Lower Drift, near the coast; No 3 Column, led by Colonel Richard Glyn, would ford the Buffalo at Rorke's Drift and advance into Central Zululand; and No 4 Column, under Colonel Evelyn Wood, VC, would attack into the north from the Transvaal. If Cetshwayo did somehow slip by all three columns and attacked Natal, a small third column, under Colonel A. W. Durnford, and a fifth under Colonel Hugh Rowlands, VC, would wait at Rorke's Drift and in the north respectively, ready to deploy at short notice. The aim, of course, was to bring the main Zulu army to action as soon as possible, but if the columns failed to flush out Cetshwayo, all three would unite and march on Ulundi, the king's kraal, roughly 70 miles away from each of them.

After a prodigious effort, all was ready by the second week of January 1879. Chelmsford had a total of 16,800 men under his command. He was still unhappy that he had only just under 6,000 Imperial regulars in the force, but, as an old India hand, he saw no reason to doubt the efficacy of the considerable number of black Natalians he had been given, nor that of the auxiliary white units who had volunteered. When the deadline arrived without response from Cetshwayo, he gave the order to begin the invasion. He put himself with the central and largest column at Rorke's Drift and, at 4.40 a.m. on 11 January, in drizzling rain, the crossing began.

Cetshwayo, 70 miles away at Ulundi, was also ready – but only by the coincidence of the first fruits ceremony having already gathered his army together. The king, however, was still horrified at the thought of going to war with the British. Even as the Redcoats were crossing his borders, he sent messengers begging for more time to consider the ultimatum and sent parties to hasten the gathering of the cattle to pay the fine. Nor was he urged on to war by his advisers, great through the provocation was agreed to be. Cetshwayo and his *ibandla* (war council) were mature men, well aware of the firepower of the whites and of the difficulties of living with them in Natal in the future, even if the invasion were repulsed. As the columns, advanced, however, it became clear that there was no choice but to defend the homeland.

Cetshwayo had his strategy planned. The invaders were to be defeated and driven out of Zululand. But he would not invade Natal. His hope was that, rebuffed, the British would retire and that it would be possible to negotiate a peace which would confirm Zululand's independence. But first, the battle. His army numbered about 40,000 effective warriors. Some of them had firearms of a sort, but these were mainly old flintlocks or early percussion muskets. This would have to be a war of traditional weapons. It went without saying that traditional tactics would be employed also. The king was well aware that Chelmsford, with his ponderous supply trains and vast number of oxen to feed, would be vulnerable to guerrilla warfare. But there was no question of using scorched earth tactics. The Zulus were pastoralists who could not afford to destroy their land, crops and cattle. And, anyway, the young men were yearning to wash their spears: morale was high and they would be unleashed to attack as Zulus always did – frontally and openly.

Cetshwayo shrewdly assessed that the central column posed the greatest threat. He therefore ordered the *abaQulsi*, a strong tribe in the north, to

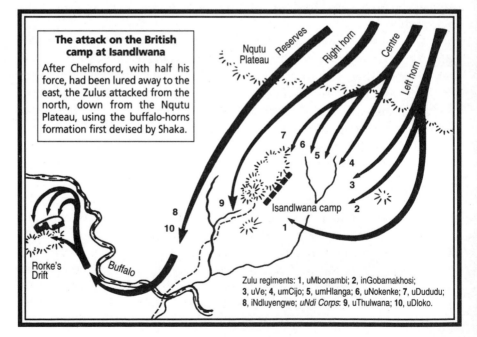

The attack on the British camp at Isandlwana

After Chelmsford, with half his force, had been lured away to the east, the Zulus attacked from the north, down from the Nqutu Plateau, using the buffalo-horns formation first devised by Shaka.

Zulu regiments: 1, uMbonambi; 2, inGobamakhosi; 3, uVe; 4, umCijo; 5, umHlanga; 6, uNokenke; 7, uDududu; 8, iNdluyengwe; *uNdi Corps*: 9, uThulwana; 10, uDloko.

oppose Wood's column; a smaller *impi* was directed merely to contain the coastal column; and the main army, some 20,000 strong, was dispatched against Chelmsford and Glyn. Before they set off, however, the king addressed the warriors personally. He told them that they must eat up the white men but not follow them back across the river into Natal. They should conserve their energy by travelling easily to the battle and, if possible, they should take the enemy in the open, for it was a mistake to attack the white man once he had thrown up defensive positions. And the priority for the *iklwas* should be the men in the red coats – they were the professional soldiers and the real danger. It was a down-to-earth eve of battle briefing.

Chelmsford's column was well equipped and experienced – at least in its regular troops. These were the 1st and 2nd Battalions of the 24th Regiment, who, to their joy, were serving together abroad for the first time. They formed the core of the column and the General was relying on their disciplined firepower. Additionally, he had a battery of six 7-pounder guns, two battalions of the Natal Native Contingent (NNC), a squadron of mounted infantry, various detachments of Natal volunteers, most of them mounted, and a company of Native pioneers. It was a force sufficiently powerful to beat the Zulus, if only he could find them.

There were no roads in Zululand and the column found the going very slow through a succession of downpours which turned the tracks into red mud. After a sharp but conclusive clash with the tribe of Sihayo, during which 400 cattle were captured, Chelmsford pressed on towards Isandlwana, whose rocky crest seemed to beckon him across the unlevel plain. By noon on 20 January, camp had been established at the foot of the great rock and throughout the remainder of the day, the column straggled in.

It had taken nine days to travel about ten miles. There had been the encounter with Sihayo's men, but it was clear to Chelmsford that his rate of progress would have to improve if he was to reach Ulundi before his supplies ran out. He needed to camp for a couple of days to concentrate his attenuated column and scout the way ahead. It was not a bad site. There was wood for fuel, water in a nearby donga and, although the ground sloped somewhat, it was level enough to pitch tents. There wás no cover for an attacking force for about one and a half miles to the north and north-east, where the Nquthu escarpment dominated the skyline, and even farther to the east and south. The only blind spot was the direction from which they had come, where a high saddle or *nek* blocked the view to the west and south-west. Lookouts placed there, however, could give clear warning in the unlikely event of an attack from that quarter. When the wagons were parked and the tents pitched, the camp stretched for about 800 yards along the eastern slope of Isandlwana. The Boers had warned Chelmsford of the need to laager wagons at night to prevent the camp being overrun in a sudden attack. Indeed, the General had issued precise regulations to the Field Force, demanding just such precautions. But at Isandlwana the camp was allowed to remain in a long, unprotected line. This was pointed out to Chelmsford but he decided that, as long as pickets and vedettes were thrown out far enough, the camp could not be surprised. The ground was too stony for entrenchment; wagons were continually toing and froing to Rorke's Drift, so making the complicated business of laagering very inconvenient; and, anyway, the firepower of the two line battalions alone would provide sufficient protection.

Chelmsford knew that he was taking a risk and it is not difficult to imagine the temper of the British command at this point: a mixture of confidence in the outcome, frustration at not having already found the main Zulu army; and unease at sitting in this wild, difficult country, knowing the enemy were out there somewhere but not at all sure where. The General had received intelligence that Cetshwayo's army was on the move, but he knew little more than that. Common sense dictated that it would be coming directly from Ulundi, the route to which lay to the east, beyond the plain and through the mountainous country of the strong Sithole clan. After a brief, abortive reconnaissance himself, Chelmsford dispatched sixteen companies of the NNC, under Commandant Rupert Lonsdale, and a mounted detachment of Natal Mounted Police and Volunteers, under Major Dartnell, to comb this difficult terrain.

At first, the scouting party found nothing, but then, in the late evening of the 21st, Dartnell's advance party discerned a large host of Zulus at the head of the Mangeni Gorge. Reinforced by the NNC, Dartnell gingerly pushed a patrol towards the Zulus, who immediately threw out horns and rushed to engulf the horsemen, forcing them to retire. Dartnell estimated that he had encountered a Zulu *impi so* he withdrew, entrenched for the night and sent back to Chelmsford for reinforcements.

At Isandlwana, the request immediately posed a problem for the commander. To meet it would mean splitting his force in the face of the enemy, a fundamental transgression of all text book teaching. On the other hand, Dartnell could have stumbled on the main Zulu army, the finding of which was Chelmsford's dearest wish. Clearly, the party could not be left there. If it was facing the main Zulu force, the whole column would be needed, but it would take hours to limber up, by which time the Zulus might have slipped away or, worse, engulfed the scouting party. Chelmsford decided to take Glyn and a strong but mobile force, leaving half of his column back at camp with the wagons.

At dawn on 22 January Chelmsford's force fell in and set out across the plain to the east. Left behind in the camp, under the command of Lieutenant-Colonel Henry Pulleine, the experienced CO of the 1/24th, were five companies of that battalion, one company of the 2/24th, two cannon, four companies of the NNC and about 200 assorted Natal volunteers and regular soldiers on specialist duties. It was a force sufficient to defend the camp, but to make certain Chelmsford decided at the last minute to order up from Rorke's Drift Colonel Durnford's small No 2 Column. This numbered about 500 men, all Native levies except for Major Russell's tiny rocket battery. This operated three devices firing 9-pounder rockets, whose inaccuracy caused great hilarity but also loud pyrotechnics which, it was felt, would scare the loincloths off the Zulus. With Durnford's force, then, Pulleine had some 950 Europeans and 850 blacks under his command.

With his mates, Private Johnson watched the General and his force disappear across the plain towards the rising sun and then settled to daily duties under canvas. The morning was uneventful until, about four hours after Chelmsford's departure, firing was heard from his direction and, at the same time, reports came in of Zulu activity in the Nquthu hills to the north. At this point Durnford and his command rode into camp. The orders which Chelmsford had sent had merely instructed him to move forward to the camp, giving him no further role. But Durnford, who had already received a reprimand for impulsiveness, was never one to hesitate. He immediately told Pulleine that he would take his column to reinforce the General, who had clearly met the main enemy, and asked Pulleine to give him reinforcements. Although Durnford was the senior of the two, Pulleine demurred, pleading that it was his duty to defend the camp with every man. Durnford did not argue but rode off. Moving east and then slightly north, the mounted men pulled well ahead of the plodding rocket unit and Durnford sent a party under Lieutenant Raw to climb the Nquthu escarpment and scout the plateau beyond, which was, of course, out of sight of the plain below. When Raw and his NNH scouts reached the top they saw a small herd of cattle being driven through the waving grass by young Zulus, who almost immediately disappeared into a fold in the ground. Spurring after them, Raw reined in at the lip of a steep slope which became a long, narrow valley. Looking down, his jaw dropped. Lining the walls, as far as he could see, were Zulu warriors – 20,000 of them, crouching and sitting. He had found the Zulu army.

Even as Raw's eyes took in the scene, the Zulus sprang to their feet and began scrambling up the valley sides and pouring over the edge. With his men, Raw turned and fled, halting once distance had been gained to fire volleys into the black host coming on at a fast trot. But the carbines were powerless to deter the charge and Raw sent riders to warn Pulleine in the camp and Durnford on the plain below and then fell back, firing as he went.

Durnford, advanced along the plain and quite exposed, saw the Zulus pouring over the edge of the plateau only a few minutes after the rider reached him. He had time to send a warning back to Russell's rocket battery but now all he could do was to deliver a couple of volleys into the first wave of the attacking tide and then retire himself. Russell stood no chance. Bravely, he and his men fired one, ineffective salvo of rockets before they were engulfed.

As chance would have it, it was the *umCijo* regiment, with Uguku among them, who were the first out of the valley on to the plateau. Mostly young men, eager to fight and knowing that they were discovered, they rushed after Raw, and in this were partly responsible for the fact that the Zulu charge was initially an undisciplined scramble. The *indunas* were able only to hold back for a moment the *uNdini* corps, at the end of the valley, to receive instructions. But it was of little consequence. The warriors knew what they had to do, and by the time they had reached the edge of the plateau they had assumed the pattern of the buffalo formation. To the left peeled off the *uMbonambe*, *inGobamakhosi* and *uVe* regiments, running in a wide crescent to take the camp from the south-east. The chest of the buffalo comprised the *umCijo*, *umHlanga*, *uNokenke* and the *uDudundu* and they ran directly to the north and centre of the camp. The right horn, made up of the *uThulwana*, curled round behind the mountain to cut off any escape. The loins, comprised mainly of the *uNdini* regiment who had been last to leave the valley, trotted along at the right rear as reserve. The formation was perfectly formed as soon as the plain was reached.

Writing his memoirs later as a general (*Memories of 48 Years' Service*, 1925), Lieutenant Horace Smith-Dorrien recalled the discipline and speed of the attack:

'They were coming over the hills in thousands. They were in the most perfect order and seemed to be about twenty rows of skirmishers, one behind the other. They were in a semi-circle around our two flanks and in front of us and must have covered several miles ...'

Before Durnford had left the camp, Pulleine had sent Lieutenant Cavaye and a company of the 1/24th up towards the Nquthu hills and they were the first to engage the Zulus. Pulleine could not see Cavaye but he could hear the firing, so he sent another company under Captain Mostyn to support him and then threw out all of his men in a line to the east of the camp, curving west in the north towards the mountain. His two guns he placed on a rocky knoll halfway along the line and these, directed by Major Stuart Smith, RA, now began a steady fire at the Zulus who were debouching on to the plain and nearing the camp at a fast pace.

Out on the plain, a solitary company of the 2/24th on picket duty under Lieutenant Charles Pope, hurried back to camp and fell in near the guns. A unit of Natal Carbineers, similarly exposed, joined up with Durnford, who had now dismounted to make a stand in a large donga about a mile from camp. Up on the spur to the north of the camp, Mostyn and Cavaye had found it hopeless to stem the attack, so Pulleine sent another company, under Captain Younghusband, to cover their retreat. The three companies fell back steadily to form the north-western end of the long line which now curved down to contingents of the NNC in the south, Durnford, out in the donga, forming a salient unconnected to the main line. The battle was now fully joined.

Pulleine knew that it was a less than ideal defensive position. His line was about 800 yards from the camp and too far from the ammunition supply; it was too thin and extended; and its ends were vulnerable to the Zulu rapid flanking movements. But the speed of the attack, the need to protect the wagons and to support Durnford denied him the chance to form a square. Yet he had placed his guns shrewdly and the Martini-Henrys of the 24th were taking great toll of the Zulu centre and Durnford and his native troops had pinned down the left horn for the moment.

The Zulu tidal wave had stopped at distances between 60 and 300 yards from the British line as the warriors sheltered as best they could from the fire. Uguku had charged with the rest of the *umCijo* and, after having covered four miles at a fast lope, his breast was heaving and his face perspiring as he crouched opposite the thin scarlet line of the 24th. This was formed in two ranks, the front kneeling and the second standing, taking it in turns to fire and reload, the blue smoke stabbed through with flame as the volleys thundered out. The cannon down the line were firing case shot at the warriors still running across the plain, but the Zulus had noticed that the gunners stepped aside when they pulled the lanyards, so they flung themselves down to let the shot explode behind them; '*uMoya*' ('just wind'), they cried in derision. Then, Uguku and his brothers realised that the dreadful rifle fire was beginning to slacken; pauses between the volleys enabled them to scramble forward. They didn't know that the British troops were beginning to run short of ammunition. Durnford had already sent riders back for carbine cartridges but they had been refused replenishments from the infantry supplies ('Hang it all man, you don't want a requisition now, do you?' snarled Smith-Dorrien at a quartermaster at one stage). The 24th were running low, too, and those ammunition boxes were proving difficult to open; their wooden lids resisted bayonets, and screwdrivers were few and far between. The Zulu left horn was edging round Durnford at the southern end of the line, which was too extended anyway, and Pulleine realised that he had to shorten it. Doing so in the face of the enemy with poorly armed Native levies manning part of its length was going to be difficult, but it had to be attempted. So he gave the order to fall back.

Just as the 24th's companies were beginning to move back, a voice rose from where the *umCijo* were sheltering among rocks and in long grass. Giving Cetshwayo the name he had earned when he defeated his half-brother, it cried: 'The Little Branch of Leaves Which Extinguished the Fire gave no such order as this.' Growling approval, the *umCijo* shed their cover, raised their spears and charged, shouting the Cetshwayo cry '*Usuthu!*' On the British right, Durnford's men, clutching their last few cartridges, mounted their horses and galloped back to the camp, releasing the *uMbonambe* and the *inGobamkhosi* to surge after them, forcing Pope's company, in turn, to curl back to avoid being taken from the rear. In the centre, the great cry of '*Usuthu!*' and the boom of thousands of spears beating on shields was too much for the two companies of NNC. They threw down their weapons and fled. It was the turning-point.

In an instant, the buffalo was re-activated. The edge of the Zulu centre curled round behind what remained of the British left, stabbing and hacking. The left horn fell upon Pope's company before it had time to re-deploy and, in the centre, the rest of the chest streamed through the gap left by the NNC, reducing the companies of the 24th to individual islets of red in a black sea of warriors. Some did not even have time to fix bayonets. Others were able to fall back in disciplined little knots, standing back to back and coolly presenting their lungers to the Zulus who milled round them.

The hand-to-hand fighting surged now between the wagons and the tents and back up the rocky slopes and ledges of Isandlwana. The bravery shown by both sides was outstanding. Dozens of Zulus, encountering bayonets for the first time grabbed them with their bare hands in an attempt to get close enough to use the *iklwa*. Durnford, back on the *nek* with his loyal NNC, desperately tried to keep the Zulu horns apart long enough to allow some to escape. He organised a party to fire on the Zulu right horn and then stayed to bring his remnants together on the saddle. Issued with carbines, they had no bayonets so they used their guns as clubs before they went under. A few yards away, the broken debris of a couple of platoons, led by Charlie Pope and his great friend, Lieutenant Godwin-Austin, formed a tight circle behind a bayonet ring until the Zulus brought them down by using their dead as bayonet shields and hurling spears. Months later, the decomposed bodies of Pope and his friend were found lying side by side, monocles still clasped in their eye sockets.

Captain Younghusband fought long and hard. With the remnant of his company he held a position on a rocky ledge before he and a handful of others found some cartridges and climbed on to a wagon, shooting steadily from there until only Younghusband was left. He managed to scramble on to another wagon and, with rifle and bayonet, held all attackers at bay until a Zulu bullet finished him. A sailor, improbably serving as an officer's servant, stood with his back to a wagon wheel wielding a cutlass and cut down anyone who approached him until he was killed by a spear thrust through the spokes of the wheel.

Colonel Pulleine is thought to have perished in his tent while writing a last letter. Before doing so, however, he had taken the precious Queen's Colour of the 1/24th Battalion and given it to the Adjutant, Lieutenant Teignmouth Melvill, with orders to take it to safety. Melvill took the heavy standard, furled and sealed in a leather sheath, and galloped with it through the crowds of fugitives and Zulus who thronged the *nek* and trail beyond. The way to Rorke's Drift was cut off by the Zulu right horn, but strings of would-be survivors struggled to reach a ford on the Buffalo River, several miles down-stream from Rorke's Drift.

The route lay over about four miles of broken, very rough country. It became a killing ground as the Zulu right horn, fresh and comparatively uninvolved in the battle, pursued the fugitives, cutting them down as they paused for breath or queued to cross a stream or swamp hollow. Somehow the gun crews had managed to limber up their pieces and escape with them as far as a stream behind the mountain. Here they stuck and the horses were speared as they dangled in the traces. Melvill, still clutching the Colour, gained the river bank, having met fellow officer Lieutenant Neville Coghill on the way. To their dismay, they found the river swollen and in torrent and the bank precipitous, but the Zulus were among them, dodging between the boulders, shooting and spearing, so both men put their horses to the surging river. Coghill reached the far bank safely, but Melvill's horse was swept away. Exhausted but still clutching the standard, he was just able to reach a boulder in mid-river before the Colour was swept away by the current. On the rock, Melvill was an easy target for the Zulus, many of whom were firing Martini-Henrys plundered from the camp, so Coghill unhesitatingly swam his horse back to the rock. A bullet killed the horse but Coghill grasped his friend and together they were able to make the Natal shore. They crawled about a hundred yards through the thick under-brush on the rise, before, completely exhausted, they sat down with their backs to a large rock, drew their soaked revolvers and awaited their pursuers who had crossed the river. Their bloody bodies were found several days later. It was not for another two weeks, however, before the Colour was dis-covered wedged into a rock downstream. Threadbare and transparent, it now hangs in Brecon Cathedral, a pathetic relic of an act of great bravery and of a day of savage killing.

From that day the ford at the Buffalo has been known as Fugitives' Drift. About 60 white men and some 400 blacks survived the slaughter of Isandlwana and reached Natal. Of the 1,800 men in the camp, 52 officers and 1,279 other ranks perished. Not one man survived of the six compa-nies of the 24th who had been, like Johnson, in the firing line. Only five British officers escaped – thanks probably to Cetshwayo, for they were all wearing blue patrol jackets, not their red coats. No wounded were left alive. The Zulus ritually stripped and disembowelled every body to let the spirit of gallant warriors escape. They then looted the camp and, wearily, looked to their dead and dying. The field was theirs, but at a terrible cost. The exact number of Zulu dead is still unknown – probably about 2,000, with perhaps half as many again wounded and dying on the long march home. The king himself was under no illusion when he heard of the victory. 'An assegai has been plunged into the bowels of the nation,' he cried. 'There are not enough tears to mourn the dead.'

It was getting on for evening when Chelmsford received news of the disaster. He had found his scouting party unharmed and with no Zulus in sight, and decided to press on to a new camp site, sending a message back to Pulleine to strike camp and follow him. Later, several messages referring to action at Isandlwana had reached him, but they were imprecise and it was not until he went back to see for himself, that he met an exhausted and horrified Commandant Lonsdale, who had returned to the camp for provi-sions and narrowly escaped with his life. Chelmsford could not believe Lonsdale's story. 'But I left a thousand men there,' he whispered.

With his weary force, Chelmsford arrived back at the smoking rem-nant of the camp after nightfall. The stench of death told them what they could not see – but there was worse. To the south-west, the sky was lit by a flickering red glow. Rorke's Drift was ablaze and, by now, Cetshwayo's *impis* were probably racing through Natal. His career in ruins, Chelmsford led his men towards the Buffalo at dawn. On the way, in one of the most bizarre incidents of the war, the soldiers became aware that they were passing, in clear view, a Zulu *impi* heading in the opposite direction. Chelmsford's men had only 70 rounds per man – the rest of the ammunition had been left at Isandlwana – and the General was in no position to attack. It quickly became clear that the Zulus were equally disinclined to fight. Both columns therefore warily passed each other, staring stonily ahead like neighbours after a quarrel.

That Zulu force, in fact, was the loins of the buffalo, the *uNdini* corps, which had been in reserve at Isandlwana and which had swung behind the mountain and therefore missed most of the fighting. Frustrated at not washing their spears, the warriors eagerly agreed when one of them suggested 'Let's go and have some fun at Jim's place' (a reference to James Rorke, who had founded Rorke's Drift as a trading post). Led by the headstrong Prince Dabulamanzi kaMpande, the brother of the king, they trotted off – nearly 3,000 of them – to attack the post.

There is no room here to re-tell the story of the most famous defence in Britain's imperial history. The bravery displayed at Isandlwana was repeated at the little makeshift hospital when a company of the 2/24ths, supplemented by a motley crew of invalids and storekeepers, held the post throughout the night against the attacks of the *uNdini* Corps. The defenders shared eleven Victoria Crosses, Britain's highest award for valour, between them, the most ever won in a single engagement. There were no medals for the Zulus, who had repeatedly stormed through the Martini-Henry volleys to fight the soldiers with their spears. They died piled up against the barricades; about 400 were later buried but many more succumbed to their wounds. It is no wonder that Prince Dabulamanzi let Chelmsford pass in peace. He, too, was tired and dispirited.

REVENGE

Like a jangling nerve end, the name Isandlwana – usually misspelt, of course – resounded throughout the British Empire. 'There will be an awful row at home about this,' one of the survivors, Richard Williams, of the Natal Mounted Police, wrote to his family after the battle (*The Red Soldier*, by Frank Emery, Hodder & Stoughton, London, 1977). And there was. A British public brought up on a diet of jingoistic success was dumbfounded to hear of the defeat of a British column (it became an 'army' in many reports) by spear-carrying warriors. *Punch*, the English satirical magazine, carried a cartoon showing a fat John Bull sitting in the dunce's position in the schoolroom, while a very black and near naked King Cetshwayo chalks on the blackboard, 'Despise not your enemy'. Prime Minister Benjamin Disraeli, already ailing, took to his bed when he received the news, and the Opposition in Parliament made hay.

The battle, however, did not end the war. It merely began it. Chelmsford, turning at bay in Natal, where the populace trembled in its beds, found that he faced no Zulu invasion. He requested reinforcements from home and, while he waited, he relieved his coastal column besieged (in effect, if not fact) at Eshowe, in March, inflicting a defeat on the Zulus at Ginginglovu on the way. In the north-west, Wood actively sought to relieve the pressure on Pearson by 'demonstrating' rather than invading. He took a bloody nose at Hlobane, but won a defensive battle at Kambula. Cetshwayo, anxiously watching events from Ulundi, knew that he had not won the war.

In London, the Disraeli administration narrowly clung to office. To some extent, the magnificent story of Rorke's drift saved its face – and the career of Chelmsford – by redeeming the public's confidence in the guts and skill of the British soldier. Cetshwayo's hope that the defeat would bring British withdrawal was ill founded. The world was watching. Imperial honour had to be restored. The government therefore issued a stinging public rebuke to Frere but retained both him and Chelmsford in office and sanctioned the sending of more than 400 officers and nearly 10,000 men to reinforce the army in Natal. Chelmsford held his own inquiry into the disaster which, in effect, whitewashed the commanders and blamed the defeat on the NNC's 'desertion'. Then, however, the General naïvely compromised his position by writing to the Horse Guards back home suggesting that a major-general be sent out. He *meant* to assist him (his next senior officer, Glyn, only held the rank of Colonel), but the message was widely interpreted as a request to be replaced and that Chelmsford had lost his nerve. Accordingly, Sir Garnet Wolseley, popularly lauded as 'England's Only General', was given the rank of full general, appointed Governor of both Natal and Transvaal and shipped to Cape Town to crush the Zulus.

But Chelmsford had no intention of waiting for Wolseley to arrive and scoop the glory. In May he launched the second invasion, comprised of a huge central column marching directly to Ulundi and a smaller one, hugging the coast and establishing supply forts along the way. This time no risks were taken – but the Zulus, while falling back before the invading mass, demonstrated once more their capacity to embarrass the British. In a minor skirmish, the popular if headstrong Prince Imperial of France, the son of Napoleon III and the great-nephew of Bonaparte himself, was killed. He had pleaded to see action. Chelmsford didn't want him but the Duke of Cambridge had intervened. Now he had perished when, in the panic of a Zulu attack, his patrol had fled, not realising that the Prince had been un-horsed. There was a court-martial and Queen Victoria, who liked the boy, was saddened for her friend, the exiled Empress Eugénie.

It was the last straw for Disraeli, grimly surviving in office. 'A very remarkable people, the Zulus,' he mused bitterly when he heard the news. 'They defeat our generals, they convert our bishops and they have settled the fate of a great European dynasty.' (*Cambridge History of the British Empire*, vol. III, CUP, 1963)

It was an embarrassment, but no mere pinprick could stop Chelmsford's revenge. Advancing ponderously in a vast square, he brought the remainder of the Zulu army to battle before Ulundi. This time the spear-men, despite their valour, could not penetrate the wall of fire and it was all over quite quickly, the Lancers charging and pursuing the routed war-riors over the plain, sticking them like pigs on the ends of their long lances. The king's capital was put to the torch and Cetshwayo was even-tually captured and taken to Cape Town. Chelmsford had just time to complete the victory and resign before a quietly furious Wolseley arrived to assume command.

The Zulu nation was in ruins. Some 8,000 warriors had been killed and probably twice that number wounded. The house of Shaka had been overthrown, the nation's great herds of cattle decimated and Wolseley now set about breaking up the country into provinces under puppet chieftains, to ensure that the Zulu army would never again be a threat. After extensive lobbying, King Cetshwayo was allowed to visit London to plead his case. With his proud bearing and dignified mien, it became clear that this was no bloodthirsty barbarian and, to his amazement, he became a popular fig-ure, being met with cheers when, in his incongruous western clothes, he took to the London streets. He was even received by Queen Victoria who, predictably, took to him and commissioned a painting of him. Eventually, he was allowed to return to his homeland and was restored as a provincial chief but it was too late and civil war and enemies had taken root in his absence. He was found dead in 1884, probably poisoned.

Confederation died too, as did the Disraeli government. Although it lingered on throughout 1879, it never recovered from Isandlwana and it fell early in 1880. Gladstone, who had thundered loud and long against Frere's policy in Natal, took office. Liberal though he was, he did nothing to stop Wolseley dismantling the Zulu state and the country remained factionalised until well into the 20th century. Importantly, however, the royal line survived through Cetshwayo's son Dinizulu and his descendants, and played a vital role throughout this century in rebuilding the nation. The present King Goodwill Zwelithini kaBhekuzulu, crowned in 1971, is directly descended from Shaka's brother, Mpande, and plays a strong role in kwaZulu affairs. The country's Chief Minister, Mangosuthu Buthelezi, who has become a towering and controversial figure in South Africa, is himself descended, via his mother, from Mpande and is the great grandson of King Cetshwayo's prime minister throughout the Anglo-Zulu war.

So neither the British nor, later, the Afrikaaner governments succeeded in completely breaking up the Zulu state. It remains today an awkward but wholly homogeneous and vital element in the new South African nation. Its independence springs, of course, from the spirit of its people. And it is difficult to gainsay the view that that spirit was cemented on the rocky slopes of Isandlwana when Uguku and his brothers broke the British line. That victory made the Zulus famous throughout the world; it gave them an international identity which has helped them in their struggle to maintain their own voice.

Nor can it now be said that that victory was a fluke, a fortuitous piece of serendipity in catching the British when their guard was down. Modern historians now incline to the view – resulting particularly from the recent research of Professor John Laband of the University of Natal and his colleague Jeff Matthews – that the leader of the Zulu army at Isandlwana, Mshingwayo, deliberately split the British forces by decoying Chelmsford away to the east by demonstrating at the Mangeni Gorge, and then switching the main *impi* to bivouac in the Ngwebeni valley to await the rising of the new moon and then, on its second day, to attack. Raw's discovery of them in the valley, then, merely brought on the battle a little earlier than intended. This is a persuasive argument, reminiscent as it is of Shaka using cattle to decoy the Ndwande fifty years before.

It is further evidence that the Zulus of Isandlwana stand head and shoulders above other so-called primitive warriors who have distinguished themselves in the past. They brought down both a heavily armed column of regular soldiers *and* a government. They established a tradition *and* founded a modern nation.

Their battlefield on that rocky slope beneath the mountain is studded today with cairns of white rock. Many of the British soldiers killed there could not be buried when a party finally reached them five months after the battle because the ground was too hard. So they were lowered into scooped-out depressions and stones were heaped above them. With the memorials since erected there, it gives a strange air to this remote place – a touch of English churchyard beneath an African sky. Sixty miles away, at Ulundi, the Zulus have their own memorial near the site of their own massacre when they tried to break the square. Equally poignant, it reads:

IN MEMORY OF

THE BRAVE WARRIORS WHO FELL

HERE IN 1879 IN DEFENCE OF

THE OLD ZULU ORDER

5

THE PRIVATEERS
The Kaiser's U-Boat Captains

What sort of men would want to lock themselves into a steel tube, sink it deep beneath the surface of the sea and then take on the greatest navy the world has ever seen?

The answer can be seen in the pictures that illustrate the books and magazines of the First World War. The faces smiling from those old photographs are those of ordinary young men of their time. Most of them were from good families and therefore probably quite well off by the standards of the first decade of the 20th century. But fundamentally they look no different from any of the other young career officers then standing watch on the bridges of the great European dreadnoughts of that Edwardian day.

What singled out all these young sailors from their contemporaries was their decision to become submariners. To the British, the French and the Americans they became pirates. But their own countrymen and their allies were to laud them as heroes, literally pin-up-boys, and use them to inspire the German nation to even greater efforts in the First World War.

Regarding them dispassionately now, it is more accurate to describe them as the greatest privateers of all time. These were the young Teutons who introduced a bewilderingly new type of sea warfare which posed problems of technology, seamanship and morality which arouse controversy to this day. Of course they were not privateers in the classic, Sir Francis Drake sense, civilians bearing 'letters of marque' entitling them to use their vessels to destroy enemy ships. However, they *were* specially licensed by their emperor to sink without warning any ship, merchantman or warship *of whatever nationality* which sailed within the war zone. These young mariners broke every mould, but if we are looking, as we are here, to categorise them, it is the word privateer which comes nearest to describing them.

Privateers have always been controversial. Usually merchant adventurers, they traditionally engaged in maritime guerrilla warfare which sailed very close to the ethical wind. Like all forms of guerrilla activity, privateering was invariably employed by nations with weak resources against those who were stronger. A country which had command of the high seas, paradoxically, was vulnerable to the privateering activities of a state which might possess only a small conventional fleet.

So it was that England, only recently recovered from the exhaustion of the Civil War of the Roses, sniped at Spain, the world's greatest maritime power, during the Elizabethan era. Then, as England's own fleets grew, King James I shied away from the use of privateers and refused to grant further letters of marque. Their attraction, however, remained real to other nations. Although privateering was never used again as an instrument of British maritime policy, Spain, France and the USA strongly deployed this weapon to attack British trade during the wars of the late 18th and early 19th centuries.

By the Declaration of Paris in 1856, privateering was abolished as a tool of war. Whether the Imperial German Navy resurrected it in the First World War and therefore broke the code, remains a matter of somewhat arid debate. What is sure is that the *unterseeboote* and their young commanders introduced a new kind of sea fighting which changed naval warfare for ever and profoundly altered national relationships. They came within a hair's breadth of winning the war for the Kaiser – and, in the end, they almost certainly lost it for him. They were key players in a conflict the echoes of which rumble on.

'UNLIKELY TO PLAY A USEFUL PART IN WAR!'

At the outbreak of war in August 1914 the German navy had 28 U-boats in service, two nearing completion in the yards and another fourteen in advanced stages of construction. In contrast, Britain had fourteen submarines commissioned and twenty more on order, France had 70 and 23 on order, and the USA 29 and 31. Yet in no way did this reflect a deep confidence in these new craft on the part of the Allies. On the contrary, the British admiralty, with the notable exception of Admiral Jackie Fisher, the First Sea Lord, rather shared the view expressed in 1911 by Admiral von Tirpitz, Secretary of the German Naval Cabinet, that he saw no role for the submarine in naval warfare.

Throughout the first decades of the century, both sets of admirals were far more concerned with building bigger and better battleships – the Germans to challenge British maritime supremacy, the British to maintain it. Both sides had invested in these strange submersibles when the British-hating American John Holland (who had been slaving over the development of his craft since 1877) persuaded the American government to place substantial orders at the turn of the century. But both moves were purely defensive measures.

To the British, with the world's largest merchant fleet, the Navy was the key element in national defence and it had long been British policy to monitor carefully new developments in naval warfare. The country had better have the damned things, 'just in case'. The London *Times* was not impressed. Its editorial on 26 March 1901 sniffed:

'... this step does not commit us in any way to the adoption of the submarine boat as a desirable or essential component of British naval strength. The student of naval affairs learns to regard with suspicion any form of protection which is not adapted for offensive warfare, and there is no evidence available at present placing the submarine boat outside this category. In its present form it may possibly have a place in harbour defence ..... there is nothing which suggests that the submarine boat is likely to play any useful part in war.'

Another commentator at the time more succinctly put the underlying feelings of the British about the submarine: 'It is underwater, underhand and damned unEnglish.'

All of which is rather strange when one considers how devotedly the pursuit of a viable means of underwater travel had been conducted for 300 years. No single person or nation is credited with the invention of the submarine. The British, the Russians, the Americans, the Swedes and the French all took a hand from the 16th century to the 20th. The basic methods of submersion and surfacing – by forcing water into tanks and then expelling it forcefully – were comparatively soon accepted, but the ideal form of propulsion proved elusive. Over the years, it seemed that everything had been tried: rowing, treadmills with paddles, exploding gases through a rear tube, hand winches and, of course, steam, which was the favourite for years. But the breakthrough came when electric motors for underwater travel and oil-driven diesels for surface propulsion (the latter a German contribution at last) came together. It was a combination which lasted throughout two world wars, only giving way to nuclear power in the 1950s.

But the early vessels were so crude that the stiff-collared, ramrod-backed admirals of the day could not love them. Certainly, there were no tears shed in the British Admiralty when the Royal Navy's first submarine, the *Holland 1*, was accidentally rammed during her trials and went straight to the bottom. In fact she was left there until the mid-1980s when she was salvaged and installed at the Royal Navy's submarine museum at Gosport.

She sits there now on a concrete quayside, looking like a crude form of oil tank. In this primitive shell sailed two officers, seven ratings and three white mice – the latter to warn when the air became foul. Speed was a respectable eight knots on the surface but only four submerged. She took up to ten minutes to dive but could not go below 63 feet. She had no sleeping-quarters or concessions to crew comfort because she was considered to be incapable of long voyages or of withstanding high sea conditions. In short, she was not taken seriously.

Neither was *U1*, the first *unterseeboot* to be commissioned by the *Kaiserliche Marine*. More sophisticated than *Holland 1*, she too had been adapted from the Holland design, but in this case, by the Franco-Spanish engineer d'Equevilley. She went into service in 1902. With a high prow and removable air cowls fitted to the deck to give ventilation when cruising on the surface, she was considered to be of very little military value and was used as a training boat throughout the First World War. *U1* is now also on display, in Munich Museum. So neither of the precursors of these potent new weapons fired a shot in anger.

But the German High Command at least had a role in mind for the submarine, albeit a defensive one. Germany's view of the outbreak of war was quite clear. On the opening of hostilities, the mighty British Grand Fleet would immediately steam out into the North Sea and seek to engage the German battle squadrons off the Heligoland Bight. Berlin saw the British admirals as imbued with the spirit of Nelson: arrogant, impetuous and anxious for glory, with a historical prestige which would demand immediate action before a watching, waiting world. The Germans could be forgiven for taking this view. At the outbreak of war, the Royal Navy was headed, politically, by Winston Churchill as First Lord of the Admiralty, and Admiral Jackie Fisher, called out of retirement to lead the professional sailors. They made a Nelsonian pair: forthright, imaginative, fearless, adversarial; they even looked alike, with twinkle-eyed, bulldog countenances. Attack, surely, would be their policy.

The Germans had prepared carefully for the encounter, which they felt would give them the chance of delivering a crushing blow to Britain at the start of the war. The two flotillas of U-boats were moored on the surface between an outer screen of destroyers, stretching in an arc some 35 miles NW of Heligoland, and an inner line of torpedo-boat destroyers, stationed about 20 miles from the island. The plan was for the destroyers to draw the British fleet over the U-boats, which would make submerged torpedo attacks on the big capital ships, aided by surface attacks from the destroyers. Wounded and weakened, the British Grand Fleet would then be ripe for the German fleet to emerge from the River Jade in the north and finish off the invaders.

Alas, after the declaration of war, nothing happened. The Germans had over-estimated British arrogance. Churchill was confident enough but Fisher and the admirals, imbued during the last decade with the knowledge of the Kaiser's vast shipbuilding programme, developed a strong sense of caution. Of course, they would fight when the German High Seas Fleet showed itself, but it would be rash to play the first card. The British cabinet, led by the gentle, reflective lawyer Herbert Asquith, was certainly not about to order the Fleet to sea over the wishes of the Admiralty. It was already clear that the British fleet commander, with his awesome multi-million pound squadrons of dreadnoughts riding at anchor in Scapa Flow, was the only Englishman who could lose the war single-handedly in an afternoon. It was a fearsome responsibility. Things had changed since Nelson's day.

The British had good reason to be cautious. The UK entered the war possessing a dominating 47.9 per cent of the world's mercantile shipping. With less than half its food produced at home and large gaps in its range of indigenous raw materials, it depended upon that merchant fleet as, literally, an importing lifeline. Without a navy to protect the trading ships, these could be picked off and the country starved into submission with comparative ease.

Germany, however, had a similar problem, although on a smaller scale. In 1914, it possessed the world's second largest mercantile marine, responsible for 11.9 per cent of world tonnage. Although, unlike Britain, it had land routes, many of these to the south were cut off. It needed to import by sea to sustain the war effort and to feed the populace adequately. Britain's fear of committing its battleships and battle cruisers did not extend to its other surface ships, of which it had a considerable number. The Royal Navy accordingly quickly threw a sea blockade around the North Sea and the Western Approaches of the Atlantic, both to deny opportunities for German surface warships to raid the sea lanes and to put economic pressure on Germany by cutting off her sea imports. At their bases in Scotland and in the south, the British capital ships waited for the call to put to sea, should the German fleet leave harbour, while the navy's cruisers and destroyers patrolled the blockade lines.

Facing this situation, the German naval staff had little room for manoeuvre. Its battle fleet was of high quality, with many new ships, well armoured and possessing a firepower matching, if not surpassing that of the British. But the German fleet was outnumbered by the British – and

Nelson cast a long shadow. The British had not been beaten at sea for nigh on 150 years. One slip and all the careful preparation and expenditure of the last twenty years could be thrown away. The Germans *would* fight but only when they were ready and on ground of their own choosing. The British Fleet would need to be weakened before it could be confronted head-on.

Reluctantly and with no high hopes, the German *Admiralstab* ordered the U-boats to leave their moorings off Heligoland and adopt a more offensive role. On 6 August 1914 three separate groups of U-boats were dispatched on patrol to establish where the British had set up their lines of blockade and, whenever possible, to deliver torpedo attacks on British capital ships and cruisers, so beginning the operation of 'equalising' the two battle fleets.

The honour of the first patrol was given to the 1st Flotilla, commanded by Korvettenkapitän Hermann Bauer. Ten of the fourteen vessels sailed from Heligoland just before dawn, in thick, misty weather. These boats were not chosen for their reliability. On the contrary, they were old and equipped, not with the diesels of their later, sister boats, but with Körting engines which threw out thick white smoke and showers of sparks which made them vulnerable on the surface. Rapid diving was impossible because tall, deck ventilators had to be lowered and stowed before submerging. The 1st Flotilla, however, possessed the most experienced U-boat commanders and it was felt that the first patrol of the war needed that kind of mature leadership.

Groping their way through the mist and drizzle, the ten craft took up station in a 60-mile line near the Dogger Bank and began a north-westerly surface sweep, towards the Orkneys. Predictably, an engine of *U5* broke down and she had to return to base on 8 August. The remaining boats of the flotilla continued the sweep and glimpsed three British warships. An attempt at a torpedo attack was made but the enemy disappeared into the mist. That evening the little fleet turned back. At a determined latitude the line of boats hove-to on the surface, under orders to wait in the hope that British ships would cross the line. Only one did so however. She was the British light cruiser HMS *Birmingham* which, on the morning of the 10th, suddenly parted the mists of the pre-dawn and came upon *U15*, stationary on the surface. Loud bangings were coming from the submarine's hull and it was clear that the vessel was undergoing repairs and that no watch was being kept. *Birmingham* swept down on the little craft and rammed her in the stern. Foaming round in a tight circle, the cruiser opened fire with all available guns and – just as the U-boat laboriously began to get under way

– struck her amidships, neatly slicing her in two. Within a couple of minutes the two halves of the boat disappeared beneath the waves. There were no survivors.

Unknowingly, the remainder of the U-boat flotilla continued its watch. *U18* did sight a British cruiser and dived to attack but lost the quarry. There were no further sightings and the eight remaining submarines turned for home. Only seven reached the safety of Heligoland. After radioing her approach, *U13* simply disappeared. There were no minefields at this stage of the war and no Allied vessels were involved. The sea had taken its toll.

The results of the other two patrols, undertaken by the more modern U-boats, were also negative. Two boats were forced back by heavy seas and the rest failed to make contact with enemy vessels. The disastrous outcome of the operations confirmed the German High Command's view of submarines. Clearly, they were incapable of offensive action, operating far from base. Their role, if there was one, would have to remain defensive.

The failure of the offensive patrols left the *Admiralstab* in Berlin faced with the same old problem: what to do to attack British sea power without risking the High Seas Fleet? Despite the *angst* generated by his flotilla's lack of success, Hermann Bauer was promoted to Flag Officer of the U-boat flotillas (*Führer der U-Boote*) at the end of August 1914 and offered to his Admirals a determined but reasoned argument for the use of the submarines in an attacking role. It is difficult to believe that the Chiefs did not shrug their shoulders and say: 'Why not? What have we to lose?' When, then, a rumour reached the German High Command that heavy British warships were anchored off Rosyth in the Firth of Forth, Bauer was given permission to try again. Accordingly, on 2 September, he ordered two boats to attempt to penetrate the Forth and sink as many warships as possible.

On 5 September, in stormy conditions, Leutnant Hersing, commanding *U21*, sighted the small British 'scout' cruiser HMS *Pathfinder* south-east of May Island. Although his small craft was pitching and tossing in the heavy sea, Hersing was able to close undetected and fired one torpedo. It was a snap-shot but luck was with the U-boat. The torpedo hit the cruiser adjacent to her magazine and the 2,500-ton ship blew up and sank, taking most of her complement of 268 officers and men with her.

More, much more, came two weeks later when the venerable *U9*, under the command of Kapitänleutnant Otto Weddingen, encountered the three old armoured cruisers, *Aboukir*, *Cressy* and *Hogue*, patrolling off the Hook of Holland. In the early morning light, Weddingen torpedoed *Aboukir*. The 12,000-ton ship settled in the water while her sister ships, believing that she had struck a mine – so lightly was the submarine threat taken in those early days – closed her at once to rescue survivors. As they did so, Weddingen calmly picked them off in turn with his torpedoes. He took his time. *Aboukir*'s men were taken board *Hogue*. When *Hogue* was sunk, they were picked up by *Cressy*. Then a torpedo hit that ship and they were back in the water again. Only 777 of the three ships' crews were saved, out of a total of about 2,200. The loss was particularly poignant to the British Navy because this was a training cruise and many young cadets were lost.

Just under a month later, Weddingen and *U9* struck again when he sent the 7,350-ton armoured cruiser *Hawke* to the bottom just off Peterhead, only 70 of those on board being saved. The two U-boats returned to Heligoland, pennants fluttering from their periscopes, to a heroes' welcome. Bauer committed further U-boats to battle and the British submarine *E3* was sunk on 18 October to be followed, on the 31st, by the seaplane carrier *Hermes*. The Royal Navy could not remember when last it had sustained such disasters. 'More men lost than by Lord Nelson in all his battles put together,' growled Fisher. What happened the next month, however, sent even greater shock waves through Whitehall.

On 23 November 1914, the audacious Hersing, this time commanding *U18*, followed in the wake of a steamer and managed to penetrate the Hoxa entrance to Scapa Flow. Like a mouse in a cat's cradle, he cautiously scanned the vast anchorage. He had six torpedoes. With them, anchored battleships were at his mercy. He could have carried out the 'equalisation' policy single handed. He swung his periscope round to find – tugs and a few escort vessels, but no dreadnoughts. The Fleet was making one of its rare sweeps in the North Sea. The cradle was empty.

Cursing his luck, Hersing gingerly turned his boat to negotiate once again the difficult Hoxa passage. Now, however, his periscope was sighted and the hunt was on. Twice he was rammed but managed to escape, even though his hydroplanes were damaged and his boat could not maintain a constant depth. Just as he seemed to have eluded pursuit, *U18* was caught in the strong Pentland tidal current and swept on to the rocks of the Skerries. Seriously holed, the submarine was scuttled by her crew.

It was the second U-boat loss of the war, but Fisher and his admirals felt no elation. True to its conviction that submarines were not offensive weapons, the Admiralty had erected no anti-submarines nets or other defences at Scapa Flow. It had always believed that the Scottish base was too far away from Germany for there to be any danger from frail U-boats. Hersing had shown this to be a complete fallacy.

Mines were hurriedly laid and nets and booms erected around the three main entrances to the Flow, but it took until February 1915 before they were complete. For the first four months of the war, then, the British battle squadrons were vulnerable at their main anchorage. During this period, alarmed by (false) reports of periscope sightings, Admiral Jellicoe, C-in-C Grand Fleet, took his ships hurriedly to other anchorages in Scotland and Ireland. This great fleet, the most powerful the world had known, was kept nervously on the move by the threat posed by a score of flimsy craft once derided as 'unfit to play a useful part in war'. That the British fleet was not attacked by U-boats reflects, again, the Germans' over-estimation of British naval competence. They took it for granted that the British bases were as protected as the German harbours. In doing so, they lost an opportunity of crippling British naval power at the very beginning of the war. Nevertheless, in the U-boat, they had discovered a weapon the potency of which was now very clear.

THE MORAL MAZE

The German Naval High Command entered 1915 with a very different view of the U-boat than had prevailed on the outbreak of war only five months before. First, it had proved itself to have a destructive power far greater than its puny size and fragile hull seemed to promise. Secondly, it had demonstrated itself to have sea-keeping qualities which allowed it to range far beyond coastal waters. The imaginative Bauer immediately took the point that the proven capability of his boats opened up the possibilities of using them to attack Britain's mercantile fleet directly, without first having to destroy the protecting warships. Britain's shipping lanes were long. They could not be policed all the time.

Bauer formally submitted his case for targeting U-boat action against British merchantmen, with the aim of cutting the supply-lines to the United Kingdom. It was rejected. Bauer was told that it would be impossible for German submarines to carry out an aggressive campaign against the British merchant fleet and still observe international maritime law, to which Germany was bound to conform. The problem was that the old international laws of engagement at sea, agreed by all the leading powers, made no provision for submarine warfare. The basis was incorporated in Article 112 of German Naval Prize Regulations. Under it, merchant vessels could be destroyed or taken into harbour as a Prize only after the identity of the merchantman and its cargo had been ascertained and provision made for the safety of its crew, either by taking them on board or by delivering them to the proximity of a port. Given the Royal Navy's mastery of the seas and the crowded nature of the waters round the British Isles, it would be impossible for large numbers of freighters to be stopped in this way. The U-boats could not house captured crews in their confined hulls and they certainly could not put themselves at risk by towing lifeboats to friendly shores.

It looked as though it would have to be back to warship-hunting for the small U-boat flotillas. Then, suddenly, the British themselves seemed to abandon the moral high ground in this debate and give the U-boats just the excuse they needed. On 2 November 1914, the British government declared the whole of the North Sea a War Zone. It did so to tighten the blockade on Germany, by announcing that it would seize all supplies destined for Germany, even though they were carried in neutral ships which were destined for neutral ports before being shipped or transported on to Germany. At the same time, Germany declared that British merchantmen were flying neutral flags to evade attack. (The British robustly denied this at the time, but Winston Churchill, writing in *The World Crisis* between the wars, sanguinely admitted to using 'this well-known *ruse de guerre* in order further to baffle and confuse the enemy'.) Both initiatives were seen by Germany as clear violations of international law.

The obvious – perhaps the only – riposte available to the *Admiralstab* was the U-boat, deployed without the constraints imposed so far by international law. A paper was submitted to the Naval Staff, arguing that 'unsparing use' be made of the U-boat by attacking merchant ships trading with Britain, even though this meant sinking their crews, too. A blockade would be announced and neutral countries would be informed. But no individual warnings could be given to ships caught in the war zone.

The German High Command at first dithered and then pressed the solution on the government. There was no immediate acceptance. The danger of alienating neutral countries and, in particular, the United States, was seen to be very real. The difference between the British and the proposed German blockade lay in the methods of intercepting ships breaking the blockade. The British threatened to stop only German merchantmen or those with cargoes ultimately designed for Germany. With its strong surface fleet, the Royal Navy could afford to observe the niceties of boarding merchantmen, inspecting their cargoes and either turning them back, escorting them into harbour and confiscating their cargoes or, at worst, sinking them and taking their crews on board. The German 'underwater blockade', in contrast, could really only operate by sinking on sight within the blockade zone, with no effective regard for a ship's flag, her destination or even the safety of her crew.

Eventually the German Chancellor agreed, over-ruling the opposition of his Foreign Office. The argument which swung the day was the hope that the threat would be sufficient to persuade Britain to lift her blockade; if that failed, consciences would be eased and neutral opposition pre-empted by issuing loud and detailed warnings before the new policy was put into practice. It was a pious but unfounded hope. The American government, which had by no means been supportive of the British and French war aims during these early months, immediately protested to Berlin. Threatening the lives of peaceful traders on the high seas was an act unprecedented in naval warfare, said the American diplomatic note, which even went on to threaten armed intervention in the war if the threat was carried out.

This was strong meat for a German government which had been unsure about the offensive in the first place. Inevitably, there was a climb down of sorts. The beginning of the campaign was postponed until 22 February 1915, and the USA was assured that there would be no attacks on neutrals if they were recognisable as such. U-boat commanders were ordered not to attack ships flying a neutral flag unless other factors – their structure, course or behaviour – gave cause for suspicion. Hospital ships, unless they were clearly being used as troop carriers, would also be immune.

This time the outcry came from the U-boat flotillas. Impeccably disciplined though they were, the young U-boat commanders nevertheless protested strongly that it would be impossible to follow these orders. Apart from the fact that Allied boats were known to be sailing under false colours, it would be impossible to be sure of a ship's identity and course when glimpsed through a periscope lens. Surface intervention could be hazardous and even fatal in the crowded waters around the British coast.

This protest was to earn support from the Englishman A. C. Bell in his official *History of the Blockade of Germany and the Countries Associated With Her in the Great War* (HMSO) published fifteen years later. 'A handful of naval officers,' he wrote, 'most of them under thirty years of age, without political training and isolated from the rest of the world by the nature of their duties, were thus given a vague and indefinite instruction to give a thought to politics before they fired their torpedoes.'

It was, of course, a nonsense. But the German government had announced its offensive to the world and given its assurances of modifications to Washington. Further changes either way would have caused confusion and would demonstrate for world opinion the tightrope which the *Admiralstab* was walking. So it confirmed the orders to the U-boat captains but quietly assured them that they would not be held responsible if, in spite of the exercise of great care, 'mistakes should happen to be made'.

After the formal opening of the offensive, five British steamers, totalling 15,049 tons, were sunk before the end of the month. It was not quite the onslaught that had been feared. But these last five sinkings were the work of only one submarine, *U8*, captained by Leutnant Stoss, on whose young shoulders rested the complete responsibility for launching the great offensive. Beneath the fear, the forecasts, the indignation and the warnings, lay the fact that Germany had only one venerable U-boat, ineffectively powered by heavy oil-burning motors, at sea and able to prosecute the new campaign on its opening day. (One other boat was at the end of her patrol and a third had to return to port with engine trouble.) The reaction to the initial success of the U-boats had obscured the reality that these new craft were still comparatively untried, sometimes downright dangerous and demanding of high maintenance. And, of course, Germany had very few of them at the beginning of the war. Admittedly, it was unusual to have only one operational U-boat at sea, but *U8*'s heavy responsibility was illustrative of a weakness which the *Admiralstab* had to remedy quickly.

The new submarine-building programme was accelerated immediately. The capture of Belgium had secured ports from which to attack cross-Channel traffic, and new, smaller U-boats, plus larger mine-laying classes, were commissioned to exploit this. The shipyards were new to the work and production was to lag behind target throughout the war, but in the first six months of 1915, 480 freighters and twelve British warships were sunk. (I am indebted for these and other statistics used in this section to V. E. Tarrant's immaculately researched *The U-boat Offensive 1914-1945*, Arms & Armour Press, 1989.)

One of these sinkings created world-wide consternation. On 7 May 1915, Kapitänleutnant Walter Schwieger, commanding *U20*, sighted a large, four-funnelled liner steaming fast on the horizon, off the Head of Kinsale, Ireland. He identified it as either the *Lusitania* or the *Mauretania*, both Cunarders and both believed by Germany to be armed merchant cruisers. In addition, it was suspected that the *Lusitania* was carrying munitions back from New York to Britain. Schwieger had no hesitation in attacking without warning. He fired one torpedo which hit the great liner just abaft the bridge. Immediately, she hove to and heeled to starboard. There was a second explosion, although no other torpedo was fired, and within minutes the 30,396-ton ship had disappeared, leaving the sea littered with debris and the desperate figures of drowning men, women and children. Among the 1,201 passengers who lost their lives were 128 neutral citizens, including Alfred G. Vanderbilt, the American financier and industrialist.

Before *Lusitania* had sailed from New York, Germany had accused Cunard of shipping munitions in her, and the German Embassy had taken space in the city's newspapers warning neutrals not to sail in her. However, this did little to reduce the outcry which met the publication in the world's newspapers of pictures of drowned children being brought ashore. The Cunarder had not been armed. Whether she was carrying munitions remained a matter of debate. The British denied it vehemently and an American court agreed, forcing the German government to pay compensation for the American dead. The argument was important. If *Lusitania* was a covert carrier of explosives – and that second, fatal explosion seemed to give credence to the view – Schwieger's attack was legitimate. If not, he was attacking civilians, some of them neutrals, and he was a pirate. The debate has continued to this day, although strong circumstantial evidence sustaining the British denial has recently emerged, following a sophisticated investigation of the wreck on the sea bed carried out by an American diving team.

After the sinking, President Wilson immediately demanded the end of the U-boat campaign against commercial shipping and only after the payment of reparations and the assurance that there would be no more attacks on large passenger liners, even if they were flying Allied colours, was he mollified. But the *Lusitania* incident was not forgotten in the USA. Schwieger's torpedo did what the British propaganda stories about the Bosche 'bayoneting Belgian babies' had failed to do. It hit directly at American interests and alerted public opinion in the USA to the horrors of total war.

The argument flared up again five months later when two more British passenger liners were torpedoed, with a handful of Americans among the casualties. This time Berlin had to bend the knee and the *Admiralstab* withdrew all U-boats from the English Channel and the South-Western Approaches and restricted attacks in the North Sea to those which conformed to Prize Regulations. It was pleased, however, with the sinking rate. The offensive *could* work, but more boats were needed. So the building programme was accelerated again and the main offensive switched to the Mediterranean, an area less well patrolled by the British Navy.

In London, the Admiralty hung out no flags. It recognised that the main pressure which had led to the departure of the U-boats from northern waters was political. The loss of commercial tonnage to U-boat attack was mounting and worrying. Minds used to straightforward confrontations could not, somehow, grasp the realities – let alone the subtle ethics – involved in this new type of warfare. When the British transport, *Royal*

Edward, was sunk in the Aegean, carrying reinforcements for the 29th Division in Gallipoli, only 600 were saved of a crew of 220 and 1,382 soldiers. That poet of Empire, Sir Henry Newbolt, wrote: '... for the first time in modern war we suffered the cruel loss of soldiers to the strength of a whole battalion killed – not in battle, but helpless and unresisting, without the chance of firing a shot or delivering a last charge with the bayonet.' In this type of conflict, there was not even a chance of last-ditch heroism, as evinced against the Zulus at Isandlwana, to give comfort to a grieving nation.

The shift of emphasis from the North Sea and Atlantic to the Mediterranean had its compensations for the German High Command. One who revelled in the new, open conditions was the unlikely sounding German, Lothar von Arnauld de la Perière. Commanding *U35*, and operating from the little Adriatic port of Cattaro, he became the most outstanding U-boat commander of the war. By the time he returned to Germany in 1918, to take the giant *U139* to the very shores of the USA, he had sunk two warships, one auxiliary cruiser, five troopships, 125 steamers and 62 sailing vessels, grossing 453,716 tons. His total sinkings were unsurpassed by any submarine commander, on either side, in both world wars.

Within three weeks, marauding from the northern Spanish Coast to the Gulf of Genoa from 26 July 1916, de la Perière sank 54 merchantmen grossing 91,000 tons. It was the most destructive single voyage of the war and the German High Command had the good luck to choose just this mission to send with de la Perière a stills and newsreel cameraman. He captured memorable images of *U35*'s 4.lin gun being fired, freighters sinking and the crews being rescued and taken aboard the submarine. The flickering images of the U-boat's crew capering on deck under a make-shift shower, the prisoners gently exercising in the sea air (only for the camera, this – they were kept below for most of the voyage), and the handsome de la Perière smiling from his conning tower like Douglas Fairbanks, went round the world. It was a great propaganda coup for the *Admiralstab*. Nowhere was it made clear that this was the Mediterranean. It seemed as though the U-boats had the complete mastery of their home waters.

This was far from true, of course. Throughout the middle years of the war, the German government continued to agonise about the implications of launching a campaign of unrestricted sinkings and there was a half-hearted return to a U-boat offensive in home waters in February 1916. Despite the retention of constraints, enough success was achieved to encourage the *Admiralstab* in the middle of 1916 to commit its High Fleet submarines to an ambitious attack on the British Grand Fleet.

At the end of May a trap was laid, aimed at luring the British battle-ships and battle cruisers out of their Scottish bases into waiting lines of submerged U-boats. The trap was to be baited by the German High Seas Fleet itself, which would make a quick sortie to the coast of Sunderland in the North of England, where it would shell military installations. At the last minute, however, the German fleet sailed to the Skagerrak (Jutland) instead, wireless messages went astray, the waiting flotillas were harassed by patrol boats and the British Fleet was able to put to sea virtually untroubled by U-boat attack. As a result, to its horror, the German Fleet found itself facing the full might of the British dreadnoughts in the very pitched battle which its whole strategy had been designed to avoid.

In the event, it was an inconclusive engagement. More British vessels than German were lost – the accuracy of the Kaiser's gun-layers and the thickness of the German armour proving superior – but the Germans' hearts were never in it and, helped by the over-caution of the British C-in-C, Admiral Jellicoe, they broke off the battle and slipped away back to the safety of their harbour fortresses. Both sides claimed the victory, but although the German ships made one more, completely ineffectual, sortie a couple of months later, the next time they put to sea was to surrender.

The U-boats played no effective role in the Battle of Jutland and their young commanders were returned to their old task of attacking commercial shipping, with one eye on the periscope lens and the other on world opinion. In Berlin, pressure was growing again to unleash the U-boats in an all-out offensive, but the fear of causing not only the USA but also neutral Holland and Denmark to enter the war against Germany kept the lid on the bubbling pot.

Considering the difficulties under which they were operating, the U-boats were remarkably successful during the months of this last, restricted offensive in the autumn of 1916. The coastal boats, operating from the Flemish ports, targeted the English Channel traffic and the Anglo-French coal trade in particular, causing French factories to close down because of lack of fuel. The mine-laying boats (grimly known as 'The Children of Sorrow') had been profitably active throughout the imposed interregnum. And the new, big U-boats had ranged much farther afield, venturing into the deep waters off the coast of Spain, the Western Atlantic and the Arctic Ocean. In all, 768 ships, grossing one and a half million tons, were sunk between September 1916 and January 1917. During this period, Germany lost ten of the operational U-boats, or *Frontboote*, with which the campaign had begun. The success of this third restricted offensive played a strong part in causing the pot finally to boil over. There were other important reasons.

The British naval blockade had forced the German government to put the civilian population on tight rations in order to conserve food for the fighting forces. It was difficult to tether the U-boat captains with moral constraints when the urban population at home was cold and hungry. In addition, the collapse of Rumania and the growing success of German troops on the Russian front had released sufficient divisions to cope with the armies of Denmark and Holland should these small countries enter the war.

To the German High Command, still shocked by the bloody land battles of the Somme and Verdun on the Western Front, the successes of the U-boats offered a beguiling prospect of finishing the war quickly and cheaply. Admiral von Holtzendorff, Chief of the German Naval Staff, calculated that if the U-boats could increase their sinkings to the level of 600,000 tons of British shipping a month – and, freed from constraint, he argued that they could – Britain could be starved and forced to make peace within five months. Even if unrestricted submarine warfare did bring America into the war, she was not mobilised and there was no way she could train and ship sufficient troops to Europe in time to affect the outcome. The few troopships which she could fill would never run the gauntlet of the waiting U-boats.

Even then, however, the German Chancellor demurred and it was decided to try one more peace overture to London. this was transmitted on 12 December and rejected. The German politicians could no longer restrain the warlords and the Kaiser gave his assent to the waging of unrestricted U-boat warfare from 1 February 1917. No way had been found through the moral maze. The young men in the conning towers were to be given their heads. In *The World Crisis*, Churchill described the coming sea battle as ' ... in scale and in stake the greatest conflict ever decided at sea. Its declared result will for generations be regarded as a turning point in the destiny of nations ...'

FROM THE CONNING TOWER

It was a very small number of men upon whom the German nation was pinning its faith. On all fronts, 105 *Frontboote* were available to launch the offensive. This meant that, with reserves and officers nearing readiness for command, the *Admiralstab* had probably little more than 200 captains available. Very few of these were over 30 years of age. Not until the Battle of Britain 27 years later were so few to carry so much responsibility while so young.

The place to examine a U-boat captain of the Kaiser is in and on his element: on the crowded bridge of his conning tower, far out at sea, butting into heavy weather, on the surface, at night. There are five men on that small steel platform: three lookouts, starboard, port and aft, and the captain and his officer of the watch peering ahead through binoculars, straining to see through spray which flies higher than the mast tops and soaks them all. They have just surfaced and the conning tower platform is slippery with jellyfish, and golden yellow weed is still clinging to the hawsers which stretch fore and aft.

They have been at sea for nearly four days and they are rounding the northern tip of Scotland before turning south through the Irish Sea to raid shipping in the Western Approaches. The captain's rank is Kapitänleutnant. His name doesn't matter – it could be Forstmann, Valentiner, Steinbrinck or Rose. They are all great U-boat aces still alive at this stage of the war. In fact, he is Gerard Amberger, captain of *U58* and a member of *II U-Flotille*, under the command of Kapitänleutnant Von Rosenberg-Gruszczynski. He is now 27 years old, and like many of his brother officers he was a junior officer in a surface ship when the war started. Also like them, he did not relish the prospect of wearing the watchkeeper's sword on the quarterdeck of a battleship which spent the war in harbour. So he volunteered for U-boats.

There have been times when he wished he had not. Early in 1916 he had been serving in *U73* when the captain, Kapitänleutnant Siess, had brought the boat home after his full bridge complement had been washed overboard and lost. Siess had taken them to sea again the next day cheerfully calling his boat 'the floating coffin'. She could manage four knots submerged 'for an occasional fifteen minutes' and took two minutes to dive. Top speed on the surface was 9.5 knots but then she threw up such a huge bow wave that, said Siess, 'any cargo boat could bolt from us'. Later, in another command, Amberger had worked feverishly to repair leaks 50 metres down after his boat had been damaged by a mine. He had watched with fascination mixed with fear as a warrant officer had used a tin tea tray for more than half an hour to deflect gushing water away from the precious electric batteries. Had the WO relaxed for a second, the water would have hit the batteries and produced a sizzling cloud of chlorine gas which would have choked them all.

This passage has hardly been a pleasure cruise, either. Amberger had slipped out of harbour and set a south-westerly course to pass through the Straits of Dover. But he had found the Straits a mass of patrol boats and mined nets, so he had turned to make his passage the long way round, circumnavigating the British Isles around Scotland. Even then he had been hounded by destroyers in the North Sea, so that he had been forced to stay submerged for nine hours, making slow headway with his electric motors.

This had not only made for slow sailing but had turned the air below foul. There had been hardly enough oxygen to burn a match. Now the diesels have taken over and the smell of oil permeates everything. Although the spray, wind and rain up here on the bridge stings his eyes and nostrils, he can still smell the oil and hear the thump of the engines. Sometimes Amberger feels that they can be heard right across the North Sea. He does not know how the engineers stand it down there; apart from the noise, the heat of the engine-room can sometimes reach 30 degrees Celsius when the diesels are at full stretch.

He swings his glasses in a quarter arc. He knows he will be in hot water on his return, however well the patrol goes. Previously, changing course would have been a matter for his discretion, but not now. Bauer has given his captains strict orders to go through the Channel to save as little time as possible in reaching and leaving patrol sectors. Amberger shrugs his shoulders under his cape. Better to be given hell by the *Führer der U-boote* than to lie at the bottom of the English Channel. He has lost so many of the friends and contemporaries with whom he trained. Lorenz, Palis, Noodt and Nitzsche have all gone. Even early heroes like Stoss have perished. As an experienced captain, Amberger reckons now that he has only a fifty-fifty chance of surviving this war.

He used to be counted rather a man-about-town when he was serving in coastal submarines and operating from the pretty Belgian town of Bruges, lying quietly safe from bombardment up the canal from the coast. It was a drinking and whoring life then and his uniform had always been pressed. Now, based at Wilhelmshaven, in the fourth year of the war, there is no time for fun. There is little shore leave while his boat is being turned round for sea between patrols; he has to supervise the work. And life on board at sea is Spartan enough.

This trip will last almost a month – particularly now that he has been forced to go the long way round – and, during that time, he will be lucky to shed more than his sea boots. Beneath the rubber cape, which reaches nearly to his boot soles, he wears rubber overalls over leather jacket and uniform trousers. They are supposed to keep out water but they don't. Nothing stops the water seeping through. His roll-neck knitted jersey, which used to be white, is now a dirty grey and is worn over two sets of woollen underwear. Within one more day his whole wardrobe will be stiff and caked with salt again; no other member of the crew spends as much time in the conning tower. His uniform cap is faded and bent at the peak and is pulled well down jauntily over one eye. That's as near as he gets these days to any display of bravado.

To his moustache he has long since added a beard, like most of his crew. Water on board is severely rationed so that anyone who wants to shave has to do so in tea dregs. Soap has disappeared from U-boats by this stage of the war, so the captain, like everyone else on board, 'washes' in a sand and pumice mixture which does for the skin roughly what holystoning did for the decks he scrubbed during his primary training.

Food lacks variety. Amberger recalls with nostalgia the golden day when they boarded an American freighter and took a live pig. Fresh pork on patrol! They finished their fresh supplies yesterday and now they are back on hard tack. But Amberger is very much aware that he is a member of an élite force. Submariners at base, officers and men, receive special rations which are much better than the miserable fare available to civilians. The pay is good and he and his crew receive an extra two Reichsmarks bonus for every dive they make. When morale is low he will sometimes order a practice dive or two, even though they are not strictly necessary. The money helps the families back home.

He also knows that he is considered to be rather a hero. Naturally his parents back home on the farm in Bavaria think that. But if they didn't feel that way instinctively, the Government is continually persuading them of the fact. While the British maintain morale with picture postcards of the stage beauties of the day, like Gladys Cooper and Ruby Miller, the idols of the German posters and postcards are the U-boat crews, crowded in artists' impressions of storm-swept conning towers, their raised fists hurling defiance at the White Cliffs of Dover.

Gerard Amberger doesn't feel a hero. He is often afraid. Only fools are not afraid, particularly when, after a crash dive, they all have to lie still, often in the dark, waiting for the damned depth-charges to creep closer. But the mines are the worst. The British are now laying them all around the German harbour approaches and groping through them is a tense business, depending more on luck than skill. No one talks of death, of course. But the trouble is that there is not much choice of death in a U-boat. Unless you are lucky enough to be killed outright by a shell, mine or depth-charge explosion, the end is always the same: the lights go out, the water gushes in and hits the motor batteries and the chlorine gas hisses out, choking and burning as the submarine plunges down ... It's horrible and doesn't bear thinking about. But everyone does.

He now hates the British (in this sea war the French, Italians and Russians are irrelevant). The old respect for fellow professionals with which he had begun the war has long since dissipated. He regards their blockade as being unprincipled. He can harbour no respect for a nation which targets women and children on the home front and therefore he applauds the decision to sink at sight all shipping in the war zone. And he has no compunction in carrying out those orders.

His crew feel the same and this has helped to weld them together into a tight, highly-focused team. With one or two exceptions, they are now experienced submariners and most of them sport the U-boat medal awarded by the Kaiser for three successful voyages. The very proximity of their living and fighting conditions at sea gives them a unity which is almost family-like. There is affection as well as mutual respect among them and they have complete trust in their captain, who, when conditions allow, permits them to come on deck to see anything which will break the monotony of a long voyage spent below.

There is affection, too, in their regard for their boat, although this is mixed with a touch of ambivalence. They are glad they are not sailing in one of the vessels built in the Germania yard. Those craft have a reputation for being unstable. When the trim is adjusted they have been known to plunge to the bottom and then to kick to the surface for no apparent reason. This is the last thing you want when making an attack. *U58* is a bit slow and she lacks the room of the new, bigger classes, but she's reliable – and so is her captain.

After the British, the main target of derision for Amberger and his men are the U-boat crews operating from the Adriatic port of Cattaro. Viewed from the warship-studded and stormy waters of the North Sea and the Atlantic, the men on the Adriatic station are on a summer yachting cruise. Any fool can sink high tonnages in those conditions!

THE BOAT

The boat which Amberger commands is typical of the cruising (i.e., ocean-going) craft which are to be at the fore of the 1917 battle. Built at the AG Weser yard in Bremen and commissioned in the summer of 1916, she is one of the *M* class and displaces 786 tons on the surface and 954 submerged. Bigger and better boats are now being launched, but this class will prove to be capable work-horses throughout the great offensive.

U58's design shows great advances on those ugly craft of the first patrols, with their high prows and cumbersome air cowls. With a length of 220 feet and just under 21 feet in beam, she is low in the water and her bows rise slightly, giving her a purposeful look. Her conning tower is slightly cowled and its platform is flanged out at the back like a Roman chariot. She has a lean beauty on the surface although, like all submarines, in dry dock her buoyancy tanks make her look like a plump, bulbous matron without her stays.

Amberger is disappointed in *U58*'s top surface speed of 14.7 knots (she can record a respectable 8.4 knots under water), despite her being fitted with the newish MAN 4-stroke diesel engines. Even older boats can make faster times than this. But she has one very special attribute which Amberger rates above all others: she can dive in 30 seconds (to a maximum depth of 165 feet). Very few boats throughout the war are to better this.

She has already proved her worth. Amberger has yet to open his account with *U58*, but under other commanders she has so far sunk five ships, with a total tonnage of some 7,000 tons. Not high scoring, but the main battle has only just begun. Her armament is conventional for this stage of the war: two 4.1in deck guns, mounted forward and aft of the conning tower on low bases which make them look permanently in recoil; and ten torpedoes, 19.1in in diameter, fired through four tubes, two forward and two aft. She has a surfaced patrol range of 10,500 nautical miles and, overall, she is a sound, proven submarine.

From his position in the conning tower, the captain looks down forward on a deck which is so awash it is virtually under water. Occasionally *U58* lurches up in a swell and reveals about 50 metres of level wooden deck, through the basket-weave holes of which the water runs away. Although, like most of the boat, the guns have been repainted a dull grey since the last patrol, flecks of red rust are already beginning to appear on them. Above him, secured to the short masts on each side of the conning tower, stout steel hawsers run fore and aft. They serve as protection against nets and mines and also act as antennae for the radio over short distances. For long distance transmission and reception, two tall aerials have to be fitted to the diving tanks on the hull. At this point in the war, however, conditions rarely allow them to be used.

From the conning tower hatch, which is only large enough to take one man at a time, a smooth, greasy ladder leads down directly to the control room, which stretches forward. The impression is of being in a tubular power house, studded with pipes, plates, rivets, levers, dials and wheels. Here sit the steersman, two hydroplane operators, and ratings to control the air valves and ballast tanks. When he is looking through the main periscope, known as 'the asparagus', the captain stands on a circular, raised platform, around which he scurries, crab-like, as he surveys the horizon. As the periscope rises, Amberger crouches to come up with it, so that he is in a position to see as soon as the glass breaks the surface. As the tube comes up, it emits a hum from its motor and clanking from its hauling chain. It also never fails to send a trickle of water on to his head as he operates the twin focusing handles.

Forward of the control room, through a strong bulkhead door, lie the ratings' quarters. There are ten bunks for 30 men, set in a seemingly chaotic muddle of pipes, wheels, steel containers and red-nosed torpedoes. Like most U-boats, *U58* operates a 'hot bunk' system – there is always an off-watch crewman asleep between the blankets. There are no baths or showers; merely two washbasins set forward. An iron ladder leads to the forward deck hatch.

Aft of the control room, another bulkhead door opens into the officers' wardroom. This is a little wood-panelled mess, fringed with black leather sofas which also serve as bunks and which are hung with dark green curtains. The central dining-table doubles up as the navigator's chart table. To starboard, leading off the wardroom through another bulkhead, this time with a long green curtain substituting for a door, the captain has his broom cupboard of a cabin. He is the only one aboard who can find privacy. This cabin is balanced, to port, by a tiny radio room and aft of that lie the banks of greasy, smelly, booming diesels, and, aft again, the silent electric motors. A small galley, powered by the main batteries, is linked to this room. Forward and aft, the torpedoes are ranged by their tubes. Nowhere is a centimetre of space wasted.

Amberger's boat serves two purposes. As a vessel, she carries and houses his crew. But she is also a weapon, in that, when a torpedo attack is made, it is the boat itself which has to be aimed, since the tubes are part of the fixed structure of the boat and cannot be trained separately. Despite the experience gained by three years of warfare, the process of an underwater attack still remains complicated and demanding of great skill – and luck.

By early 1917, merchantmen are no longer sitting targets. In dangerous waters, they steam at maximum speed and on a zig-zag course. Underwater, a submarine is slower than most steamers. On sighting a puff of smoke, then, Amberger must shadow it on the surface at a safe distance, hull awash, pushing his diesels as hard as possible to get ahead of his quarry before diving to set up the attack. Once close and ahead, the captain will only allow himself glimpses of the steamer through 6-second periscope observations at intervals of about one minute, depending upon how near he is to his prey.

From these 'looks', he has to establish the type of ship he is attacking (he must make a detailed report later and, anyway, he does not want to waste a torpedo on a small patrol boat), estimate her course, her speed and, most difficult, the pattern of the zig-zag. The objective is to be in place to make a broadside attack at a range of about 900 metres. Nearer would make success more certain, but would also make detection more likely. The torpedo has a range of some 2,000 metres and a speed of between 35 and 40 knots – much faster than any merchant ship so that sort of range is more than acceptable.

In the Second World War, a mechanical form of computer, affectionately known in the Royal Navy as the 'is-was' or 'fruit machine', will make these calculations for the captain. But now, Amberger must do it all for himself as he scurries around his platform, catching glimpses of his target in the distance and swearing at his hydroplane operators to keep the depth right. As he plots his attack, he must at the same time maintain a vigilant watch for escorting warships (and, later in the war, aircraft). The very act of launching the torpedo imposes a further problem. The opening of the torpedo tube, the in-rush of the water and the release of the torpedo, alter the balance of the boat and can cause the submarine to break surface or even send the torpedo straight to the bottom. Therefore the boat must be trimmed to compensate as the torpedo is fired. The whole business calls for nerves cooler than an ice bucket and the guts to press home the attack in the presence of enemy warships.

Night attacks are different. Finding the quarry in the first place, of course, is more difficult and usually demands moonlight and a calm sea. But the attack is normally safer, in that the periscope is less easy to detect at night. If no warships seem to be in attendance, it also provides the option for Amberger to return to the old form of attack by surfacing and sinking the ship with gunfire, so saving precious torpedoes. Although virtually all merchantmen are armed by now, their guns and gunlayers are usually no match for a U-boat's deck armament and its trained crew. And, of course, the low-lying submarine is an extremely difficult target to hit at night.

Despite the difficulties of attack and the number of warships arrayed against them, Amberger and his comrades are entering into the last great battle full of optimism. They are no longer fettered by antiquated rules of engagement, which means that they can approach and attack without surfacing – using the submarine, in other words, as it was meant to be deployed in war. Their vessels and weapons, despite problems with some boat designs and faulty torpedoes, have been refined by three years of campaigning. U-boats no longer have to operate only in the crowded waters of the English Channel and the 'British' North Sea. They have much greater range and can hunt down British and neutral freighters on the high seas, away from the protection of patrol vessels. The captains and crews that have survived to this stage are experienced and cunning. Now, at last, they can win this war on their own!

THE LAST OFFENSIVE

The orders of the *Führer der U-Boote* to his captains for this offensive were precise and expansive. The instructions on using the Dover passage was typical of the detail. The tone was urgent and exhortational. This was to be 'ruthless U-boat warfare'. Unarmed passenger steamers, Belgian relief ships and even hospital ships, when the latter were found within the English Channel (where the Germans believed them to be used as troop transports), were to be sunk on sight. There were to be no warning shots or boardings. U-boats were to stay on station even in bad weather; no running before a storm. The aim must be to stay at sea for at least fourteen days in every month. Every effort was to be made to fire all torpedoes and ammunition effectively on every patrol. Leave was to be restricted to periods when boats were being repaired and absence caused by venereal disease was to be eliminated. 'Orders must be carried out with exactitude ...'

The war zone (*Sperrgebiet*) covered the Channel, the western half of the North Sea and the west coasts of Scotland, Ireland, England and France. It extended about 400 miles west into the Atlantic. It also included the Mediterranean, except for narrow strips near the Spanish coast and, later, a narrow corridor to Greece. Neutral governments were not notified until the day before the start of the offensive, to give maximum impact to it, even though they had many ships already at sea in the zone. Pussyfooting with uncommitted countries was now a thing of the past

The main weight of the offensive was directed towards the Western Approaches and was carried out by the High Seas Flotilla, although all sectors were involved. The 105 U-boats available at the beginning of the offensive (which rose to 117 in March and 120 in April) is slightly misleading. The demands of refitting meant that the maximum number of boats at sea in any one day in February was 44, rising to 58 in April. Nevertheless, this was the largest fleet that Bauer had mustered so far during the war and his captains went to their task with a will.

The outrage which greeted the new offensive from outside the Axis Powers was universal. Never before had privateering been carried out so ruthlessly, by vessels which were so efficient at the task and by captains so determined to carry it out. The indignation of the Allies continued long after the war was over and it lingers still, re-fuelled by the Second World War. What is difficult to comprehend over the distance of nearly 90 years, however, is the equal revulsion felt by Germany for the British blockade. Because Germany lost the war, there were fewer opportunities afterwards for this indignation to be expressed. One of them was seized, however, in 1930 by Chief Petty Officer Roman Bader, a submariner, who wrote in *U-boat Episodes* (John Constable, edited by Neureuther and Bergen):

'British ships were carrying on a system of war which thrust into the hands of innocent German children a slice of raw onion for their supper. When I travelled home on leave and often saw children whose angel-souls shone through their pale, starved bodies, or soldiers, themselves just skin and bone, carrying home their last loaf to their wives whose hour was nearly come, I was seized with fury against this inhuman enemy who had cut Germany's food imports. What I felt, all my comrades on the sea felt, too. It was the enemy's crime that forced sailors like ourselves to sink floating palaces, masterpieces of human ingenuity and workmanship.'

In fact, there were precious few palaces torpedoed. Most of the U-boats' victims were merchant ships: freighters and tramp steamers. And, of course, if Germany had possessed surface mastery of the sea, she would undoubtedly have thrown a cordon around the British Isles and imposed a blockade quite as brutal in its effect as that exercised by the Royal Navy. But indignation removes rationality. This was total war and both sides were full-bloodedly engaged in it.

The impact of the submarine offensive was immediate. From averaging sinkings totalling just over 300,000 tons a month in the autumn of 1916 – which the British regarded as being worryingly high – the U-boats sank 520,412 tons in February 1917, of which 500,537 tons represented the loss of 243 British ships. The trend continued in March with the loss of 564,497 tons, of which 556,775 tons (413 ships) were British. The U-boats were rushing towards von Holtzendorff's target of 600,000 tons, designed to bring Britain to her knees.

They exceeded it in April when shipping totalling 860,334 tons, virtually all of it British, was sent to the ocean floor. The campaign was succeeding beyond all the expectations of the *Admiralstab*. What's more, it was doing so at no increased cost in submarines. Ten U-boats, the number lost in the 1916 autumn campaign, was the price – and two of these had been lost to German mines and another had run aground. It was clear that the underwater attacks were paying off. Of the ships attacked by torpedoes in the first three months, 72.5 per cent had been sunk, while only 58 per cent of the much small number of surface gunfire attacks had been successful.

These statistics sent shudders through the British Cabinet. UK food stocks ran dangerously low – one source estimated that there was only six weeks' supply left by mid-year – and rationing was introduced for the first time in British history.

Oil and coal imports were particularly hit and the Admiralty was forced to order all Royal Naval vessels to reduce speed when not in action, in an attempt to conserve fuel. The 'U-boat Peril' featured in most newspaper headlines and it was clear in Britain that a crisis point in the war had been reached. Admiral Jellicoe, now first Sea Lord, was not amused when one earnest citizen wrote to him suggesting that Fynon's Health Salts be poured into the North Sea so that the U-boats would just pop to the surface. On 10 April, Jellicoe was forced to admit to the American Admiral Sims that Britain had at last lost command of the seas; a grim and, for him, humiliating confession to have to make.

Even the predicted entry of America into the war on the side of the Allies in April did little to cheer the Admiralty who felt that defeat was staring them in the face. It was ironic that the United Kingdom, renowned for its navy but with a comparatively poor reputation for great continental land battles, should be hanging on so tenaciously in the trenches of Flanders and France and yet be succumbing in its area of strength – the sea. In fact, America was to provide the solution. But salvation seemed far away in April 1917.

It should be said here that Jellicoe and his Admirals, for traditionalist old salts who still, in official memoranda, called warships 'men o' war', as though they were Nelson's wooden-walls, had shown a surprising inventiveness in trying to combat the U-boats. An early breakthrough when the German naval radio code was broken had helped, but the inability of the U-boats to use their radios for much of their voyages rendered this a limited advantage. Jellicoe himself had created a central anti-submarine department at the Admiralty and this proved a great step forward. It was endlessly inventive during the middle years of the war and a wide range of counter-measures were tried. These included the towing of submerged British submarines behind merchant ships; the implementation of a building programme to give the navy new, small patrol boats; the introduction of depth-charges; the invention of crude hydrophones to detect the sound of a submerged U-boat's engines; and elaborate net systems across the Channel, linked to mines and, later, lit up at night 'like Piccadilly Circus'. An attempt was even made to extend a mine curtain across the North Sea from the Orkneys to Norway.

One of the most innovative devices was the creation of the Q-ship decoy. This was usually an innocent-looking tramp steamer, her only armament seemingly a puny 12-pounder mounted aft. She would steam a straight, slow course in a main shipping lane, simply begging to be torpedoed. Once the torpedo struck, crew 'A' would make a panicky display of taking to the boats as the ship settled low in the water. But there she would stay, for an unconscionable time, refusing to sink. The reason lay with the timber which filled the hold, bequeathing a buoyancy designed to test the U-boat captain's caution to the limit. When, patience exhausted, the U-boat surfaced to finish off the steamer with gunfire, the Q-ship's crew 'B', who had been lying muscle-achingly hidden, would suddenly spring into life. Down would come dummy bulwarks and cabin sides to reveal a 4in gun and torpedo tubes, and the U-boat was finished.

The secret, of course, lay in the mongoose convincing the snake that it really was a rabbit. The Q-ship captains went to great lengths to hoodwink the U-boat commanders. They and their crews never wore uniform, ashore or afloat, and were sworn to secrecy. While on leave in their civilian clothes, some of them were handed cowardice white feathers for evading service. Some skippers went so far as to dress up a young rating as the captain's wife, nursing a doll 'baby' on the bridge. Anything to fool the watching, waiting periscope.

These decoy ships destroyed eleven U-boats in all during the war. Despite the secrecy with which they were shrouded, however, the U-boat captains finally caught on and the effectiveness of the Q-ships had diminished by mid-1917. Mines were much more effective, although the quality of British mines used during the war was not good. Several U-boats escaped after being caught seemingly hopelessly in mine-nets.

Depth-charges were more promising, although their performance did not match that promise until the Second World War. They were introduced in January 1916. Detonated by a device which activated at various depths, according to predetermined settings, they were greatly feared by submariners, to whom, previously, fathoms of deep green water had always provided ample protection. To sink a U-boat, however, the charges had to explode within about 14 feet of the submerged craft, or within about 28 feet to force it to the surface. This demanded an accuracy which was extremely difficult to achieve. And it was not until the end of the war that depth-charges became available in sufficient numbers to become a major weapon in the anti-submarine armoury.

The problem in deploying all these initiatives was that the Admiralty was pursuing the chimera of developing offensive tactics against the U-boats, when what was needed, as V. E. Tarrant argues persuasively in his book, was a defensive policy. Small boats such as U-boats, operating singly in vast areas of sea, were extremely difficult to find. They needed to be attracted, like iron filings to a magnet, so that they could be destroyed. The answer, of course, was the convoy.

The concept was not new. Sailing groups of merchantmen together, protected by escorting warships, had been practised successfully by the British in the Napoleonic Wars. But the Admiralty, and Jellicoe in particular, strongly resisted it now. Jellicoe's objections – which he was still rehearsing as late as 1934 when he published *The Submarine Peril* (Cassell) – were threefold: Britain lacked sufficient escort vessels to protect the large convoys which would be needed; there were no waters safe enough in which to assemble the large number of freighters needed to make up the convoys; such a large number of ships, moving at the speed of the slowest, would be easily found by U-boats and would form a vulnerable target.

The entry of America into the war provided the answers to the first two arguments in that the USA immediately agreed to provide destroyer escorts, and her east-coast harbours provided good marshalling grounds for UK-bound convoys. Still Jellicoe would not have it. It took a personal visit by Lloyd George, the British Prime Minister, to the Admiralty to 'persuade' him. On 27 April, the policy was accepted and put into practice immediately.

It was the beginning of the end of the U-boat offensive, although no one realised it at the time. The convoys took some time to mount. Many freighters had no rev counters or telephonic bridge-to-engine room communication. Keeping station at sea, therefore, was difficult. The organisation demanded brought mutterings of 'nationalisation' from the British Mercantile Marine. But April 1917 proved to be the high-water mark of sinkings by the U-boats. No other month in either world war matched that remarkable total of 860,334 tons, which, for the second half of the month, represented an annual sinkage rate of 50 per cent of available tonnage.

The battle continued, of course, and the British had no immediate evidence that the peak had been passed. Sinkings continued to be high and at such a rate – 616,000 tons in May, 696,000 tons in June and 555,000 tons in July – that the Admiralty concluded that there would not be enough tonnage left by the year's end to carry all the imports Britain needed. In addition, the sink-at-sight policy had had the effect of scaring off a considerable number of neutral shipping lines, whose vessels had provided an important link in the imports life-line. They returned later, but stood off during these crucial months. The stakes were still high with everything to play for.

Both sides were engaged in a desperate race to produce more vessels than were being sunk. The High Seas U-boat Fleet was responsible for the greater proportion of the sinkings, carried out in the Western Approaches. Its range was increased when the larger boats, led by the 1,500-ton *U155*, were commissioned. These had a surface cruising range of 25,000 nautical miles and carried 18 torpedoes and two 5.9in. guns. They carried the battle far out into the Atlantic and, from May 1917 until September, *U155* herself undertook a record-breaking 104-day patrol during which she sank fourteen ships, totalling 52,000 tons.

The Germans, in fact, were winning the ship-building race. The rate at which the new *Frontboote* were being commissioned was now in excess of their losses. The British had begun a programme to construct 1,200,000 tons of new merchant shipping during 1917. It was a prodigious task and it involved scouring the world's shipyards for capacity and cancelling plans to build three new battle cruisers. But the rate of construction still remained far below that of destruction.

It was against this background that the first convoys sailed. Two experimental voyages were completed and both were successful, with only one ship, which had been forced to drop out of the convoy, being lost. With an urgency born of near desperation, the British began shepherding their reluctant merchantmen into a pattern of large convoys for most of the inward-bound trade. The system demanded great organisation. The freighters – sometimes as many as 60 in each convoy – were provided with Royal Naval signalmen (and the older ones with voice pipes to link bridge and engine room) and ratings to count the engine revolutions, because keeping a constant speed to maintain station in zig-zagging was vital. The merchantmen were escorted with heavier warships in deep waters and then met with a screen of smaller, specialist anti-submarine craft nearer home.

Jellicoe's fears that such large gatherings of ships would prove almost impossible to defend proved unfounded. The first problem faced by Amberger and his colleagues was in locating the convoys. Previously, under independent passages, so many individual ships were scattered around the sea that a U-boat was fairly sure to meet one sooner or later. But even a convoy of 50 ships, plus escorts, was not easy to locate in a vast ocean. And attacking near port meant facing formidable numbers of escorts. (It was significant that all *U155*'s victims were ships sailing independently, far from home.)

An attack on a well-protected convoy proved to be extremely hazardous. The wolf-pack tactics of the Second World War could not be employed because of the difficulties of making radio contact to call the pack together once a convoy was sighted, although one ineffectual attempt was made. Single submarines, on the other hand, once they had found a convoy, experienced great difficulty in ducking under the escorting cordon and then creating time and space in which to mount flank attacks on tightly controlled vessels, zig-zagging in formation.

The statistics which began to emerge proved to be the writing on the wall for the U-boat flotillas. From May to July, 8,849 ships were convoyed but only 27 were sunk. As the Admiralty, belatedly, extended the system to outgoing ships and also to the Mediterranean, the loss rate stayed acceptably low: only 49 ships being lost from 12,098 convoyed, while 221 were lost from independent voyages in the same period. The case had been proven and by November 1917, 90 per cent of British ocean-going shipping was sailing in convoy.

The U-boat captains kept probing at the system, looking for weak links. They switched to coastal waters and did well for a time, feasting on smaller vessels outside the ocean-going convoys. The British losses stayed high, averaging more than 400,000 tons a month from August to December. But this was far short of von Holtzendorff's magical 600,000 tons. The corner had been turned and it was plain that Britain would not now be starved into submission within six months.

Coastal convoys were inaugurated and a new and most effective anti-submarine weapon joined the conflict in its closing stages: the aircraft. The *Admiralstab* sacked the imaginative Bauer, but stuck rigidly to its perceived solution of building more and better U-boats, while failing to solve the crucial question of how to attack escorted convoys. As the weary combatants entered the last year of the war, the Allies' shipping losses fell further: from 296,558 tons (139) ships in May 1918, to 115,237 tons (73 ships) by October.

U-boat losses now began to mount. In all, 45 U-boats were sunk in the last seven months of the war. They included that of the promising young captain, Karl Dönitz, who was to lead the U-boat fleet in the Second World War and, eventually, take over the leadership of a defeated Germany from Adolf Hitler. Dönitz fell victim to the imperfections of the boats from the Germania yard when his submarine popped to the surface amidst enemy ships in the Mediterranean and he was forced to surrender. It was a mine in the Dover barrage which accounted for the great ace Max Valentiner, who had sunk 141 merchant ships, grossing nearly 300,000 tons. And Gerard Amberger? With his crew, he went down just off Milford Haven in November 1917, while attempting to avoid a depth-charge attack. By that time, *U58* had accounted for eighteen ships, grossing 29,352 tons. But, like so many of his colleagues, Amberger had failed to survive that fifty-fifty chance.

DEFEAT AND AFTERMATH

Mainly because of the convoy system, the U-boats failed to prevent two million American troops from crossing the Atlantic to reinforce the hard-pressed Allied troops in France and Flanders. They arrived only just in time.

The drained German Army made one last great effort, the *Kaiserschlacht*; on the Western Front in the spring of 1918 and made surprising inroads before being halted and then turned back in August by the French and British Armies, with the rookie Americans in strong support.

In October the German Chancellor sought an armistice from President Wilson. The American President replied that talks could not even begin while German U-boats were still sinking passenger ships. The *Admiralstab* argued fiercely that to withdraw the U-boats would be to 'lay aside our chief weapon', but it was overruled and, on 20 October, all U-boats at sea were recalled.

The defeat of the army in its last great push, the failure of the U-boats to prevent American troops reaching Europe and the cumulative effects of the British blockade produced conditions of near revolution among the German civilian population. These soon spread to the armed forces and a desperate attempt by the *Admiralstab* to put the High Seas Fleet to sea to fight a last, great Valkyrian surface battle with the British Fleet led to a mutiny which spread throughout the fleet.

But not the whole fleet. Not one U-boat crew mutinied. They kept station and obeyed orders until the end. Indeed, only two days before the Armistice was signed on 11 November, *UB50* sank the old 16,350-ton British battleship *Britannia*. To press the point home, she did so off Cape Trafalgar, only twenty days after the anniversary of Nelson's famous victory there.

The German battle fleet sailed to Scapa Flow to surrender formally and, once within the harbour, the crews scuttled their great vessels. It was a last act of defiance from a fleet which had shown very little of that during the war. The U-boat captains, who had fought so valiantly, carried out no scuttling. Perhaps they loved their boats too much. The U-boat flotillas were handed over to the Royal Navy with dignity, mainly at Harwich, over twelve days in November 1918. In a conflict which had seen so much hatred, chivalry returned at the end. Commodore Tyrwhitt, the English commander at the surrender, ordered that his crews maintain strict silence as the U-boats steamed past. The U-boat men were not to be humiliated in any way.

One last batch of statistics sums up this strange story of the war beneath the waves.

Amberger and his colleagues remain the most successful submarine commanders the world has so far seen. Although nearly three times more U-boats were deployed in World War Two, proportionately they sank far less tonnage. The exchange rate in the first war was 29 merchant ships lost for every U-boat sunk. In 1939-45 it was just under four ships for every submarine.

That 50-50 survival estimate of Amberger's was roughly correct. Germany built 374 U-boats just before and during the war. A total of 178 of these were sunk by enemy action and 30 others were lost by other means. But, to sink those boats, it took in anti-submarine deployment, from the British alone: 277 destroyers; 194 aircraft; 49 armed yachts; 844 trawlers; 77 decoy ships; 44 P-boats; 867 drifters; 68 coastal motor-boats; 30 sloops; 338 motor-launches; 65 submarines; 50 airships; 24 paddle minesweepers.

It had been a close run thing. If the U-boats had been able to maintain for a further few months their sinkings at the level of March-April 1917, a weary and starving Britain, with a battered army propping up, on the Western Front, a French force on the verge of mutiny, could well have been forced to sue for peace. But then if the U-boat captains had not been allowed their heads and caused an aggrieved America to enter the war, enabling, in turn, the convoy system to be introduced, the war might well have not been lost by Germany. It is difficult to avoid the conclusion that the U-boat commanders very nearly won the First World War – and certainly lost it.

As privateers, they were more professional than Drake's men of Devon, more destructive than the corsairs of North Africa and certainly more catalytic than Napoleon's interceptors operating from Brest and Cherbourg. On the quayside in Kiel a stone imperial eagle stands in tribute to the U-boat crews. But their mark on history is etched deeper than the words on that memorial.

Before the First World War, the USA was a nation with isolationist views. It had no desire to become involved in foreign wars nor, in fact, did it show signs of becoming a militaristic power. Its relations with the British Empire were, if not cool, then certainly not close. The two countries had been at war with each other only a hundred years before, and Britain's sympathy for the South in the Civil War still rankled. By forcing a reluctant USA to enter the war on the side of the Allies, the Kaiser's submarine captains were the catalyst in not only creating the 'special relationship' between Britain and America which has been a strong ingredient of both countries' foreign policies throughout the rest of the century, but also in hastening the process by which the USA has become the strongest player in world affairs.

The British decline, on the other hand, has been profound. The British merchant fleet, of course, had borne the brunt of the U-boat attacks and more than 4,200 ships had been sunk and thousands more damaged.

No other nation's loss approached this and the British never recovered; the depression of the inter-war years, the loss of the Empire, and the growth of flags of convenience, helping to reduce its once proud merchant fleet to a nominal number of tankers, cruise ships and fishing vessels by the early 1990s.

Amberger and his colleagues have one last, further claim to have altered world events. By their controversial, courageous and skilled work in their primitive craft, they took naval warfare beneath the waves. With monster, nuclear-powered submarines now regarded as the capital ships of the 21st century, that seems likely to be where it will stay.

6

THE ARMOURED ONES
Hitler's Panzer Commanders

G ermany is the only nation to have provided two of the warriors featured in this narrative. This distinction is earned because within the space of one generation that nation twice developed tactical weapons and the men to use them that revolutionised warfare and changed the world. Hardly had the shock and controversy surrounding the U-boat died down, when an Austrian ex-corporal hit on a method of by-passing fixed land defences which made a virtual mockery of the bloody but static confrontation of the First World War. Just as the U-boat captains so nearly delivered victory to the Kaiser, so did the tank commanders, who were the key elements of Hitler's panzer divisions, present the Führer with the opportunity of re-drawing the map of Europe.

That Adolf Hitler failed in the end to turn that opportunity into permanent reality lay with his own arrogance and incompetence – plus the corruption endemic in the Nazi creed of National Socialism. It was certainly not the fault of his tank commanders. They, more than any other single branch of the German war machine, brought about the collapse of France, Holland, Belgium, Denmark and Norway in 1940; the retreat of the British army in Egypt back to its Suez Canal base a few months later; the overthrow of Greece and the old Balkan regimes in 1941; and the surrender of five million Russian troops in the lightning campaigns of 1941.

It was a magnificent display of imaginative soldiering; of what could be called old-fashioned *élan* – if it was not so coldly modern in its weaponry, tactics and brutality. The brutality, it must be said, came mainly from the *Reichscommissars* of the Party, who moved into occupied territories after the panzers had swept on and treated both the civilian population and captured troops – particularly the Russians – with mindless brutality. The tank commanders and their crews were no more or less chivalric than any other modern warrior, killing and being killed at a distance.

But they had no time for niceties either. Their byword was speed: keep moving at all times; don't let the enemy regain his breath or build his defences; motor fast and deep behind his lines; cut off his communications; pin him into defensive pockets and then sweep on, letting the following infantry mop him up or starve him out; spread panic and disruption; halt, fire and then accelerate. So the tanks, followed by their own assault guns and grenadier infantry and supported closely by the Stuka dive-bombers, all operating as an integrated whole, rolled up the armies of France, the Low Countries and Britain in six weeks in 1940. That campaign and that of Rommel in 1941-2 and of the panzers in Russia in the same period, set the world by its ears and earned the admiration – grudging or otherwise, depending upon nationality – of professional soldiers everywhere.

Hitler's tank commanders used their machines in the same way that the armoured knights of medieval times deployed their own armour and mobility to create fear and havoc among massed infantry and civilian populations. In terms of their effect upon the world and of the innovative way they swept aside the old order of defensive land warfare, the panzer men must be regarded as the most impressive 'armoured ones' the world has ever seen.

'THE NECESSITY FOR MACHINE-GUN DESTROYERS'

The idea of employing a self-propelled, armoured gun on the battlefield demanded no great leap of the imagination. It was no more than a logical development of the war chariot and the armoured elephant, and the arrival of the internal combustion engine put the concept within the range of nations who had the political will to overcome the many problems inherent in the development of such a weapon. For it wasn't easy. Carrying protected firepower around a battlefield churned up by high-explosives shells begged many expensive questions. Before the answers could be chipped out of granite, the need had to be there to justify the expensive effort involved. In some ways, the tank was a solution waiting for a problem to be posed with sufficient urgency.

That moment came about a year into the First World War. By 1915, an infantryman equipped with a bolt-action, magazine loaded rifle could fire fifteen rounds a minute, a machine-gun 600 and a cannon, launching shrapnel shell filled with particles of steel, twenty rounds. This fire power was prodigious and no army on either side could advance into it across open ground without sustaining terrible losses. Within months of the opening of the war, both sides – matching each other roughly equally in armament and heroism – had been forced to adopt static defensive positions. The trenches stretched from the Belgian coast to the Alps and there seemed no way of breaking the stalemate.

The conventional solution was an escalation of artillery power. The war factories pumped out the shells but however heavy the barrages, somehow the defenders still contrived to scramble out of their dug-outs to man the trench parapets when the inevitable infantry attack came. More and more the machine-gun, firing from a protected bunker behind the cruel barbed wire, came to dominate No Man's Land. To advance into its arc of fire and then, unprotected, try to clamber through the wire entanglements was to invite death.

It was against this background that the tank was born. The man who has the most claim to being the father of the ugly infant was a British officer named Ernest Swinton, who, at the outbreak of the war had graduated – via a Distinguished Service Order in the Boer War and the authorship of the official history of the Russo-Japanese war – to the post of Deputy Director of Railway Transport. But he was also a member of the Committee of Imperial Defence and had been posted to the Western Front to observe and report on the conditions there.

The domination of defences quickly became apparent to Lieutenant-Colonel Swinton and it did not take him long to come to the conclusion that the best way of breaking the stalemate was to devise a power-driven, bullet-proof, 'armed engine', capable of destroying machine-guns, crossing broken country and trenches, breaking through wire entanglements and climbing earthworks. Armoured cars existed, but conventional transmission and tyred wheels could not give the traction required to power the machine through mud and across trenches. What was needed was a caterpillar track similar to that used on agricultural tractors.

Swinton was not alone in thinking this way. An Australian engineer, Lancelot de Mole, had abortively put forward a similar idea to the British army before the war and the Royal Naval Air Service had been taking tentative steps down the same road. If it seems improbable that a branch of the Navy dedicated to flying machines should be involved in armoured land warfare, a reminder that the First Lord Of the British Admiralty at this time was Winston Churchill should be sufficient explanation. This man of boundless energy and fecund imagination could no more confine himself to his formal, naval brief than water could stay in a colander. After Swinton had codified his proposals in a memorandum submitted to the General Staff in France entitled 'The Necessity for Machine-Gun Destroyers', Churchill seized the initiative and diverted £70,000 of Admiralty funds to develop the idea. If Swinton is acknowledged as the father of the tank, certainly

Churchill must be regarded as its midwife. The Admiralty's role in the birth was acknowledged in the title 'Landship' used to describe the infant, although the emergence of the clumsy, ponderous prototype inevitably led to the use of the shorter, more descriptive epithet of tank.

The project took on a momentum of its own which survived the falling from grace of its sponsor, Churchill, after the Dardanelles campaign. Prototypes 'Little Willie' and, more satisfactorily, 'Big Willie' were produced in 1915. 'Big Willie' metamorphosed into 'Mother', which became the prototype for all Mark I British tanks, the first to go into action. In fact, there were two genders: the female tanks were designed to carry only machine-guns, while the males were fitted originally with two 6-pounder cannon. Whatever the sex, the babies would win no beauty prizes. They were steel-plated, flat-sided and lozenge-shaped, their caterpillar tracks running right round the edges of the hull. Their noses pointed in the air and they travelled at a stately but menacing four miles per hour. By early 1916, trials had won over most of the British top brass (including King George V, who was given a special demonstration) and 100 models were ordered. Equally importantly, Swinton was selected to raise and command the first 'Tank Detachment' with the task of training it to go into action on the Western Front.

The only other nation involved in developing tanks at this time was France, whose interest lay – and remained for many, misguided years – in producing a light machine which could be used in supporting infantry attacks. The Germans and their Austrian allies had no tank building programmes of their own and, indeed, had no idea that their enemies were so engaged.

The British work was ahead of the French and, when Haig's huge offensive on the Somme began to go badly in July 1916, the British Commander-in-Chief seized on the tank as a possible saviour. Ignoring Swinton's arguments that he should wait until crews were better trained and more tanks were available so that they could be used in depth, Haig committed each of the 49 machines at his disposal in small packets of twos and threes, across the entire front of his new, planned attack. So began a debate about tank deployment in battle which was to continue in Europe for the next 25 years and end to Germany's advantage.

The first action of what was called 'The Heavy Section' took place on 15 September 1916 towards the end of the sprawling Battle of the Somme, when a section of three tanks was assigned the task of clearing a pocket of Germans between Ginchy and Delville Wood. Two of them broke down and the third, *D1*, commanded by Captain H. W. Mortimore, was disabled by a shell but not before clearing out the enemy pocket convincingly. The other tanks virtually fought singly, so diluted were they across the width of the front. But, despite breakdowns, they did well enough and their very presence, looming out of the dawn mist, had a frightening effect on the German defenders. One German war correspondent reported them approaching 'slowly hobbling, rolling and rocking ... Someone in the trenches said: "The devil is coming" and the word passed along the line like wildfire.'

Haig was pleased enough, although Swinton knew that his machines could have done so much better had they been used selectively in groups, on terrain better suited to them. A hundred more tanks were ordered for immediate delivery, the designs of the old Mark Is were improved and production of a further 1,000 ordered. The twelve tank companies in France were increased to four battalions and a further five were formed in the UK. Swinton was a casualty of the expansion. He was regarded as insufficiently experienced in front-line fighting to be given the task of leading in France and, unsung, he was returned to duties at the War Cabinet Secretariat, his role in creating the tank only being recognised after the war when, as a respected major-general, he became one of the first Colonels Commandant of the Royal Tank Corps.

One of Swinton's last acts was to appoint Lieutenant-Colonel Hugh Elles to command the Heavy Section in France. Elles, feeling his way, developed into a first-class tank commander and, although his machines were still used piecemeal, they did well enough in a series of engagements in 1916 without producing the coup which everyone awaited. His command grew into three brigades, although GHQ deliberately seemed to snub the new force by holding back the promotion of its key officers. Elles himself was not appointed brigadier-general until May 1917. He was commanding ten battalions before he became a major-general.

The French, meanwhile, had formed their own tank arm, equipped with their own machine, the lightly armoured Schneider tank. On 16 April 1917, at Berry-au-Bac on the River Aisne, they went into action in force, just six months after the first British engagement. It was a disaster. Two columns of 132 Schneiders assembled in broad daylight and were caught by the German guns, directed by spotter aircraft. After their experience with British tanks, the Germans had widened their trenches and the Schneiders found difficulty in crossing them. Their armour proved vulnerable to German fire and 76 tanks were lost, 57 completely destroyed by shellfire. It was the ease with which this massed attack was defeated which strongly influenced the Germans' decision not to begin a tank building programme of their own.

During his first year of command, Elles had had no more luck than Swinton in dissuading Haig and his commanders from frittering away his tanks' effectiveness by committing them in small numbers. Casualties were accordingly high and, even though the Heavy Section had become the Tank Corps in July 1917, its further growth was halted. Then Haig agreed to give the new Corps a chance – to fight in its own way on terrain of its own choosing, if Elles could sell the idea to an army commander. The saviour of the British tank took the unlikely form of General Sir Julian Byng, whose Third Army faced the Germans south of Cambrai, in firm, rolling countryside comparatively unbroken by heavy artillery fire. Byng persuaded Haig to let him upgrade the tank attack into a planned battle and the challenge was on.

Elles had grouped about him a small but distinguished group of staff officers, foremost among whom was a young GS02, G. F. C. 'Boney' Fuller, who was to prove a master tank strategist and have a profound effect upon the development of German tank warfare in the Second World War. Although the Cambrai ground was good for tanks, the objectives were protected by the Hindenburg Line, a defensive maze of wire and support trenches. To penetrate this, Fuller evolved his famous trench crossing drill whereby three tanks would advance in arrowhead formation, each carrying a fascine – a giant bundle of brushwood bound with chains and designed to be dropped into a trench from the front of the tank to provide a causeway. The first tank would break the wire and then turn left, its fascine undropped, and move parallel with the front line German trench, but on the British side, riddling the trench with bullets. The following tank, some 200 yards behind, would cross the first trench by dropping its fascine, and also turn left, firing from both sides into the first and support trenches. The third tank would drop its fascine into the support trench and follow the others until the lead tank returned to cross the first trench across the dropped fascine, saving its own bundled causeway for a later trench crossing.

These tactics were used throughout the battle, except in the line occupied by the 51st Highland Division, whose commander, bewildered by talk of brushwood and geometric choreography, rejected them as being 'too unmilitary'. His was the only area where the attack failed. To preserve surprise, a preliminary bombardment was eschewed and the entire Tank Corps, of three brigades of three battalions each – 476 tanks in all – was committed. Elles, who led the attack in a tank from the centre – a most unusual gesture from an officer of general's rank in modern warfare – would have preferred to have had his tanks concentrated in depth, rather than spread across the entire 6-mile front. But he had been given his chance and he took it.

The attack began shortly after 6 a.m. and by 1600 hrs the battle was won. The most rapid advance of the entire war had been achieved. A gap some five and half miles deep had been torn through the Hindenburg Line at a cost of 6,000 casualties. Previously, such an advance would have been prefaced by weeks of expensive bombardment and the loss of a quarter of a million men. Alas, the prepared cavalry breakout through the gap was mishandled, the Germans quickly regrouped and, as on so many occasions in the Great War, the advantage was lost. But the tanks had proved themselves. Haig's dispatches recorded that their value had been displayed beyond doubt.

Between Cambrai and the end of the war, tanks were rarely absent from any major Allied attack. The French fought and secured a narrow victory at Soissons in July 1918 and the Germans belatedly attempted to build their own tanks, the A7Vs. But it was too late and, when the Armistice came on 11 November 1918, the General der Infanterie A. W. H. von Zwehl is said to have claimed that his nation was defeated 'not by the genius of Marshal Foch but by "General Tank"'.

The tank's effectiveness had been proven but so too had its vulnerability. Perceptive observers, among them the young military historian Captain Basil Liddell Hart, noted that controlled speed was the key to success. If the tanks moved too slowly, they could be picked off by enemy artillery, particularly when special armour-piercing shells were used. If, on the other hand, they sped ahead too fast and out-distanced their following infantry, the foot soldiers met difficulty in consolidating the territory the tanks had won. Less objective observers had moved not one inch from their view that tanks were ugly, noisy, messy things, lacking the grace and manoeuvrability of cavalry. This type of warfare was not soldiering. If tanks had their place it was in support of the infantry. And, dammit, it was time they *knew* their place!

If this attitude sounds Blimpian and definitively British, it was to find a surprising echo in Germany.

PANZER

The Treaty of Versailles emasculated the German Army. It reduced it in size to 100,000 men, banished a General Staff and forbade the use of tanks. Among the professional German soldiers who survived both the war and the heavy redundancies was a 31-year-old ex-*Jäger* (light infantry) officer who had spent much of the war in signals and then as a general staff officer.

Hauptmann Heinz Guderian had had a full war, serving as a cavalryman, fighting in the trenches and once even acting as an observer in an aeroplane. But he does not record in his war memoirs *Panzer Leader* (Michael Joseph, London, 1952) any personal encounters with tanks, although he was serving along the River Aisne in 1917 when the French's first attack with tanks was summarily repelled by German artillery. Like many young staff officers of the time, however, he was dismayed by the aridity and waste of modern defensive warfare and felt that there had to be a better way. In searching for that way, Guderian was to play the single most important role in the creation of the Panzer concept.

After the Armistice, Guderian spent a difficult period on the old Eastern Front, fighting to restore order against anarchists and communists. At this time he nearly resigned his commission but was saved by an order to return to his old regiment to command an infantry company – the last time for many years that he was to command infantry. An appointment to a motorised transport battalion followed and, then, in 1922 a transfer to the Defence Ministry as part of the Motorised Troops Department. This seemingly gloomy assignment to a desk was the making of him. In the next few years, the junior staff officer (he spent twelve years as a *Hauptmann* or captain) put together all his experience – of the trenches, his months with a cavalry regiment, and his time as a signals specialist – and matched it with his observation of what could be done with modern motorised transport. During this period he began reading prodigiously, particularly the writings of the British tank men, Fuller, Martel and the new guru, Basil Liddell Hart. He became convinced that tanks should form the basis of a new, highly mechanised army, fast-moving and committed to deep attacks through and behind defensive positions. If strongholds could not be taken, they should be bypassed. Guderian was a Prussian and the son of a conservative, conventional army officer, but he was no reactionary. If he had been born 50 years later he would have been called a lateral thinker. He envisaged a total integration of forces to make up his fast-moving columns. Motorised reconnaissance units would scour the territory ahead, the Luftwaffe would dive-bomb strongpoints, self-propelled artillery would protect the tanks which, as the main vanguard of the column, would be served by close-support supply and repair units, and coming along closely in the rear would be the column's own grenadiers and infantry. The keys to the success of these flying columns were command exercised from as far forward as possible, to cope with events as they occurred, and radio to link the elements of the attack together.

Most of this was in the future, but in the twenties this straight-talking, coolly determined junior staff officer seemed to be everywhere, mocking-up cardboard tanks on car chassis for exercises, using his radio expertise to create forward command posts in bouncing motor cars and, once his ideas had been formed, always projecting them: presenting papers, writing monographs, continually proselytising and never fearing to disagree with his superiors. Despite the lessons of Cambrai, the British staff still believed that tanks should be used as infantry support units. Guderian studied exercises in England featuring tanks in this role and found to his dismay that this view was also entrenched among senior officers in the painfully re-emerging Wehrmacht. In 1929, Guderian conducted a field exercise using part of an imaginary armoured division (motor cycles, wooden anti-tank guns and cars with bolted steel plates to simulate tanks), but the Inspector of Transport Troops forbade even the theoretical employment of tanks in units of greater than regimental strength.

Guderian became even more determined. He writes in *Panzer Leader*: 'In this year, 1929, I became convinced that tanks working on their own or in conjunction with infantry could never achieve decisive importance. My historical studies, the exercises carried out in England and our own experiences with mock-ups had persuaded me that tanks would never be able to produce their full effect until the other weapons on whose support they must inevitably rely were brought up to their standard of speed and of cross-country performance. In such a formation of all arms, the tanks must play the primary role, the other weapons being subordinated to the requirements of the armour. It would be wrong to include tanks in infantry divisions: what was needed were armoured divisions which would include all the supporting arms needed to allow the tanks to fight with full effect.'

The ardour with which Guderian expressed these views earned him a reputation as a pushing, over-ambitious officer, albeit an efficient one. His retiring General, Otto von Stülpnagel, told him: 'You're too impetuous. Believe me, neither of us will ever see German tanks in operation in our lifetime.' But the new Inspector of Motorised Troops, General Lutz, who had already promoted Guderian and given him command of a motorised battalion, had long been a convert to the cause. He made Guderian his Chief of Staff and allowed him to develop his ideas, now codified as the creation of Panzer Divisions (*Panzer*: armour, armour plate). In 1933, Guderian had the opportunity of demonstrating the concept to the new Chancellor, Adolf Hitler. At Kummersdorf, he was allowed just half an hour to show how a motor-cycle platoon, an anti-tank platoon, a platoon of tanks and two platoons of armoured reconnaissance units would work together in attack. But it was enough for Hitler to be impressed by the speed and precision of the units. 'That's what I need,' said the Chancellor. 'That's what I want to have.'

It was the breakthrough and by the end of the year, the Chief of the General Staff, Generaloberst Ludwig Beck, agreed to the setting up of two Panzer Divisions, although Guderian wanted three. The agreement was reluctant: 'I don't want to have anything to do with you people,' said Beck. 'You move too fast for me.' And when Guderian explained that, thanks to wireless, even divisional generals could command from forward positions with their troops, the General exploded. 'But you can't command without maps and telephones,' he cried. 'Haven't you ever read Schlieffen?'

Hitler's election as Chancellor – and particularly his acquisition of complete power after Hindenburg's death in 1934 – ended any pretence of adherence to the confines of the Treaty of Versailles. Germany now prepared for war and the modest tank building programme already in place was expanded. Panzer training courses, originated in 1925, were established at a new school in the garrison area of Wünsdorf-Zossen, thirty miles south of Berlin, and tank gunnery was taught separately at Putlos on the Baltic coast.

The original programme of tank construction, begun in the 1920s, had envisaged a 27-ton medium machine (a Panzerkampfwagen Pz Kpfw) armed with a 7.5cm gun, plus a lighter tank fitted with a 3.7cm weapon. This proved difficult to produce and, ironically, it was the British who came to the rescue. Discreetly and indirectly, British Carden-Loyd chassis were purchased and these became the basis for the prototype of a new, 6-ton tank, manufactured by Krupp, styled the Pz1 and intended as a training vehicle. A second, 10-ton model was made by MAN, equipped with a 2cm cannon and a coaxial machine-gun, and these two machines were used to equip the first panzer regiments forming at Zossen and Ohrdruf. By the end of 1934, six panzer regiments (four battalions of four companies, with 32 tanks each) were raised and incorporated into three panzer divisions. The following year, a panzertruppen command was established, so creating the panzer grenadiers.

The pace of armoured development now increased through the thirties. Despite Hitler's patronage, it was hampered by manufacturing difficulties and, still, opposition from within the German High Command, not least from the cavalry, but a raft of tank protagonists were coming forward to argue the cause – von Kleist, von Manstein, Hoepner and the young Rommel among them – and the number of panzer divisions had increased to five by the end of 1938, with a sixth forming. In 1937, Guderian, now a major-general and still encouraged by his mentor, Lutz, had published a book, *Achtung, Panzer!* This delineated the panzer approach and, the following year he developed this further with a long article which appeared in the journal of the National Union of German Officers. It is significant for its evangelical language – revealing the resistance to the idea which still permeated the German High Command – and also for its Prussian air of certainty and Hitlerian note of impatience. Extracts (from *Panzer Leader*) reveal both the tone and the core philosophy:

'...the chances of an offensive based on the timetable of artillery and infantry co-operation are even slighter today than they were in the last war. Everything is therefore dependent on this: to be able to move faster than has hitherto been done; to keep moving, despite the enemy's defensive fire and thus to make it harder for him to build up fresh defensive positions: and finally to carry the attack deep into the enemy's defences.'

On the need to drive a hole quickly through defences so that reserves can pour through:

'We want these reserves to be available in the form of Panzer Divisions, since we no longer believe that other formations have the fighting ability, the speed and the manoeuvrability necessary for full exploitation of the attack and break-through.

'We will in no circumstances agree to time-wasting artillery preparation and the consequent danger of losing the element of surprise, simply because the old maxim says that "only fire can open the way to movement". We believe, on the contrary, that the combination of the internal combustion engine and armour plate enable us to take our fire to the enemy without any artillery preparation, provided always the important conditions for such an operation are fulfilled: suitable terrain, surprise and maximum commitment.'

These conditions were ideally provided when Hitler decided to attack Poland in 1939. At dawn on 1 September, two German Army Groups crashed across the Polish Frontier. Spearheading both Groups were two panzer corps: XIX, led by Guderian, in the north, and XVI, commanded by General (later Field Marshal) Paul von Kleist, in the south. Both Groups – but definitively Guderian's, for von Kleist was more cautious – employed the *Blitzkrieg* tactics devised by Guderian in the preceding months he had spent as Chief of Mobile Troops and General of Panzer Troops.

The corps were led by reconnaissance forces, usually armoured cars on the main roads and motor-cycle units on the side tracks, accompanied by artillery observation officers and forward air controllers. These units were in close radio contact with their commander, travelling just behind the vanguard of his tanks, and the mobile artillery and the corps' own support aircraft. The latter were usually the new Stuka Junkers Ju 87 dive-bombers, which dived vertically from about 15,000 feet before releasing their bombs – usually with remarkable accuracy – at 3,000 feet. The Stukas and the self-propelled guns were mobilised to concentrate on the strong-points encountered in the great sweep forward, blitzing them in a concentrated bombardment and leaving them to be mopped up by the panzer grenadiers and troops in the rear, while the tanks swept forward to attack lines of communication and cut off troops behind the lines.

The Poles, with little armour – and what they had mostly split up ineffectually among infantry divisions – fought with great bravery but they were overwhelmed. Outnumbered anyway, the speed, concentration and ferocity of the attack took them by surprise and their fate was sealed when Russia, acting in secretly prepared agreement with Hitler, struck from the east. On the 27th day of the campaign, Warsaw fell and the campaign was over. The watching world recoiled in horror. Nothing quite like this kind of warfare had been seen before. It was as though Napoleon had been reincarnated and given modern technology to play with.

Overwhelming though it was, the Polish victory had not been without its lessons for the Germans. The war machine had not operated as smoothly as Guderian, for one, would have wished. He had been the only general to go into action just behind his lead tanks, commanding from an open car, equipped with radio, coding and de-coding machines, typewriters and protective armour. The tanks, the early Pz Kpfw I and II, had proved to be under-gunned and too lightly armoured, and the infantry too slow in following the tanks. This time, however, Guderian was not a lone voice. The Commander-in-Chief of the German Army, Walter von Brauchitsch, had always encouraged motorised developments and changes were put in hand immediately.

Improved Pz Kpfw III tanks, with thicker armour and a heavier 5cm gun, were introduced, as were the Pz Kpfw IV models, which were to prove the great armoured work-horses of the German army throughout the war, although their new, long-barrelled 7.5cm guns could not be fitted in great numbers until 1942. Few armoured personnel carriers had been available to carry the motorised infantry, and overloaded standard trucks had limped along behind the tanks. New APCs were now produced, carrying better armour as protection for their passengers, and these were to bestow much greater speed and mobility on the motorised infantry which were so vital a part of the panzer divisions.

Not all the necessary improvements were in place, nor were sufficient tanks available to give Germany superiority in armour over the Allies when Hitler chose to attack next, in May 1940. The combined Anglo-French forces in the west had just under 4,000 armoured vehicles. The Germans had 2,800, including armoured reconnaissance cars and, when the attack was launched, only 2,200 of these were available. French tanks on paper were superior to the Germans' both in armour and gun calibre. In the event, however, operating usually in support of non-motorised infantry, they proved to be no match for the panzers.

The cohesion and self-sufficiency of a typical panzer division is illustrated by the war establishment of 1st Panzer Division, in Guderian's XIX Corps, on 9 May 1940. It comprised: one panzer brigade of four tank battalions, plus a supply unit; one rifle brigade, made up of motorised troops, including a motor-cycle battalion and special machine-gun companies; an anti-tank battalion; an armoured reconnaissance battalion, containing armoured cars and motor-cycle companies; an artillery regiment; an anti-air-craft battalion; a signals battalion; an engineer battalion; an air reconnaissance squadron of nine aircraft; a supply battalion and an administrative service section. It was a highly mobile and almost self-contained miniature army. Napoleon would have been delighted with it.

In fact, these divisions were rarely fully equipped. German industry never became geared to meet the demands of total warfare as presented by the vastly expanded panzer divisions, the Luftwaffe and the U-boat fleets. Whatever they lacked in machinery, however, the German forces now poised to attack France were far superior in terms of leadership, tactics and determination than the Allied armies facing them.

After the *longueurs* of the 'Phoney War', the German attack which began the Battle of France was stunning in its force and speed. Ten panzer divisions, deployed into three army groups, led the attack. In all, the Germans had 120 divisions opposed to 83 French, nine British, 22 Belgian and ten Dutch divisions. The Allies had an advantage in armour, but the Luftwaffe quickly attacked French airfields, destroying hundreds of aircraft on the ground, so gaining air superiority.

The Allies, still thinking in terms of the past, had anticipated that the Germans would attack, as before, through neutral Belgium. When, therefore, von Bock's Army Group 'B' attacked over the Dutch and Belgian borders, the main French and British forces moved north-east to face the threat. But Bock's move was only a feint (for all that, it was to prove a most successful operation in its own right) and the main attack came from von Runstedt's Army Group, centred on the Ardennes, which was supposed to be impassable by tanks. The third group, Army Group 'C' (von Leeb) huffed and puffed in front of the Maginot Line along the extended German border, sufficiently convincingly to keep large French forces committed there.

The tactics first tentatively tried in the Spanish Civil War and honed in Poland worked impressively well. This time the opposition was equal in numbers and, indeed, superior in armour, but the breakthrough was incisive. The French and British armour was distributed in First World War 'penny packets' in support of non-motorised infantry across the widest of fronts. In contrast, the panzer divisions were powerful concentrations of armour with close Luftwaffe support and they forced crossings of the River Meuse and struck west through France, punching deep holes in the French defences. The corridors they created were filled by motorised and then marching infantry, freeing the armour to sweep on towards the Channel ports, cutting off the British Expeditionary Force and, with von Bock's infantry moving through Holland and Belgium, encircling large contingents of the French army.

The advance of the panzers was so rapid across the northern plains of France that the lead tanks of von Ravenstein's Battle Group swept into Le Catelet on 18 May and captured the entire staff of the French Ninth army in a hotel in the town square. Had they been half an hour earlier, they were told, they would have bagged Marshal Pétain too. Similarly, Guderian's 2nd Panzer Division captured a British battery in the town square of Albert. The battery was only equipped with training ammunition because their commander believed they were too far behind the lines to be in action that day.

Holland had fallen almost immediately to an attack led by paratroops and glider troops and the Belgian troops put up little resistance, surrendering on 28 May. Much of northern France was occupied by 24 May and the British Expeditionary Force was penned into a pocket round Calais and Dieppe and totally cut off from its Atlantic coast bases at Cherbourg and Brest. It was now that Hitler made a mistake which was to cost him dear later in the war. Impressed but made nervous by the speed of his armour, he held back his tanks from delivering what must have been the *coup de grâce* to the beleaguered British force. He told Guderian that he wished to preserve his tanks from fighting among the ditches of Belgium. But the General believed that Hitler drew back to allow the Luftwaffe to defeat the British on its own. It failed and 320,000 men somehow got back to England aboard the 'Little Ships' fleet. They were to form the nucleus of the army which was to return to Normandy four years later.

So Hitler missed the chance of making Britain completely defenceless before mounting his Operation 'Sealion', the invasion across the Channel. The moment never returned. Göring failed to gain air superiority and the operation was dismounted, the panzers benefiting merely by the introduction of amphibious tanks which were to prove useful in crossing Russian rivers. For it was to the east that Hitler now looked, horrifying the older generals on his staff (he assumed the title of Commander-in-Chief of the army himself on December 1941) by revealing his intention of attacking Russia and so resuming the First World War burden of a war on two fronts.

It seemed, at that time, as though Adolf Hitler could do no wrong and that, in military terms, his Midas touch was conveyed through his panzer divisions. When his erstwhile mentor, Benito Mussolini, began an ill-prepared war of conquest in the Balkans, Hitler came to his aid and once again the panzers made lightning advances. The 2nd Panzer Division swept from Novo Selo to Salonika and during the advance the entire Macedonian Army surrendered to the 2nd Division. Similarly, when Mussolini ran into trouble in North Africa following the defeat of his army by the British Western Desert Force, ten times smaller in number, the Führer created the Afrika Korps and gave it two panzer divisions. Under its brilliant general, Erwin Rommel, this tank-led force swept the British back almost to the Suez Canal. It was later to bend the knee in turn to superior and better-equipped British and American armies, but not before it had shown just how formidable these German tank commanders had become.

For the first time the men who actually commanded the tanks individually began to be lionised in Germany. The speed of their campaigns and the invincible way they had swept across the plains of Poland and France and then the sand dunes of Libya had caught the imagination of the German nation and, of course, the Goebbels propaganda machine leaped into action. Pictures and posters of the new 'Knights of Our Times' appeared everywhere, showing lean jawed young men, in their distinctive black uniforms and rakish berets, riding high in their turrets – swashbucklers in casual control of their monstrous machines.

Nor were these young men taken lightly by their superiors. At first, the main route for tank commanders lay through the cavalry. But, as the panzer divisions expanded and the requisite qualities became refined, so recruits were welcomed from all sections of the motorised army. Non-commissioned officers became tank commanders and even section and company leaders. Promotion from within the tank crews was also encouraged and such promotion could be spectacularly quick, once the Russian campaign began to exercise its grim toll.

From the outset, the Germans fostered the sense of team spirit which was vital in bringing out the best in five men crouched in a noisy, smelly, steel shell. The stiff formality usually attributed to an army still led at the top by Prussian officers is not much in evidence in these first four 'leadership requirements' laid down in an early German Panzertruppe manual:

1.   A leader is one who makes followers of his troops through his ability, conduct and character.
2.   Willingness to accept responsibility is the most outstanding leadership quality. This must not be allowed, however, to lead to arbitrary decisions made without regard for the whole. Priggishness must not be allowed to take the place of obedience or independence permitted to become arbitrariness.
3.   In addition to physical and military training, it is moral and emotional strength which determines a soldier's worth in combat. Increasing this worth is the task of soldierly education.
4.   Comradeship is the tie which binds the troops together in any situation. Each man is responsible not only for himself but for his comrades as well. Those who are more able or capable must assist and guide the inexperienced and weak. From such a basis grows a feeling of close comradeship, which is as important between leader and soldier as it is between the men of the unit.

These admonitions, while perhaps ponderous in their phrasing, are also touching in their anxiety to inculcate care for others. It is clear that panzer commanders recognised that their new type of warfare needed rather special kinds of men to carry it out successfully. These young men were to be tested to the full in the Russian campaign, Operation 'Barbarossa', which was launched by Hitler at 0300 hrs on 22 June 1941.

Most historians now agree that, despite the importance of the campaigns in North Africa, Italy and Normandy, and the battles fought in the skies over Europe and on the waters of the North Atlantic, Hitler's war was won and lost in Russia. Hitler grossly under-estimated the size of the Soviet army and its ability to absorb punishment from the best and, until then, most successful army in the world. He launched the attack with 153 divisions – only 140 of which were actually German – and 3,417 tanks. He estimated that the Soviet Union possessed 150 infantry divisions, of which fifteen were motorised, 32 cavalry divisions and 36 motorised brigades. They had, he believed, some 10,000 tanks. It didn't take long to discover how wrong he had been. Within four months, some 360 Russian divisions had been identified. And yet at first it seemed as though another panzer triumph was in prospect.

The campaign was launched, with the by now customary complete surprise, with armoured thrusts from three army groups. Army Group North was commanded by von Leeb and, led by Hoepner's 4th Panzer Army, had Leningrad as its objective. Army Group Centre, under the command of von Bock, had two panzer groups, led by Guderian and Hoth respectively, and was given Moscow as a (vague) directive. Von Runstedt's Army Group South, had von Kleist's First Panzer Army in the van and was targeted towards Kiev and Rostov. It was a remarkably ambitious, even amateurish, plan. The distances involved, both in terms of length of front as well as depth of penetration demanded, was prodigious. The objectives lay hundreds of miles away and their distance from one another meant that the nearer the individual army groups got to them, the much more would they be operating independently with little chance of support from their neighbours. That this demanding plan nearly succeeded, once again speaks volumes for the ability of the tank commanders who led the attacks.

The strongest German forces were concentrated in the centre and here progress was rapid. Smolensk was taken on 15 July, bringing the panzers to within 200 miles of Moscow. By this time, Army Group North was advancing on Leningrad and Army Group South was threatening Kiev, the capital of the Ukraine. Within three weeks, the tanks and support troops had advanced some 700 miles. In the first two weeks alone, more than 300,000 prisoners had been taken and 3,000 tanks destroyed as a result of the classic panzer tactics of quick penetration and encirclement. The Russians, who had large masses of troops in forward positions, had been taken completely by surprise. Their forward tank units were inexperienced, they lacked time and experience to group properly and fell easy prey to the panzers. The Russian Marshal Pavlov was executed for incompetence. By September, however, as the penetrations had the effect of broadening the front, Hitler was forced to amend his plans.

Guderian's panzers were diverted to help Army Group South in its attack on the Donetz industrial area, and Hoth's Third Panzer Army was also partly switched from the centre to aid von Leeb's investiture of Leningrad. In the south, the move succeeded and Kiev was taken, with thousands of prisoners and much booty. Then von Kleist's First Panzer Army crossed the Dnieper and took Rostov, the gateway to the Caucasus and its much coveted oilfields. There the penetration ended, however, and von Kleist was forced back to the River Mius. In the north, Leningrad held out grimly (it was never to fall), so Hitler resumed the central thrust towards Moscow. But the Russian winter now approached and rain, frost and snow bogged down the tanks and the motorised columns. By now, Russian resistance had hardened perceptibly. Shortened lines of communication meant that winter supplies and equipment could be brought up quickly, reinforcements were pouring forward from the Soviet Union's deep resources, Russian morale was stiffening – not least because of the stories of atrocities being perpetrated on Russian prisoners and the civilian population by the German *Reichscommissars* – and, significantly, the Soviet T34 tanks now being deployed were showing themselves a match for the German Pz Kpfw III and IV. By December, panzer divisions had reached to within twenty miles of Moscow, but they could penetrate no farther.

Hitler had gambled all on accomplishing the destruction of the Soviet Union within a three-month summer campaign. As a result, his troops lacked the vital components with which to fight a winter war: warm clothing, anti-freeze for tanks and mechanised transport, and a sophisticated supply line with which to keep the army in the field along a front which stretched for 2,000 miles. The initial *Blitzkreig* was over, but the Germans were by no means yet defeated on their eastern front. The war settled down into a heroic struggle between two comparatively evenly matched sides. As the massive Russian production machine slipped into gear, however, the scales inevitably began to tip in favour of the Soviet Union. A counter-offensive in defence of Moscow saw Guderian forced to fall back, in defiance of a 'stand or die' order from Hitler. He was quickly retired – not the last time this would happen to a general on the Russian front. Both sides suffered in the severe winter of 1941/2 and both made strenuous efforts to re-arm and re-equip, the Germans improving the armour of their Pz Kpfw IVs and up-gunning them. More importantly, in 1942 the first of the new 60-ton Tiger tanks, designed to out-gun the T34s, began to trickle to the front.

In the spring of 1942, the Russians counter-attacked across most of the front. The Germans on the whole held firm and then, in June, launched their own offensive in the south. This was to prove the last hurrah of the *Blitzkrieg* and at first it seemed as if the clock had been turned back. The tanks rolled across the plains towards the Caucasian oilfields and Stalingrad, cutting down all before them. Then Hitler interfered and made redeployments which delayed the advance and enabled the Russians to re-group. Stalingrad itself was an important manufacturing centre, but it was not as vital as the oilfields beyond it. Yet Hitler insisted on its investment and Stalin, in turn, saw it as the symbolic point of Russian resistance. For eight months both nations poured virtually all their resources into what became a titanic struggle of artillery duels and hand-to-hand combat in the streets. It became Germany's second Verdun. Short of provisions and ammunition, the besieging Germans in turn became encircled. On 2 February 1943, having suffered some 120,000 casualties, Field Marshal Friedrich Paulus surrendered with 24 generals and 91,000 men.

It was a shattering defeat and it set up the greatest tank battle of the war, at Kursk. It is time to look at the type of man who will fight there and who had been largely responsible for taking the panzer divisions to their tragic tryst on the southern Russian steppe.

THE 'KNIGHT OF OUR TIMES'

By 4 July 1943, on the eve of the great battle of Kursk, *Unteroffizier* Hans Muller is tired. He has been fighting in tanks on the Russian front for exactly two years and now, as he bivouacs beside his Tiger, on the edge of a remote plains village just south of Orel, he counts himself lucky to be alive. In the morning he may not be. He leads a platoon of four tanks in 505 Heavy Panzer Battalion, part of Field Marshal Walter Model's Ninth Army, which is due to attack tomorrow from the north to cut off the Kursk Salient. It's all to be part of Operation 'Citadel', but he doesn't much care what fancy name they've given it. He's been in so many Operations. They all now come down to dog-fights with other tanks or scraps with dug-in anti-tank guns. The last are the worst, because you can't always see the gun.

Muller is sitting on the ground, leaning against the knobbly tracks of his Tiger, reflectively sipping coffee from a tin mug. He is a small man, which helps in the confined interior of a tank, but the only noticeable feature about him are his eyes. He is only 22 but these are the eyes of an older man: always narrowed, they seem strained and wary. They look about him now but note little to impinge on a brain still weary from the strain of leading his four tanks for days on end. There are a few low peasant huts, some stunted trees and the never-ending plain. Nothing like the sylvan settings of those 1938 cigarette cards which showed laughing tank crews lounging under willows by a stream in 'Summer Bivouac'. Muller glances towards the setting sun. It will be an early start tomorrow, of course, an hour before dawn. They won't have the luxury of attacking with the sun behind them this time but there will be plenty of dust.

Dust ... that always reminds him of his first campaign, when he had set off two years ago with 'Hurrying Heinz' Guderian near Brest-Litovsk to invade Russia. That was Operation 'Barbarossa' – there's another fancy name for you – and young recruits have often asked him what it had been like, that great advance: cutting through the Russian infantry and old tanks like a knife through *Wiener Schnitzel*, rolling up the kilometres day after day in the hot sun. And the dust!. He had been a loader then, which meant the worst seat in the tank, sitting uncomfortably by the gun with his back to the advance, not seeing anything but choking with the dust, despite wrapping his mother's old scarf round his mouth. So, to him, that had not been a glorious campaign, just the most uncomfortable three weeks of his life.

Having said that – Muller tips the coffee dregs away and tosses the cup to his loader – the dust and heat was better than the cold of 41/42. Reactively, he pulls at his jacket collar, although it is not at all cold. He is dressed now in a well-worn, two-piece mouse-grey overall, worn over his panzer uniform. The exaggeratedly full beret of the propaganda posters has long since gone and been replaced by a serviceable peaked cap. In fact, he is over-dressed for the current climate. But even in mid-summer the nights on the Russian steppe can be cold and you never know.

The winter of '42 had nearly killed him and his fellow crewmen. Even by mid-January, they were still dressed in their thin denim summer uniforms and cotton underwear. Rumour had it that, despite his junior rank, Guderian had flown back to Berlin to protest personally to the Führer about it. Not that that had done any good. They survived by digging the tanks into the ground as best they could during the night, lighting a paraffin lamp inside the tank (strictly forbidden) and keeping a fire kindled under the engine. It was risky but it was the only way of preventing the 120-litre radiator from freezing, for there was no issue of anti-freeze liquid. They were in constant dread of running down the battery and not being able to re-start. An immobile tank is a vulnerable tank and dependent upon that battery were the radio equipment, the inner and outer lights, the ventilator and the electric ignition for the gun. Starting by hand required two men getting out to crank the engine with a tool similar to that used to start old aircraft – or, if you were lucky, getting a push start from another tank in the platoon.

Muller swings himself up on to the body of the tank and, with a practised movement on to the turret and then down through the cupola. He stands for a moment, his head and shoulders protruding through the top. The Tiger has improved since its introduction. For instance, its cupola hatch used to stand up vertically when opened, so that, if it were left that way, a high-explosive shell bursting overhead would be diverted downwards by the 'lid' on to the commander's head. Now the hatch swings right down flush with the turret top, though the commander can feel very exposed during the moment when he must lean over to close it.

Muller now feels that he knows the Tiger well. He was lucky to be selected, back in 1942, to go on the first training courses with the prototype Tigers in Normandy. Lucky because he had no officer's braid to give him preferment. Impressed by the glamour of the posters and of what he had read of the Battle of France, he had volunteered for the panzers and been selected because of his experience as a motor mechanic. From loader he had progressed to driver and then to tank commander. Strange, it was usually the drivers who became commanders, rarely the gunners; probably because the drivers often had to act instinctively in battle, positioning the tank before the commander had time to give the orders. Good drivers, then, usually developed a sense of tank tactics, and, he smiled to himself, he *had* been a good driver.

Sitting in his familiar seat in the commander's cupola, Muller makes a final check. Below him, to his right, on the far side of the gun breech which dominates the interior, sits the loader, beside whom hangs the canvas sling which catches the shell cases. In front, glued to his eye pieces when in action, sits the gunner and, one step down and farther forward, the driver, and the radio operator who also serves the forward machine-gun. Beside Muller's head in the turret are clipped hand-grenades and demolition charges. He has taken out one of the charges and the empty clip holder neatly takes his schnapps bottle. Priorities are important in war!

The prevailing impression, sitting inside the commander's cupola with the lid closed, is one of claustrophobic loss of the outside world. There is a periscope, and eight vision slits, each about eight millimetres deep, run horizontally around the cupola. They are narrow to prevent shrapnel coming in, but this means that only by pressing one's face close against the steel does one get any view – and this is inevitably restricted. Sight, of course, is all-important. Sound plays no part in tank warfare – except that all messages from outside, and most of the conversation and commands within the tank, are relayed by radio. The earphones and the noise of engine and tracks cuts off other sound from the exterior. Nor would the report of an anti-tank gun be of much use if they could hear it; the shell would have already arrived. No, vision is all-important and that is why Muller and his colleagues prefer to keep the lid open as long as possible, to optimise the chances of seeing the low outline of a dug-in T34 or the long barrel of an anti-tank gun peeping through foliage before they come into range.

But given the way the Russian campaign has developed, this is a luxury mostly denied them once they are in action. Then, their Tiger becomes an all-embracing universe in which they live, travel, fight and – at times – defecate. During the 41/42 winter campaign, Muller carried out his ablutions outside the tank only after dark. The smells during the day added to the noise, cold and general discomfort in the stuffy interior of the tank, but it was better than being dead. 'Outside' in the combat zone was dangerous. This proved literally so for four infantrymen to whom Muller's commander in that campaign gave a lift. They had climbed on to the rear deck of their panzer III, and were found dead on arrival at base. They had sat on top of the cooling vents where warm air was expelled from the engine and had all succumbed to carbon-monoxide poisoning from the exhaust fumes. Yes, to a tank man, 'outside' is hostile, alien territory.

As Muller's eye wanders around inside the cupola it catches sight of a tattered booklet tucked behind one of the demolition charges. He extracts it, opens it at random and smiles. It is the Tiger's training manual which was belatedly issued to commanders long after the first tanks had gone into action. In fact, as Muller remembers only too well, not even technical instruction books were available to the crews when first the Tigers went into battle at Leningrad (unsuccessfully, thanks to Hitler's impatience in hurrying his new weapon into action before it was ready). After the first Tiger was captured by the Russians, they issued to their own tank and anti-tank crews a Russian instruction manual defining the strong and weak points of the new enemy tank. Capturing this in turn, the German Tiger commanders translated it and found it immensely useful in understanding and handling their new vehicles!

Now Muller leafs again through the training manual. In its way, it is a kind of breakthrough for this kind of German material. It uses a mixture of photographs, humorous drawings, mottos, technical passages and straightforward prose but it is the American-style but ponderous cartoons and mottos which now cause Muller's face to slip from smile to frown as he flips over the soiled pages. On re-fuelling: 'fill it, don't spill it'. On firing: 'the way Max Schmeling throws his right, you throw the shells in a fight'. On vehicle care: 'one thinks, when a track chain rips, if only I'd looked after it!'

To Muller, the banal phrasing is an insult to fighting men. It's typical of the Goebbels domination of every level of formal communication in the Third Reich: superficial, slick and demeaning. Muller, like many – but by no means all – of his fellow tank commanders, no longer believes that the war can be won. He has lost his former solid confidence in Hitler as the saviour of Germany. True, the Führer had done magnificent work in taking Germany out of the recession and in rebuilding the economy, and the war in the west had had to be waged to redeem the disgrace of Versailles. But it had been a mistake to attack Russia and even Muller has heard mutterings about Hitler's disastrous interference in purely military affairs. Muller is no Prussian but he believes that the German army has proved itself the best in the world and the generals should be left to fight the battles. Although he has never served under him, the commander Muller respects most is Rommel, an infantryman who has become a great panzer general. Now, Rommel's magnificent Afrika Korps has been forced to surrender in Tunisia and, it is rumoured, Rommel had flown home to persuade the Führer to negotiate peace.

A particular bone of contention to Muller and his Wehrmacht officers is the preferential treatment now being given to the special SS panzer divisions. These have been created by Hitler to serve directly under the overall command of SS chief Heinrich Himmler, as a counter-balance to the Army. As the war has continued, so Hitler's paranoia about the loyalty of the traditional Wehrmacht has increased. As a result, the black-and-silver regiments have come into being, as a kind of private army within an army, designed to house officers and men whose loyalty is as much to the Nazi Party as to the fatherland. The trouble is that these SS divisions are now tending to receive the better equipment and weapons. They certainly take priority in terms of the new Tigers. And, of course, as with Hitler, Himmler never comes to the front to see action for himself.

Muller makes to throw the manual out of the cupola, then, shrugs and places it back behind the demolition charge. The thing might make an amusing souvenir after the war – if he survives. He stands to look ahead, over the familiar outline of the Tiger. If he lives to see the end of the war, he will owe it to the long barrel protruding before him, the great 8.8cm gun of the Tiger. For the first time the Panzers can take on the Russian T34s and T43s on equal – if not advantageous - terms. Before, Muller and his brothers, fighting in their ubiquitous but out-gunned Pz Kpfw IIIs and IVs, had to rely on the greater experience and skills of their crews to outwit the Russians. By 1941, the panzer commanders had become the best in the world. Their experience in the widely differing conditions of Poland, the Battle of France and the Russian campaigns, plus the very priority they received in most battle plans, had honed their skills to an extent not matched by the tank men of the Allies – even though, for much of this time, it was they who had the best tanks and equipment.

To stay alive, Muller and his like had had to think faster, fire more quickly and more accurately, and move with greater alacrity. They had also had to improvise. A colleague of his, Unteroffizier Hermann Bix, kept a Russian fur hat in his tank. Once, in unknown territory at night, in his open cupola, wearing his captured hat, he was waved carefully over a difficult bridge by a Russian sentry. Muller himself always reversed the peak of his distinctive cap when conning his tank through a battle zone at night.

In those pre-Tiger days, the panzers had one advantage over the Russians. All the German tanks had a five-man crew, the Russians only four.

This meant that the Soviet tank commander had to double up as gunner, so despite being out-ranged and usually out-armoured, the German crews could fire more quickly and accurately.

As platoon leader, Muller's job is to get his four tanks into the best position to attack a defined enemy. He prefers to attack in a wedge-shaped formation, but when moving up, they travel closed up in single file. (This will not be so later, in the Normandy campaign, when Allied air superiority will force the Tigers to space themselves out.) In the heat of battle, however, he has to revert, perforce, to tank commander, giving directions to the driver, feeding him information about the terrain and taking the tank to the best position for firing. Like most of his comrades, Muller prefers the tank to be stationary when firing, so as to give the gunner a better chance. But it is his job to decide the target and ammunition to be used – usually high-explosive (against infantry and anti-tank guns) or armour-piercing (against tanks or armoured anti-tank guns). The key to success is speed and precision. It is something which Muller has had to learn the hard way.

He has had many narrow escapes. The crash of an armour-piercing shell hitting the tank is unnerving enough, but its entry is catastrophic. There is little chance against a direct hit, but equally dangerous are the splinters of steel and rivets – the 'flashings' – flying about within the confined space of the tank hull and turret. The greatest danger is if the fuel tanks are hit, resulting in the tank 'brewing up' in a ball of flame, which was the reason for the constant practising of 'abandon tank!' back in training at Paderborn.

But Muller is philosophical. If it happens tomorrow – it happens. He climbs out of the cupola as the sun at last slips below the plain and spreads its red glow along the horizon. He walks once more round the machine, looks carefully at the tracks and then, giving the tank an affectionate kick, goes off to the barn to have his evening meal. He has done all he can. The rest is up to Providence – and his Tiger.

TIGER!

In the spring of 1941, when the Germano-Russian honeymoon was still a warm reality after the successful division of Poland between the two aggressors, Hitler allowed a Soviet military mission to visit Germany and be shown over tank manufacturing plants and training schools. Despite the imminence of his attack on Russia, he gave instructions that nothing should be withheld from the visitors. At the end of the visit, the Russians complained that German heavy tank production had been hidden from them. The truth was, however, that there was no German heavy tank, either on production line or drawing-board. Germany was relying completely on the Pz Kpfw III and IV medium tanks.

These performed extremely well until, several months after the invasion, they encountered the Russian T34, arguably the most successful all-round tank of the Second World War. Designed in 1939, this medium tank, mechanically simple and capable of mass production, was fast, mobile and diesel-engined, which gave it greater range than its German counter-parts – a vital factor in the immensity of Russia. Between 1941 and 1945, 39,698 were built, representing 68 per cent of Soviet tank output. They showed their real worth for the first time on 6 October 1941 when 4th Panzer Division was savaged just south of Mzensk. The T34s had rounded turrets (ironically, produced on German hydraulic presses delivered just before the war) off which the shells from the short-barrelled 7.5cm cannon of the Pz Kpfw IV were deflected. They and the later, improved T43 models, were armed with long-barrelled 7.62cm guns and the only way the IV could be sure of destroying a T34 was by hitting it in the rear. Only the introduction of the long-barrelled German 7.5cm and the greater skills of the panzer commanders made it a contest.

It was clear that the Germans needed a heavy tank – and quickly. In late 1941 the well-established firms of Porsche and Henschel were ordered to develop competitive prototypes for a 43-ton tank. Competitive development programmes were wasteful and the time-scale imposed was ludicrously short, but it was met. Henschel won the contest and Porsche's designs were converted to carry self-propelled guns. The first pre-production vehicle left the factory in August 1942 and a half-company of Tigers was rushed into combat at Leningrad in September.

The Tiger had grown into a comparative monster of 60 tons, mainly because the main armament had been increased to a long-barrelled gun of 8.8cm, with consequent growth in turret size, superstructure and track width. Compared to other tanks in service at the time, the Tiger I was outstandingly well armed and protected; the gun was mounted in a fully traversing turret and it was the first German tank to carry armour of a greater thickness than 50mm. With Russian rivers in mind, the first 400 models were made to be fully submersible, with a collapsible telescopic snorkel tube fitted to the rear engine deck. In this and in many other ways, the Tiger was to influence European tank design for many years after the war.

The model (Tiger I, or Type E) which Hans Muller was to take into action at Kursk still had to win its great reputation against the enemy. But Muller and his colleagues knew that they had a formidable machine. There had been time to eliminate some of the faults detected at Leningrad, but the vertical steel plates, which did nothing to deflect armour-piercing shells, remained; later they would be replaced by sloping panels. Petrol consumption was still high and the radius of action consequently limited, but the tank was easy to drive and operate.

Before the coming of the Tiger, it took a lot of strength to steer a panzer tank. The newcomer, however, had a steering wheel, power-assisted steering and, with his finger-tips, the driver could shift 700bhp and steer 60 tons. The V12 cylinder petrol engine performed best at 2,600rpm, for at 3,000 it soon became hot. Top speed was 45kph on roads and 20 cross-country. The transmission functioned semi-automatically and had eight forward and four reverse gears, which could be pre-selected. A steering gear enabled the power to be removed from one track and transferred to the other, so enabling the tank to turn almost on its own axis. The overlapping suspension had eight axles on each side, each axle being attached to three road wheels which ran on the track.

Larger tanks would be fielded before the war's end – in fact, Hitler developed a fixation with them – but the Tiger's overall dimensions were impressive, mainly because of the great 8.8cm gun. With the barrel lined fore and aft, the tank's overall length was 8.2 metres; hull width 1.8 metres; overall track width 3.7 metres. Firing height, however, was comparatively low at 2.2 metres. The tank could span ditches of 2.3 metres and climb a gradient of 35 degrees.

Both specification and performance were good for its day, but the Tiger was also well armoured and – its main asset – extremely well armed. Armour thickness ranged from 110 to 90mm at the front of the turret to 26mm at hull top and bottom. The long 8.8cm gun produced a muzzle velocity of 810mps, throwing a 10kg anti-tank shell which could penetrate 82mm of armour at 2,500 metres' range. A good Tiger gunner felt that he could destroy a T34 at 900 metres if he caught it right.

The gunners loved the Tiger. Their feet rested on a tilting platform. If they pressed the tip of the foot towards the front, the turret turned to the right. If they pressed with their sole to the back, it revolved left. The harder the platform was pressed, the quicker the turret turned. The movement was not fast. At its slowest, the 360-degree revolution took an astounding 60 minutes; at its fastest, 60 seconds. It was, therefore, extremely sensitive and the electric ignition system ensured that the slightest pressure of the finger fired the round, thereby eliminating inaccuracies resulting from the gunner snatching at the trigger.

The secondary armament consisted of two MG34 7.92mm machine-guns, fitted in the turret for the commander and in the hull where the radio-operator also acted as gunner; the commander also had a machine-pistol. These MGs were not decorative toys. (Other heavy tanks were produced without such secondary armament – much to the chagrin of Guderian, recalled by Hitler from enforced retirement in March 1943 to be Inspector-General of Armoured Troops and, later, to be Chief of the Army General Staff. They proved vulnerable to close attacks by infantry and reverted to becoming virtually self-propelled artillery.) The machine-guns, then, were vital for close-quarter fighting. A Tiger carried between 3,920 and 4,500 MG rounds and 92 anti-tank or high-explosive shells.

Such a sophisticated machine carried with it the kind of endemic problems with which we are familiar in today's computer age. There were more and more complicated things to go wrong. In fact, there were so many breakdowns in the Tiger's early days that it was nicknamed 'The Furniture Van' by its crews and service engineers. The servicing demands were exigent. The main engine held 28 litres of oil, the transmission 30 litres, the reduction gears 12 litres, the tread power system five litres and the ventilation motors seven litres. The latter were vital. According to Otto Carius (*Tigers in the Mud*, J. J. Fedorowicz Publishing Inc., Winnipeg, 1962), on a move of only seven kilometres, 170,000 litres of air was sucked into the engine. In the arid conditions of the Russian plains in mid-summer, the dust of almost four acres of land was stirred up by one Tiger. Air filter cleaning was therefore necessary before every move.

There is no doubt that the Tiger, formidable though it appeared and impressive as its reputation became with the Allies, contained faults which put even greater strains upon its commander and crew. In particular, it had limited range and its heavy armour and armament meant that it was not a fast tank. Each Tiger cost approximately half a million marks to put into commission. This, plus the complications of its design and the many other demands on German's industry, meant that only 1,995 of all types were produced, of which 1,350 were Tiger Is. This compared with the 6,000 Pz Kpfw IIIs manufactured. The Tiger, then, was definitely an 'élite' tank. Much was expected of it and of its commanders. The Battle of Kursk was to be its first and greatest test.

THE KILLING FIELDS OF KURSK

The Battle of Kursk lasted ten days and was fought during July 1943 on a central/southern sector of the long Russian front, some 200 miles south of Moscow. It developed into the largest tank battle ever fought, involving more than 5,000 tanks, some 4,000 aircraft and more than two million men. It proved to be the turning-point of the Russian campaign and must, then, be regarded also as the turning-point of the Second World War.

Stalingrad had been a bitter defeat for Hitler but it did not quite mark the end of success for him on the Russian front. As the victorious Red Army pressed forward to eliminate German positions before Stalingrad in February 1943, the offensive was halted by the First and Fourth Panzer Armies, under Field Marshal Erich von Manstein, a cool, skilled strategist. The counter-attack pushed north-east, cutting off the Soviet 6th Army, recapturing Kharkov on 12 March and going on to take Bjelgorod, an important rail junction. Inspired by this success, the German Army Staff planned a great summer offensive, Operation 'Citadel', to regain the initiative on the Eastern Front.

Von Manstein's counter-attack had left a large Soviet salient centred on Kursk, north of Bjelgorod, and some 100 miles deep north-south and east-west. The plan was to cut off this bulge by launching a pincer attack from the north and the south, using classic panzer break-through tactics, led by the new Tigers and the even newer Panther, a 50-ton tank with a 7.5cm gun and intended as a replacement for the Pz Kpfw IV. But only 146 Tigers and 40 Panthers were available to lead the attack. Aware of this – and with intelligence revealing that the Russians were preparing in-depth defences exactly where the offensive would be launched – Guderian opposed the plan and even von Manstein was ambivalent about it. But Hitler approved and 'Citadel' was launched on 5 July, five days before the Allies began their invasion of Sicily.

Guderian recalls in his autobiography that 'everything that the German Army could muster in the way of attacking strength was committed to this offensive'. From the south, in the Bjelgorod area, ten panzer, one panzer grenadier and seven infantry divisions attacked, while in the north seven panzer, two panzer grenadier and nine infantry divisions went in from the area west of Orel. Stukas fell from the skies in close support. But the Soviets had withdrawn all but a minimum force from the western line of the bulge and, precisely anticipating the German plan, had reinforced the northern and southern sides of the salient (after all, they had had plenty of experience of panzer tactics over the previous two years).

As Muller and his colleagues in the lead tanks rumbled in from north and south, they found the Russians ready, waiting and quite prepared to fight a defensive battle from carefully prepared positions consisting of dug-in tanks, well-concealed anti-tank and heavy artillery batteries, and entrenched infantry lines studded with concrete pill-boxes and machine-gun cupolas. The Germans committed a total of some 2,000 tanks and 800 assault guns from north and south, but found that they were heavily out-numbered by the Russian armour and artillery.

As ever, Muller and his fellow tank commanders fought magnifi-cently, devising new tactics on the spot to compensate for their inferiority in numbers. Faced with tanks which would not leave their safe, dug-in posi-tions, unable to bypass them or penetrate the wall of fire, the Panzers aimed high-explosive shells to explode just in front of the defensive posi-tions. Under cover of the dust clouds that blinded the Russian gunners, the tanks surged forward, laid their guns on the muzzle flashes through the dust and, when visibility was clear, blasted the defences from close range. It was dangerous, but it was the only way that the out-ranged IIIs and IVs could operate.

At the end of the first day, the German tanks had penetrated only 22 kilometres in the south and even less in the north. Guderian's fears about committing the new Panthers, with their inexperienced crews, were con-firmed, and these new machines – later to win a high reputation manned by experienced crews fighting on the defensive – suffered heavily. The 90 Porsche Tigers which fought on Muller's flanks in Model's army attacking from the north also justified Guderian's strictures about their lack of machine-guns. They proved incapable of close-range fighting. Once they had broken through into the enemy's infantry zone they were forced, in Guderian's words, 'to go quail shooting with cannon'. Their only arma-ment, the big 7.5cm, could not deal adequately with dug-in riflemen and machine-gunners, with the result that the infantry following up were met by fierce small-arms fire.

As the battle progressed, the conventional Tigers, few though they were, came into their own. The Tiger crews found that they were at risk to the Soviet T34s and T43s from about 600 metres to the front, 1,500 metres to the side and as far as 1,800 metres to the rear, but that they could out-range the Russian tanks consistently if the Tiger were handled adroitly. The gunners found that the T34's armour was particularly vulnerable where the turret met the hull and this became their target. A direct hit could blast off the T34s' turrets so that they gambolled like schoolboys' caps across the plain. After Kursk, the phrase 'the T34 raises its hat whenever it meets a Tiger' became the toast in the German tank messes.

The Battle of Kursk came to a head on 11 July. Then, in an amazing confrontation in an area between the railway line and the Psyol, just north of Prokhorovka, and measuring only about 500 metres wide and a kilome-tre deep, the two tank corps of the Soviet 5th Tank Army drove out to meet the panzers. Like knights of old, the squadrons of tanks charged at one another, breaking through one another's lines, wheeling and firing in a holocaust of fire and smoke. Tanks, denied room to manoeuvre, collided, turrets were blown off and screaming men tumbled out of wrecks with their overalls on fire. The temperature inside the tanks reached 60 degrees Centigrade as they rumbled and wheeled across the plain, firing as soon as they could re-load. Above, the Stukas joined in until they were driven off by Soviet fighters which then, in turn, became locked in dog-fights with the Messerschmitts. On the edges of the amphitheatre the opposing ground troops fought, too. It was, in fact, total war. For three hours the battle raged until the area had become a tank graveyard, shrouded in a dense cloud of dust and oily, black smoke.

Both sides fought with a valour never exceeded in the war. It was here that young Michael Wittman, a panzer commander who was to become the most famous Tiger leader of them all before his death in Normandy, made his name. He destroyed 30 enemy tanks, 28 anti-tank guns and put out of action two heavy batteries with a total of eight guns. But the Germans could not sustain confrontation on this scale. They lost 300 tanks in the Prokhorovka engagement alone, including 70 of the precious Tigers – half the total complement on the Eastern Front at that time.

After ten days Hitler, now concerned about the threatened Allied invasion of the Italian mainland, called off the offensive. On 15 July the Russian counter-attack began and within days Orel had been re-captured and then Bjelgorod. Across the whole Russian front, the exhausted Germans began to fall back. They were never able to launch another offensive.

In *Panzer Leader* Guderian wrote:

'By the failure of "Citadel" we had suffered a decisive defeat. The armoured formations, reformed and re-equipped with so much effort, had lost heavily both in men and equipment and would now be unemployable for a long time to come. It was problematic whether they could be rehabilitated in time to defend the Eastern Front: as for being able to use them in defence of the Western Front against the Allied landings that threatened for next spring, this was even more questionable. Needless to say, the Russians exploited their victory to the full. There were to be no more periods of quiet on the Eastern Front. From now on the enemy was in undisputed possession of the initiative.'

Hans Muller – we must admit now that he is a fictional figure, but representatively based on research of the men who commanded the Tigers – most probably died in the first few days of the offensive. Given the casualty rate of the Tigers and as a platoon leader in the van of the attack, he is unlikely to have survived the courageous drives on the dug-in defences of the Russians, let alone the holocaust of Prokhorovka. His grave would have been unmarked. The Russians had neither time nor inclination to observe such niceties.

RETREAT AND DEFEAT

There were to be many more brave battles fought by the panzer men before the end of the European war in May 1945. But with the possible exception of von Runstedt's brilliant but short-lived 1944 counter-attack in the Ardennes, they were never again to break through in the classic manner of 1940 and 1941. The Germans fought with remarkable tenacity on three fronts – Russia, Normandy and Italy – once the Allies had landed in France, fighting classic defensive battles in which the Tiger and Panther tanks, although sorely outnumbered, became greatly respected by the forces opposing them.

German tank construction throughout the war never reached its targets and never exceeded 200 a month. The records of Albert Speer (Hitler's Minister for Armaments and War Production) show that total production of tanks and assault guns during the war did not reach 39,000. From 1939 to 1945, the USA alone produced 88,000 tanks and the tank factories of Russia and Britain were producing highly efficiently by the war's end. Given the forces arrayed against it, it is amazing that Hitler's Germany first conquered so much of Europe so quickly and then, faced with overwhelming odds of manpower and equipment, was able to contest for so long every inch of ground occupied.

The distinguished American historian, Stephen E. Ambrose, writing an introduction to Colonel Hans von Luck's memoirs *Panzer Commander* (Praeger, New York, 1989), attributes the reason to the German soldier. He writes:

'The German soldier of World War II is universally agreed to have been the best soldier in the war. German training was tougher, more realistic, and lasted longer than that of their enemies. German soldiers were in superb physical condition, accustomed to long night marches and the sound of live ammunition whistling over their heads, long before they reached the front lines. ... what the Germans had that their enemies never matched was unit cohesion and, as a consequence, a strong sense of comradeship. Infantry and armoured combat are above all a matter of teamwork and no army anywhere, since the days of the Roman legions, has been so successful in establishing and maintaining teamwork as the German army of the first half of the twentieth century. That is why the Germans, twice came within sight of complete domination over all of Europe.'

A more specific tribute to the part played in the war by the panzer troops and by their creator, Heinz Guderian, is offered by the British historian, Captain B. H. Liddell Hart, in a foreword to Guderian's autobiography. He writes:

'... in 1939–40 Germany's forces in general were not sufficient to overcome any major Power. Her opening run of victory in the Second World War was only made possible by the panzer forces that Guderian had created, and trained, *and* by his audacious leading of those forces in disregard of his superiors' caution as well as Hitler's fears. Guderian's break-through at Sedan and lightning drive to the Channel coast virtually decided the issue of the Battle of France.

'A year later, the drive he led into the East came close to producing the complete collapse of Russia's armies, but this time renewed hesitancy on top imposed a delay that spun out the campaign until winter intervened, and gave the Russians a breathing-space for recovery...Thus the victories that Guderian had made possible proved more fatal than if no victory had been gained. Early blossom turned into bitter fruit.

'That retributive sequel to his work, however, does not affect his historical significance – in the moulding of history by the application of a new idea, of which he was both the exponent and executant. The conquest of the West did not last, but it changed the shape of Europe and has profoundly affected the future of the whole world. That is clear, although we cannot yet tell what will emerge.'

It must be admitted that the story of the panzer commanders, like that of the U-boat captains, is one of might-have-been. If only. Yet the qualifications for entry into this book do not include that of continued success. The panzer men had their moment – and not so brief – when, by their actions, they changed the map and the course of world events. Had Hitler sat on the laurels of conquest in the west which they delivered to him in 1940 and not embarked upon his suicidal attack on the Soviet Union, Britain might well have been subdued and the other dominoes of America's and Japan's entries into the war might not have fallen into place. We shall never know.

Nevertheless, the Mullers and the Wittmans, riding high atop their caterpillared steel machines, must stand foremost among the great armoured warriors of the past. They accomplished more than the armoured knights of William the Norman, the crusaders, Saladin or those steel-clad captains whose exploits flicker through to us from the formative days of China and the other great nations of the East. The early heroes of tank warfare from the First World War were never employed in significant enough numbers to win a campaign on their own – despite General von Zwehl's rueful compliment to 'General Tank'. And, although tanks have featured in every major conflict in the world since 1945, the exploits of their commanders and crews do not stand out as starkly as those of the panzer men. What could they not have accomplished had their leadership been balanced and their cause just!

POSTSCRIPT

Are there any lessons to be learned by considering the lives and triumphs of the warriors in this book? After all, history can warn, as well as divert, and all the gurus at the world's great military academies earn their living by demonstrating daily that it is certainly not bunk. Apart, then, from flippant truisms – such as, it is best not to annoy a Plantagenet, and *Danegeld* may buy you time but little else – there are several serious points to be drawn from the exploits of these fighting men.

With the exception of the Vikings, all the protagonists were undervalued by their opponents. The English bowmen were regarded with derision ('men without worth and without birth') by the French; John Burgoyne condemned the revolutionary American soldiers as 'rabble'; before Isandlwana, Chelmsford believed that the only problem in defeating the Zulus would be in bringing them to battle; the U-boats were 'unlikely to play a useful part in war'; and the Allies in the Second World War began the conflict dismissive of the panzer concept and still firmly believing that tanks should be used only to support infantry.

In each case, the come-uppance when it came was devastating. The old adage that time spent on reconnaissance is never wasted certainly can be extended to apply to a study of the enemy. Wellington is arguably the greatest British general ever to command in the field, although he never seems to have been rated so highly in other countries (Napoleon called him 'that Sepoy General' and revisionists have even tended to award Waterloo to Blücher). Yet, throughout a very active career in the field, the Duke never lost a single battle. His secret lay in carefully estimating his enemy's strengths and making his plans accordingly. His long Peninsula campaign consisted of a succession of brilliant defensive moves and battles. Usually outnumbered, he won by counter-punching. A feature of virtually all of the warrior stories in this book is the arrogance of their opponents.

What else? Well, in singling out interesting 'specialists' as the finest fighters of their type, perhaps this narration has rather neglected the exponents of mainstream warfare – the infantry, the cavalry, the men who manned the ships of the line and so on. Of course, wars could not have been won without them. Yet in concentrating on the specialists, I have not done so just because they were, and are, more interesting, but also because they demonstrate how the strange and the new can influence events.

The determined but anxious congressmen in Philadelphia who sent out that first call for frontier riflemen, presciently sensed that something other than line militia was needed to fight King George's Redcoats. The accuracy of Morgan's skirmishers at Saratoga swung the battle, I have no doubt about that. And Saratoga swung the outcome of the rebellion.

Similarly, the sea still frightened all but a few hardy souls in the Europe of the 9th century. To the Vikings of Scandinavia, however, it was not just a way to travel but a means to attack and to conquer – so they became the first true practitioners of amphibious warfare. The painful lesson administered by those few thousand axe- and swordsmen had the effect of creating effective navies and, of course, marines. But breaking the mould can be a painful as well as an exhilarating experience.

It would be a comforting thought to end with the conclusion that these studies also prove that virtue always wins in the end. Alas, as we all know, the world is not quite like that. By conventional mores, three of the six protagonists in this book are less heroic than the others. The Vikings were brutal even beyond the barbaric standards of their day. The Kaiser's U-boat captains and Hitler's panzer commanders were controversial figures in their own times who have received a very mixed Press ever since. The Norsemen had two hundred years of domination; the Germans, in comparison, only a fragment of time. Yet, for those times, they *were* dominant, seeming to show that the strong and inventive will always dominate the placid and peaceful.

Whether these great soldiers and sailors changed the world for the better in the end is a matter for debate. What they all did, however, was to irradiate it for a time and to show once again the capacity of ordinary people to do extraordinary things when the call comes.

SELECT
BIBLIOGRAPHY

The Marines:

Bronsted, Johannes. *The Vikings*. Penguin Books, 1965.

Crumlin-Pedersen, Ole. *The Ships of the Vikings*. Uppsala, 1978.

Enterline, J. Robert. *Viking America*. Doubleday, New York, 1972.

Farrell, R. T. (ed.). *The Vikings*. Phillimore & Co., London, 1982.

Foot, P., and Wilson, D. M. *The Viking Achievement*. Sidgwick and Jackson, London, 1970.

Graham-Campbell, James. *The Viking World*. Francis Lincoln, London, 1980.

Haslock Kirby, Michael. *The Viking*. Phaidon Press, Oxford, 1977.

Instad, Helge. *Westward to Vinland*. St Martin's Press, 1966.

Jones, Gwyn (trans.). *Erik the Red and Other Icelandic Sagas*. Oxford University Press, 1961.

Wernich, Robert. *The Vikings*. Time-Life Books, Amsterdam, 1979.

Whitelock, Dorothy (ed.). *The Anglo-Saxon Chronicle*. Rutgers University Press, 1968.

The Artillerymen:

Allmond, Christopher. *Henry V*. Methuen, 1992.

Barber, Richard. *Life and Campaigns of the Black Prince*. Folio Society, 1959.

Bradbury, Jim. *The Medieval Archer*. Boydell Press, 1985.

Hardy, Robert. *The Longbow*. Mary Rose Trust, 1986.

Heath, Ernest G. *The Grey Goose Wing*. Osprey, 1971.

Hibbert, Christopher, *The English. A Social History*. Grafton Books, 1987.

– *Agincourt*. Collins.

Hodgkin, A. E. *The Archer's Craft*. Faber.

Johnson, Paul. *Edward III*. Weidenfeld & Nicholson, 1973.

Keegan, John. *The Face of Battle*. Jonathan Cape, 1976.

Prestwich, Michael. *The Three Edwards – War and the State in England*. Weidenfeld & Nicholson, 1980.

Tannahill, Reay. *Food in History*. Penguin Books. 1973.

The Skirmishers:

Bird, Harrison. *March to Saratoga*. Oxford University Press, New York, 1963.

Black, Jeremy. *War for America. The Fight for Independence 1775–1783*. Alan Sutton, London, 1991.

Creasey, Sir Edward. *The Fifteen Decisive Battles of the World*. Richard Bentley & Son, London, 1851.

Dillin, John D. W. *The Kentucky Rifle*. Rifle Association of America, New York, 1928.

Elliott, Lawrence. *Daniel Boone. The Long Hunter*. George Allen & Unwin, London, 1977.

Fischer, David Hacket. *Albion's Seed*. Oxford University Press, New York, 1989.

Furneaux, Rupert. *Saratoga. The Decisive Battle*. George Allen & Unwin, London, 1971.

Higginbotham, Don. *Daniel Morgan. Revolutionary Reformer*. University of N. Carolina Press, 1961.

Kelley, Kenneth W. *What is Distinctive About the Scotch-Irish?* University Press of Kentucky, 1991.

Ketchum, Richard R. *Men of the Revolution.* vol. xxvii, American Heritage, 1976.

LaCrosse, Richard B. Jnr. *The Frontier Rifleman.* Pioneer Press, Union City, Tennessee, 1989.

Middlekauff, Robert. *The Glorious Cause.* Oxford University Press, New York, 1982.

Mintz, Max M. *The Generals of Saratoga.* Yale University, New York, 1990.

The Spearmen:

Ballard, Charles. *The House of Shaka.* Emoyeni Books, Cape Town, 1988.

Barthop, Michael. *The Zulu War.* Blandford Press, London, 1980.

Emery, Frank. *The Red Soldier,* Hodder & Stoughton, London, 1977.

Knight, Ian. *Brave Men's Blood,* Greenhill Books, London, 1980.

– *Zulu. The Battles of Isandlwana and Rorke's Drift,* Windrow and Greene, London, 1992

Laband, John. *Kingdom in Crisis.* Manchester University Press, 1991.

– *Fight Us In The Open.* Shuter & Shooter, Pietermaritzburg, South Africa, 1985.

Laband, John, and Thompson, Paul. *Kingdom and Colony at War.* University of Natal Press, Cape Town, 1990.

Lloyd, A. *The Zulu War 1879,* Hart-Davis, London, 1974.

McBride, Angus. *The Zulu War.* Osprey Publishing Company, London, 1976.

Morris, Donald R. *The Washing of the Spears.* Jonathan Cape, London, 1966.

Taylor, Stephen. *Shaka's Children.* Harper Collins, London, 1995.

Vijn, Cornelius. *Cetshwayo's Dutchman.* Greenhill Books, London, 1988.

The Privateers:

Bell, A. C. *History of the Blockade of Germany and the Countries Associated with her in the Great War,* HMSO, London, 1930.

Campbell, Gordon. *My Mystery Ships.* Hodder and Stoughton, London, 1928.

Churchill, Winston. *The World Crisis.* Odhams Press, London, 1939.

Dönitz, Karl. *Memoirs.* Weidenfeld and Nicolson, London, 1956.

Jellicoe, Lord. *The Submarine Peril.* Cassell, London, 1934.

Jones, Archer. *The Art of War in the Western World.* Oxford University Press, 1987.

Keegan, John. *A History of Warfare.* Hutchinson, London, 1993.

Newbolt, Sir Henry. *Submarine and Anti-Submarine.* Longmans Green, London, 1918.

Neureuther C. and Bergen C. (eds.). *U-boat Stories.* John Constable, London, 1930.

Rössler, Eberhard. *The U-boat.* Arms & Armour Press, London, 1981.

Tarrant, V. E. *The U-boat Offensive 1914–1945.* Arms & Armour Press, London, 1989.

Thomas, Lowell. *Raiders of the Deep.* Garden City, New York, 1928.

The Armoured Ones:

Carius, Otto. *Tigers in the Mud.* J. J. Fedorowicz Publishing Inc., Winnipeg, 1989.

Edwards, Roger. *Panzer – A Revolution in Warfare.* Arms & Armour Press, London, 1989.

Forty, George. *Tank Commanders. Knights of the Modern Age.* Firebird Books, Poole, 1993.

– *German Tanks of World War Two.* Blandford Press, London, 1988.

Guderian, Heinz. *Panzer Leader.* Michael Joseph, London, 1952.

Gudgin, Peter. *The Tiger Tanks.* Arms & Armour Press, London, 1991.

Keegan, John. *A History of Warfare.* Hutchinson, London, 1993.

Kurowski, Franz. *Panzer Aces.* J. J. Fedorowicz, Winnipeg, 1990.

Klein, Egon, and Kuhn, Volkmar. *Tiger.* J. J. Fedorowicz, Winnipeg, 1989.

Liddell Hart, Basil. *The Tanks,* vol. II. Cassell, London, 1959.

Luck, Hans von. *Panzer Commander.* Praeger, New York. 1989.

Macksey, Kenneth. *Guderian — Panzer General.* Macdonald and Jane's, London, 1975.

INDEX